*Biomechanics
of Women's Gymnastics*

Biomechanics
of Women's Gymnastics

Gerald S. George
University of Southwestern Louisiana

Prentice-Hall, Inc., Englewood Cliffs, N.J. 07632

Library of Congress Cataloging in Publication Data

GEORGE, GERALD S.
  Biomechanics of women's gymnastics.

  Bibliography: p. 215
  Includes index.
    1. Gymnastics for women—Physiological aspects.
I. Title.
GV464.G46   796.4'1   79–18854
ISBN 0–13–077461–8

Printed in the United States of America

10   9   8   7   6   5   4

Editorial/production supervision by Frank Hubert
Page layout by Rita Kaye Swartz
Cover design by Michael Clane Graves
Manufacturing Buyer: Harry P. Baisley

PRENTICE-HALL INTERNATIONAL, INC., *London*
PRENTICE-HALL OF AUSTRALIA PTY. LIMITED, *Sydney*
PRENTICE-HALL OF CANADA, LTD., *Toronto*
PRENTICE-HALL OF INDIA PRIVATE LIMITED, *New Delhi*
PRENTICE-HALL OF JAPAN, INC., *Tokyo*
PRENTICE-HALL OF SOUTHEAST ASIA PTE. LTD., *Singapore*
WHITEHALL BOOKS LIMITED, *Wellington, New Zealand*

To my wife, Janet, and to my children,
Tasha, Jimbo, Jonathan, and Michael

Contents

vii

9

ANALYSIS OF CORE UNEVEN PARALLEL BAR SKILLS   *151*

Foreword

One basic need in the overall development of a sport and the continued improvement of the method in which skills are performed is the devotion of those who have had a beneficial relationship with that sport activity and are dedicated to the teaching and training of others. During my many years of association with gymnastics and trampoline, I know of no one better qualified to undertake the august task of putting into the written word a new comprehensive approach to this very complex sport of gymnastics. Gerald George is among the few people who have carefully observed and studied human motion as applied to gymnastics, and he has successfully imparted his knowledge in this very intriguing and refreshing book.

Practical biomechanical principles are innovatively employed and purposely developed to be expedient in nature from the teacher or coach's point of view. Dr. George's timely and imaginative concepts give new meaning to the gymnastic world.

The section on movement principles is unique in that it defines and outlines gymnastic movement as implicit in nature, and it transcends the currently established criteria for today's performers.

Of particular interest is the chapter on "The Mechanics of Rotation" where Dr. George brings to the gymnastic world a time-tested system of twisting so necessary to the growth of the gymnastic athlete. These twisting techniques, as pioneered by the American trampolinists, open up a whole new era in the history of the sport of gymnastics. The number of skills that can be accomplished with this system of twisting is indeed infinite.

The book is a needed and long-awaited contribution to the existing literature of sport and physical education for which we the readers are grateful.

Jeff T. Hennessy
Technical Committee Chairman
Federation International Trampoline

Acknowledgments

Having been involved in almost every phase of the gymnastic spectrum over the past twenty years, it would indeed be an impossible task to credit accurately all the wonderful and dedicated people who, either directly or indirectly, contributed to the writing of this book. For the enriched experiences they provided as well as for their continued encouragement and friendship, the author is forever grateful.

In addition, the author would like to extend his very sincere thanks to:

Fred Martinez, E. D. "Buddy" Wood, and Dr. William H. Bankhead, who helped a clumsy little kid find himself through the magic of gymnastics.

James H. Stephenson, an artist of the first order, who took the author's rather stilted line-and-angle drawings and masterfully shaped them into meaningful form.

Jeff Hennessy, a world-renowned trampoline expert, who readily made available his vast knowledge and experience upon which a major section of the text was based.

Myrtice Blanchard, who unselfishly devoted many long hours typing and retyping the manuscript.

And finally to Janet, Tasha, Jimbo, Jonathan (now deceased), and Michael, who endured without complaint the disruption of their family life so that this book might be written.

G.S.G.

1
Introduction to Gymnastic Movement

Simone Chappuis, Acadiana Gymnastic Club, Lafayette, Louisiana.

The sport of gymnastics, perhaps more so than most activities, encompasses a seemingly endless quantity of movement skills and innovations. Even more incredible are the numbers and varieties of information put forth to define and clarify these movements. One need only compare descriptive mechanical analyses of almost any given skill presented by any number of gymnastic authorities to discover that interpretations are strikingly divergent. To compound the problem further, skills are often viewed and presented as separate entities, each distinctly different from all others. While such efforts to further our knowledge and practices in sport technique are indeed commendable, a critical review of contemporary methods leaves little wonder why gymnastics mechanics and techniques appear, at best, to be perplexing!

Actually, this should not be the case at all. Unlike many sport activities, a majority of the movements in gymnastics are both symmetrical in pattern and simplistic in nature. Although it might be argued that skills differ according to their objectives, close observation clearly reveals that a vast majority of such differences exist more so in terms of degree and not kind. In fact, the similarities found in gymnastic movement patterns far outweigh the differences. The mechanics involved to execute even the most basic skills are precisely the same as those used in the advanced skills. Many backward moving skills are simply the mirror image of forward moving skills. The mechanical principles utilized in landings are merely the reciprocal of those seen in takeoffs. In this light, the contents of this book are based upon the premise that movement skills can and should be conceptualized and taught according to their technical and mechanical similarities.

The perspective for the correct technical execution of any movement arises out of the performer's current, yet continuously evolving, concept of what is considered to be the "ideal model." Relying upon available information and experience, the mind's eye attempts to create the best model it can possibly conceive and then to utilize that model as the basis for formulating correct technique. As the conceptual model becomes more and more refined, practical execution of the actual skill can more readily approach perfection. For example, if a child were to be taught the concept of a straight line, it would be wise to provide her with a model of as straight a line as possible! In so doing, she would have a better opportunity to more closely approximate the desired objective, identifying a truly straight line.

While in no way final or absolute, the illustrations presented in this book are an attempt to provide the readers with "ideal model" concepts. Their underlying purpose is to serve as a basic framework upon which even more "ideal models" can be developed. *It is extremely critical to ultimate gymnastic success that an ongoing effort be made by teachers, coaches, and gymnasts alike to continuously refine and improve upon all existing skill models as well as to innovate new and untried models.* While a working knowledge of the biomechanical principles observed in gymnastics is essential to this end, it in and of itself is not enough. One must also be able to employ these principles accurately. And this is unquestionably dependent upon the quality, accuracy, and exactness of the model.

Another area of concern which directly influences the rate of progress and degree of success one can ultimately hope to achieve in gymnastics centers upon the *appropriate use of skill progressions.* In an attempt to lend a better insight into the word "appropriate," the following guidelines are offered:

To ensure a maximum rate of progress, the difficulty level of the task must be commensurate with the experience and ability level of the performer.

Since the concept of "difficulty" is a direct function of the degree of task complexity *as perceived by the performer,* we should guard against the tendency to categorize skill progressions based solely on the Federation of International Gymnastics' (F.I.G.) rating scale. It would also be wise to consider the relative difficulty level of task progressions in terms of the experience and ability level of *each individual performer.* This will help to ensure more efficient and productive use of one's time.

Even a cursory review of studies on "psychological readiness" and "critical learning periods" supports the theory that quality learning and performance are largely dependent upon maturational readiness. Why then should we persist in the *untimely* pursuit of difficulty at the expense of technical excellence? Inappropriate use of skill progressions, more than any other reason, is the major factor limiting ultimate success.

Task mastery of the essential basic movement patterns is the single most important criterion for prediction of future success.

How often, in our blind aspiration for short-cut success, do we fall prey to the misuse of this well-known, yet seldom followed, guideline? The *difficulty syndrome* appears to have permeated every facet of the gymnastics world. All too often we mistakenly employ *task complexity techniques* rather than *task execution techniques* in search for the spectacular. Difficulty levels are prematurely advanced at the expense of execution, natural mechanical progression, and a totality of experience in basic movement patterns and sequences.

Task mastery of basic level skills prior to reasonable increments in difficulty will significantly facilitate achievement of the ultimately desired level of performance.

The degree of ultimate success in actual performance inevitably depends upon the degree of basic-to-complex task mastery. Since advanced skills are, for the most part, an integrated series of elementary movements, the necessity of mastering the "basics" initially should become quite obvious. This is precisely why many ineptly trained, elite-level gymnasts, regardless of their efforts after the fact, are never fully capable of truly maximizing execution in the advanced skills. As the skills increase in complexity, the underlying problem is compounded until finally these performers are confronted with having to relearn basic skills, often times with limited success.

Mastering basic skills serves to increase significantly the degree of performance consistency.

Gymnastic training sessions should provide for and emphasize successful experiences. In so doing, *consistency becomes a learned trait initially* rather than finally. Hence consistency (that infallible badge of every champion gymnast) need no longer be considered as a problem, rather it becomes an asset. There is an old Chinese saying: "It's never too early to start winning." Think about it.

Mastering basic level skills significantly reduces the frequency and intensity of injuries.

Injury consumes potential at a rate similar to that of fire consuming fuel. It has neither memory nor conscience. Even minor injuries, although seemingly healed, often return to plague the gymnast at a time when her body is called upon to sustain the enormous stresses inherent in advanced level skills. Again the implications are obvious. No one can deny that the inevitably nagging fly of injury is a major stumbling block to long-range success. All too often have we heard it said: "She could have been an Olympic champion. Too bad she's a Band-aid gymnast . . . comes apart too easily." Let's stop for a moment and ask ourselves *why*. Why does she come apart so easily? In most, if not all, instances, poor training methodology rather than all the other explanations combined is the root of the problem.

In viewing Olympic and World Championship competitions, have you ever considered why a chosen few gymnasts stand far above all others? What is that seemingly indefinable quality that characterizes their performances and that accounts for the differences between the champions and the would-be champions? The discernible difference is found in the *degree of matured movement patterns*. Difficulty per se is of little consequence, especially in the final analysis. All the finalists possess "difficult" routines, yet the *margin of victory* is inevitably awarded based upon the degree of *correct technical execution*.

Work hard to continually improve upon your "ideal model" concepts, rely heavily upon the practical principles and relationships revealed in the science of biomechanics, exercise patience in the use of skill progressions with emphasis on correct technical execution. Do these things and you shall find that the answer to success has been secretly lurking in your own backyard ever since the beginning of time.

> . . . And now the silence of the crowd becomes deafening. Electricity permeates the air as the performer walks onto the floor. The awesome, bland countenance of the "technical evaluators" seems to employ X-ray vision as they pointedly stare through the performer's eyes and into the back of her skull. The stage is set and irrevocable judgment will now be rendered. That automatic pilot inherent in all great gymnasts is now called upon to tell its story. . . .[1]

[1]Salmela, John H., ed. *The Advanced Study of Gymnastics*. Springfield, Ill.: Charles C Thomas, 1976.

2
Basic Principles for Refining Gymnastic Movement

Simone Chappuis, Acadiana Gymnastic Club, Lafayette, Louisiana.

To say that success in gymnastics is dependent upon what skills a performer can execute is but a story half-told. The very word "skill" implies not merely *what* is done but more importantly the *way* in which it is done. Experienced coaches, teachers, and gymnasts are all well aware that refining basic gymnastic movement is a critical first step in the learning process toward more advanced skills. With this in mind, let us then look to a set of fundamental principles that serve to refine gymnastic movement; perhaps then we can begin to account for why one performer looks significantly better than a second performer even though it "appears" that both execute the same skills in exactly the same way!

2.1 Amplitude: The greater one's amplitude, the greater one's potential for realizing maximum execution of the skill.

Almost all gymnastic enthusiasts are at least vaguely familiar with the concept of amplitude. Essentially, amplitude refers to the "range" through which a body moves and can be subdivided into two basic types. The first type, "external amplitude," is used to describe the range through which the *total* body unit moves relative to the ground and/or apparatus. For example, figure 2.1 illustrates a comparison of the airborne phase of two gymnasts executing the Yamashita Vault. More external amplitude is observed in the second illustration because the vaulter attained greater vertical height and horizontal distance from the apparatus. Obviously, to attain this additional external amplitude, the gymnast must coordinate each phase of the vault

FIGURE 2.1. A comparison of external amplitude in executing a Yamashita Vault.

7

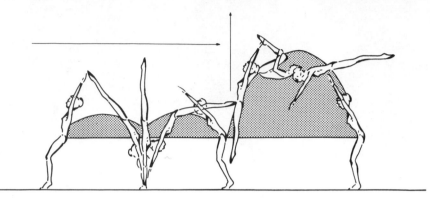

FIGURE 2.2. A backward handspring into a tucked backward somersault. (Horizontal amplitude is emphasized in the handspring whereas in the somersault vertical amplitude is emphasized.)

using proper technique. However, the "hidden component" that allows the gymnast to take full advantage of technique is her own internal *power*. A very fast approach and hurdle, an instantaneous takeoff, and a most powerful repulsion from the horse itself are the underlying factors that characterize this concept we call external amplitude.

It is interesting to note that the objective of the gymnastic skill will dictate the desired "direction" of external amplitude. Although the objective of most vaulting skills is to attain the maximum amounts of *both* horizontal and vertical amplitude, many gymnastic skills are characterized by external amplitude primarily in *one* direction. The backward handspring into a tucked backward somersault seen in figure 2.2 illustrates the point. Since a large amount of *horizontal* amplitude is desirable in the handspring phase, the observed movement pattern is long and low to the ground. In the somersault phase, however, the reverse is true in that the objective is to obtain great *vertical* amplitude or "lift" from the ground. Hence, the desired direction of external amplitude is dependent upon an accurate understanding of the skill's objective.

The second type of amplitude, "internal amplitude," focuses upon range of motion *within* the joints of the body. More specifically, it refers to the range through which one or more of the individual body segments move relative to each other. Figure 2.3 depicts two performers executing the step-out phase of a front walkover. The additional ranges of motion in the shoulder, back, and hip areas observed in the second example serve to illustrate greater internal amplitude. In addition to its aesthetic appeal, this fuller utilization of the appropriate joint ranges has an important functional value. Because the lead foot can now be placed much closer to the support hands, the weight transfer from hands to feet will not only be easier to accomplish but will also be significantly smoother! The aesthetic and functional values demonstrated in this example can be applied to numerous skills including back walkovers, cartwheels of most types, and related skill variations.

FIGURE 2.3. A comparison of internal amplitude in the step-out phase of a front walkover.

Just as power is the hidden component underlying external amplitude, joint range of motion or *flexibility* is the key factor for obtaining maximum internal amplitude. Although many performers find it particularly difficult to obtain full joint ranges of motion (not to mention the muscular capability of controlling these numerous ranges), the fact still remains that, without sufficient flexibility in all of the major joints of the body, the internal amplitude component of every movement pattern will suffer.

There are many gymnastic skills which depend upon a close interaction between internal and external amplitude. To demonstrate this relationship, compare the two techniques used in executing the forward headkip shown in figure 2.4. In the first example, the performer displays limited internal amplitude in that the maximum appropriate range of motion at the hip joints has not been fully utilized. Consequently, the hip extension or "kip" action is something less than what it could have been. This set of affairs reduces the potential for realizing maximum external amplitude. Such is not the case in the second example. In the kip phase, this performer uses the fullest appropriate hip joint range of motion. This increase in distance through which force can be applied improves the potential for a more vigorous and effective kipping action. Because maximum internal amplitude is employed, the opportunity for realizing maximum external amplitude becomes readily apparent. Compare the relative body shapes at the instant each performer makes foot contact with the ground.

FIGURE 2.4. Two techniques used in executing a forward headkip.

In these examples, as well as in all gymnastic skills, attaining maximum amplitude is of prime importance. The movement patterns will then appear larger than life, be more aesthetically pleasing, and have a sound functional base. One need only look to any championship performance at any level in gymnastics to discover that this principle is used time and time again.

2.2 Segmentation: As skill proficiency increases, the number of segmental body parts used in its execution decreases.

Before considering how to apply this principle, it is necessary to have a clear understanding of what is meant by the term "segment." Any body shape that forms a symmetrical line can be called a segment. The first example in figure 2.5 illustrates a body that is essentially in a 1-segment shape. A single straight (and therefore symmetrical) line can be drawn from the top of the performer's hands, through the entire length of the body and down to the bottom of the feet. As seen in the second example, when an obvious part of the body changes position to the point such that the line appears broken or lacking in symmetry, a 2-segment shape is then formed. The remaining examples demonstrate that the number of segments formed is simply a matter of the number of symmetrical lines or shapes observed.

The symmetry formed by the various body parts need not necessarily be straight lines to qualify as segments. *In fact, a majority of the movement patterns observed in gymnastics is characterized by dynamically curved lines.* Yet these curved lines should be as perfectly regular in nature as possible. Any rather abrupt irregularity in a single curved line becomes, by virtue of the original definition, a 2-segment shape.

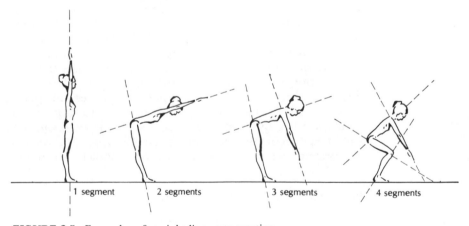

| 1 segment | 2 segments | 3 segments | 4 segments |

FIGURE 2.5. Examples of straight-line segmentation.

The three sets of body shapes revealed in figure 2.6 serve not only to illustrate the use of both curved and straight line segments but also to compare the numbers of segments actually needed to execute each skill properly. Careful observation will reveal that, in each instance, the more aesthetically pleasing position is the one which employs the *fewest* number of segments!

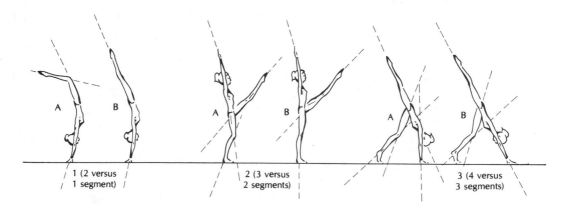

FIGURE 2.6. Examples of straight- and curved-line segmentation: (1) hand support phase of a backward handspring; (2) standing leg lift; (3) imput phase of a forward handspring.

The beginning of the second half of a backward handspring is presented in the first example. Because of the abrupt bend in the knees of performer A, a 2-segment motion (one curved line segment and one straight line segment) is observed. In addition to affecting the symmetry of the body, this untimely knee bend often interferes with the rhythm or tempo of the movement. When properly executed, however, this dynamic tumbling skill requires the use of only a single curved segment.

The standing leg lift example is essentially a 2-segment movement. Again, the unnecessary knee bend in the support leg of performer A creates an aesthetically questionable, nonfunctional third segment. Inadequate flexibility and muscular control about the hip joints are generally the factors affecting this type of mechanical compensation. Looking at perfomer B executing the very same skill using only the necessary 2-segment involvement demonstrates proper utilization of the segmentation principle. In this case, the gymnast possesses a more pleasing symmetry, is able to stand taller, and has additional freedom to maximize the movement pattern.

Although the input phase of the forward handspring illustrated in the final example can be reduced to a 3-segment motion, the exaggerated bend in the shoulder joint angle of performer A produces an additional, yet again unnecessary, segment. Since proper execution of the skill requires only momentary hand contact, this unwarranted bend at the shoulder joints results in limited repulsion or push-off from the ground. Correct alignment of the arms, trunk, and lead leg demonstrated by performer B serves both to raise the body's mass center further away from the ground (initially increasing height) during the input phase and to place the entire body unit in a more mechanically advantageous position for a powerful repulsion.

Motor skill learning is a process rather than a product. It involves more than mere repetitious practice and the inherent capabilities of the performer. One must have a clear understanding of the maximum execution potentials characteristic of each individual movement. In this way, gymnastic training becomes a continual process of motor skill refinement. *Performing the skill is a product, refining the performance is a process!*

FIGURE 2.7. Segmental comparison of two techniques used to execute a step-up to a handstand: (1) a 1-3-5-3-1 segmentation; (2) a 1-2-2-2-1 segmentation.

It is this "process" of refining performance that lends real substance to the segmentation principle. The comparison of two techniques used in executing a kick or step-up to a handstand revealed in figure 2.7 illustrates this application of the segmentation principle to the learning process. The first example shows a typical technique observed in a beginning level performance. As the gymnast proceeds through the skill, notice the rather large number of segmental components employed in its execution. Regardless of this fact, it cannot be denied that the performance of the skill, the final product, has been achieved. At this level of learning, use of numerous segmental components to realize success is usually necessary if not essential. However, the key to championship gymnastics is found in the never ending process of continually refining the performance.

Application of the segmentation principle provides the gymnast with a more accurate understanding of "how" to refine the movement. In the second example of figure 2.7, observe that the number of segmental components used in executing the very same skill has now been decreased to the necessary, critical few. Obviously, such a procedure requires an exceptional amount of flexibility, particularly in the hip joints. Yet the net effect of this 2-segment system renders a longer, smoother flowing body line, allows for maximum internal amplitude, and is more mechanically simplistic. With this knowledge at hand, the beginning level gymnast can now embark upon a road, the only road, to elite level performance.

It must also be pointed out that as the number of segmental components employed in the execution of any skill is decreased, the physical demands placed upon the body itself correspondingly increase. Included among these demands are increases in total body flexibility, power, timing, and balance. *The implication here is that "difficulty levels" should be conceived in terms of the quality or degree of skill execution rather than the degree of skill complexity.*

2.3 Closure: As skill proficiency increases, use of the maximum tolerance limits of closure also increases.

Closure refers to the degree to which a performer alters body shape in the execution of a skill. Essentially, the principle of closure implies that, in the broad category of skills characterized by very obvious or extreme changes in body shape, such changes should occur as fully and as completely as possible. At the other end of the continuum, there is another wide range of skills that call for unobvious, scarcely discernible changes in body shape. In these instances, such body shape changes should be as slight and as discreet as possible. Again, the gymnast must have a clear understanding of the nature and objectives inherent in the "ideal model" of each skill to apply the principle effectively.

With this in mind, observe the forward hip circle on the uneven parallel bars presented in figure 2.8. The initial front support position reveals that the gymnast has a fully extended body shape which is situated in a fashion such that the bar (axis) lies slightly below the body's mass center. This uneven weight distribution in favor of the upper body causes the gymnast to begin rotating about the bar in a forward direction. The fully extended body shape is maintained until the performer approaches illustration B. All of a sudden, the body begins to undergo a rapid and highly obvious change in shape. This deep "piking action" seen in illustrations C and D drives the head and feet toward each other causing the upper half of the body to move faster, and

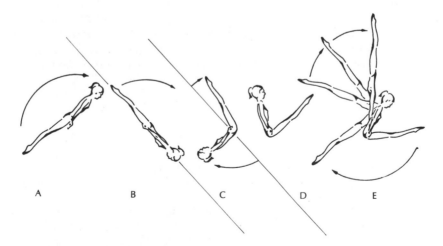

FIGURE 2.8. The forward hip circle cast to handstand is in that category of skills requiring highly *obvious* changes in body shape.

therefore to cover a greater rotary distance, than the lower half. Because the deep pike (fully closed body shape presented in illustration E) is maintained until the gymnast again arrives in a front support, the trailing lower half of the body is in the proper position to cast effectively to any of the sequentially related skills.

By the very nature of the observed movement pattern, it becomes apparent that the forward hip circle would be placed in that category of skills characterized by extreme changes in body shape. Consequently, the closure principle implies that *such changes* must be appropriately timed and *should occur as fully and as completely as is mechanically possible*.

The application of this important principle to those skills which utilize very slight and unobvious body shape changes can also be demonstrated. Figure 2.9 provides a comparison of two techniques for obtaining proper body shape during the takeoff and preflight phases of a handspring vault. The performer in the first example requires the use of both the takeoff phase *and almost the entire preflight phase* to assume a body shape that should have been initially assumed upon becoming airborne, i.e., a fully extended, yet slightly hollowed, shape. The reason for such a predicament can be

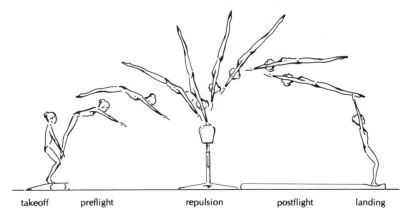

takeoff   preflight   repulsion   postflight   landing

FIGURE 2.9. The handspring vault is in that category of skills requiring highly *unobvious* changes in body shape: (1) poor closure; (2) good closure.

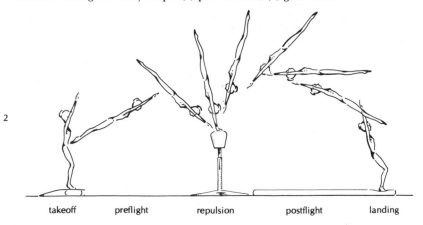

takeoff   preflight   repulsion   postflight   landing

found by a close examination of the actual takeoff itself. Because the feet are in contact with the vaulting board for less than a fraction of a second, there is not sufficient time for this compressed body shape to be fully and completely extended during the takeoff phase alone. Consequently, the performer has no choice but to exhaust much of the preflight time attempting to make up for this initial error.

The experienced gymnast, presented in the second example, knows that proper mechanics at takeoff are characterized by a body shape that *already* most closely approximates the ultimately desired extended body position. The implication here is for the performer to stand as tall and as elongated as is mechanically possible *during takeoff* so that the observed changes in body shape (occurring from the takeoff phase to the initial aspect of the preflight phase) are as instantaneous and *as scarcely discernible as possible*. This use of the closure principle maximizes both the aesthetic and mechanical potentials not only for vaulting takeoffs but also for the wide range of skills whose common thread is highly unobvious movement pattern changes.

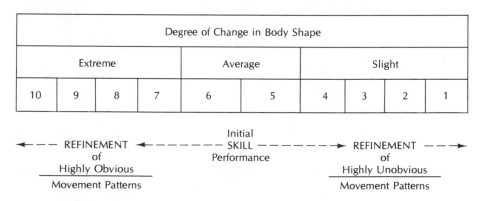

FIGURE 2.10. The Closure Continuum. (Number 10 and Number 1 represent the maximum potential levels for highly obvious and highly unobvious body shape changes respectively.)

The closure continuum, presented in figure 2.10, illustrates that the "degree" of body shape change used in the performance of a skill serves as an excellent measure for evaluating the quality or level of execution. During initial learning and performance, the observed body shape changes in a vast majority of gymnastic skills are neither highly obvious nor highly unobvious in terms of degree, but rather they appear to cluster together in the average range. Because of this, noticeable differences in movement shapes are often difficult, if not impossible, to ascertain. With appropriate training habits, however, the various movement patterns become further and further refined. As a result of this refinement process, the degree of change in body shapes becomes *either* more apparent *or* less apparent until the maximum potential level characteristic to each skill is finally realized. This goal of ultimate technical execution requires full and complete utilization of the closure principle.

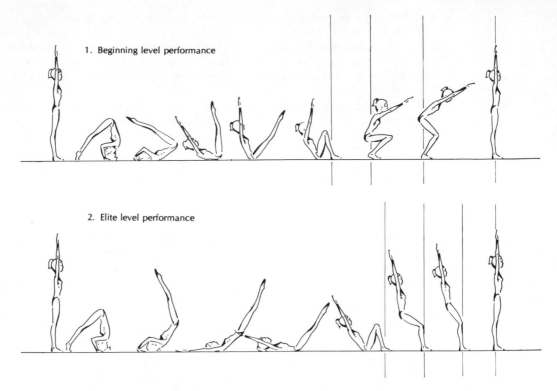

FIGURE 2.11. A comparison of two techniques used in executing a forward roll: (1) poor peaking; (2) good peaking.

2.4 Peaking: As skill proficiency increases, the use of peaking techniques correspondingly increases.

Peaking can be defined as a technique of "timing" accuracy used to achieve the maximum execution tolerance limits of a skill. To demonstrate the concept, observe the comparison of the two forward roll techniques shown in figure 2.11. Because of insufficient forward momentum in the first example, the performer has no choice but to wait until the body's mass is centered directly over the feet (final base of support) before attempting to stand. This inappropriate timing results in the head, trunk, and arms moving "backward" in the final stand-up phase of the "forward"roll. Notice that the performer in the second example assumes a rather extended body shape during a large portion of the actual roll sequence. Such a procedure provides the necessary forward momentum to initiate, execute, and complete the final stage of the skill *without* having any of the various body parts transcend the vertical. Precise timing of the movement allows the performer to "swing up" *to* a stand rather than rolling *through* a tucked balanced position and then standing.

The very same movement objective exists for hand-support skills in apparatus work. Figure 2.12 presents a comparison of two techniques used in executing a free backward hip circle on the uneven parallel bars. Although attaining a vertical handstand position is the final objective, the principle of peaking requires careful consideration of "how" this ultimate objective is achieved. In the first example, observe that the feet and legs transcend the vertical on the upswing phase of the backward hip circle. Since this action occurs *prior* to final completion of the skill, these body parts must ultimately *reverse* direction to attain the appropriate vertical handstand position. Such is not the case in the second example. Using a large amount of backward circular motion, the performer is able both to complete the entire hip circle and arrive at the desired handstand position without any of the various body parts having to transcend the vertical. Swinging up *to,* rather than *through,* the vertical not only eliminates unnecessary adjustments used in arriving at the handstand position but also affords the performer additional time so critical to maximum execution of the sequentially related skills.

Nearly all gymnastic enthusiasts have at least some understanding of how to speed up and slow down rotation while in the air. Even the very first attempt at performing a somersault in tumbling, for example, makes the gymnast well aware that tucked or compressed body shapes rotate much easier and quicker than extended or elongated body shapes. Although very important, this level of understanding is sufficient only during initial learning. It tells the performer little in terms of how to maximize the rotational aspects of the skill.

FIGURE 2.12. A comparison of two techniques used in executing a free backward hip circle to the handstand on uneven parallel bars: (1) poor peaking; (2) good peaking.

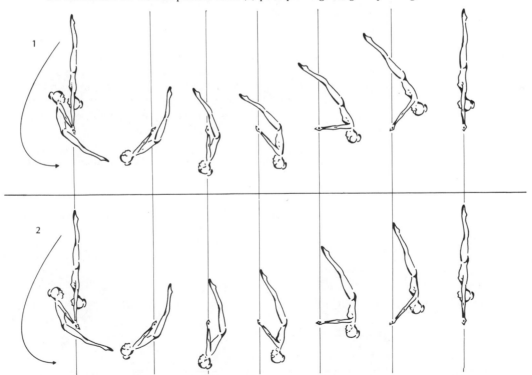

Consider the comparison of a tucked backward somersault presented in figure 2.13. Assume that both performances result from identical approach techniques in the preparatory Round-off–Backward Handspring phase. In the first example, the rotation appears to be diluted or spread throughout a majority of the airborne trajectory. Although the body is somewhat compressed (shortened radius of rotation) to ensure that the gymnast can rotate easier (increased angular velocity) and therefore complete the somersault, the "timing" of this movement sequence is neither exacting nor accentuated.

While it must be emphasized that rotation occurs continuously throughout the entire airborne phase of any somersault, proper application of the peaking principle renders the illusion that the performer is capable of initiating, executing, and completing the entire rotation during the apex of the skill. Because the gymnast in the second example assumes a fully elongated body shape (large radius of rotation) during major portions of both the ascent and descent phases, there is little apparent backward rotation (small angular velocity). *Yet during the apex phase of the skill,* observe that the instantaneous change to a fully compressed or tucked body shape greatly increases the speed of rotation. This "timely" shortening of the body's radius of rotation causes a majority of the somersault to occur at the very "peak" of the skill rather than having it spread throughout the entire trajectory. The ultimate objective in terms of further refining the skill is, of course, *to contain the greatest percentage of the somersaulting action within the smallest portion of the apex phase!*

It is important to emphasize that all gymnast skills can be reduced or described in terms of these four basic movement principles: *amplitude, segmentation, closure, and peaking.* Their central purpose provides a conceptual framework for refining all movement technique and, as such, has universal application to the broad spectrum of gymnastic skills. In this way, the *process* of skill refinement becomes characterized by an *ongoing evaluation* of the maximum execution potentials for virtually every movement pattern. Such an approach not only enhances performance quality based upon the presently conceived skill models but also ensures that these models will continuously evolve into ever more "ideal" models!

FIGURE 2.13. A comparison of two techniques used in executing a tucked backward somersault: (1) poor peaking; (2) good peaking.

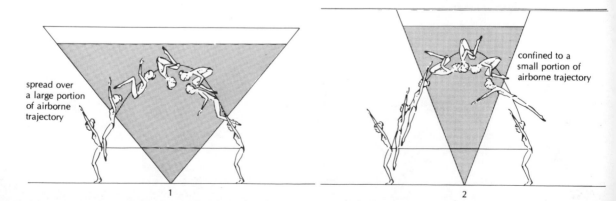

spread over
a large portion
of airborne
trajectory

confined to a
small portion of
airborne trajectory

1   2

3
The Mechanics of Swing

Diane Ellingson, University of Utah, Salt Lake City, Utah. Photo by Paul Jackson.

From a mechanical standpoint, "swing" is essentially a form of rotary (angular) motion. It can be defined as the circular movement of an object about some axial line in a fashion such that all parts of the object travel through the same angle, in the same direction, in the same amount of time. This line, often referred to as the axis of rotation, always lies at right angles to the object's plane of motion.[1]

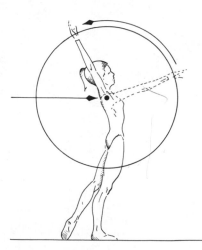

FIGURE 3.1. An example of internal swing occurring at the shoulder joint.

The human anatomy, with its numerous joints and segments, can be thought of as an articulated system of swinging levers which circle about one another in coordinated sequence to produce a desired movement. Yet, to qualify as swing, the movement need not necessarily be complex. Any joint motion of one body segment about another can be considered an elementary form of swing. Notice in figure 3.1 how the shoulder joint serves as the axis of rotation for swinging the arm above the head. Because this type of rotary motion occurs *within* the physical limits of the body, it is called "internal swing."

[1]James G. Hay, *The Biomechanics of Sports Techniques* (Englewood Cliffs, N.J.: Prentice-Hall, 1973), p. 12.

20

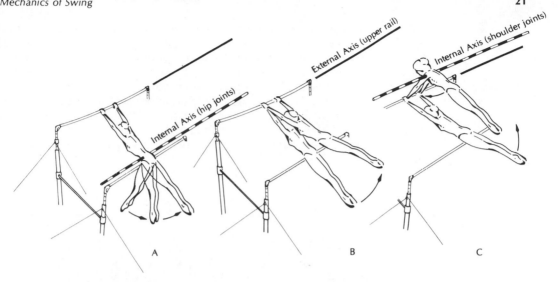

FIGURE 3.2. An example of the interrelationship between internal and external swing in executing a belly whip uprise on the uneven parallel bars.

In the performance of many uneven parallel bar skills, the gymnast is often required to undergo a somewhat different form of swing. It is different in that the axis of rotation lies *outside* rather than within the body's physical limits. As shown in figure 3.2, the upper rail of the apparatus serves as an external axis of rotation for executing a Belly Whip Uprise. Whenever the entire body unit is attached to and circles about a fixed axis, the realized movement is termed "external swing."

It is both interesting and important to understand that a close interrelationship exists between these two fundamental types of swing. In the Belly Whip Uprise sequence, for example, observe how the internal rotary motions, first of the legs about the hip joints and then the trunk about the shoulder joints, are used to direct and control the extent of the total body motion (external swing) about the upper bar. The timely interplay of these rotary motions, together with proper utilization of the elastic properties inherent in the bar rails themselves, collectively determine the quality of this and, in fact, all "swing-oriented" skills. In this light, it would be helpful to consider carefully how to take maximum advantage of these variables as well as to understand how to establish the most appropriate trajectory of those "airborne" skills that are initiated from swing mechanics, i.e., release-regrasp skills and dismounts.

3.1 INTERNAL SWING

It is a well-known fact that, although force may be present without motion, motion can never be realized without sufficient force. In addition, the greater the amount of force applied, the greater will be its resulting effect. Consequently, to produce a desired internal swinging motion, an appropriate amount of muscular force must be exerted by one body part on another. Whenever such an action occurs, an equal reaction occurs *simultaneously* in the exact opposite direction. Consider the first example presented in figure 3.3 and assume that the performer is free from all outside influences. In swinging from a piked to an extended body shape, notice that as the legs and feet move in one direction (clockwise action), the head and trunk simultaneously move in the exact opposite direction (counterclockwise reaction). Since the amount of mass above and below the hip joints is comparatively similar, the *observed effect* of the applied force is motion in *both* directions.

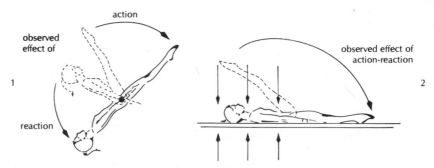

FIGURE 3.3. Example No. 1: The observed effect of action-reaction when the performer is free from all outside influences. Example No. 2: The observed effect of action-reaction when the performer is in contact with the mat.

The very same movement principle can again be demonstrated in the second example and yet the *observed effect* of the applied force is decidedly different. In this instance, the performer's upper body remains in contact with the ground while the lower body is free to swing about the hip joints. The force exerted through the upper body and against the enormous mass of the earth is not, to say the least, of a sufficient magnitude to produce motion in this direction! As a result, the net effect of the applied force is received by the freely swinging lower half of the performer's body with motion being observed in *one* direction only—the clockwise rotation of the legs and feet.

Once an internal swinging motion has been developed in one body part, its momentum can then be transferred into other body parts. Take, for example, the basic "kip action" sequence pictured in figure 3.4 and assume that the central objective is to proceed from position A to position E in a most effective way. Notice that the hip joint angle is fully closed (deep pike) in the initial illustration. This body shape is most advantageous in that it provides for the greatest potential distance through which force can be applied. In order to insure a large quantity of internal swinging motion, the hip joints are then forcibly extended throughout their range to a point just above the surface of the mat (illustration B). The idea here is to generate the fastest possible swing so that a proportionately greater quantity of motion can ultimately be transferred into the upper body. Just prior to contacting the mat, the rapid motion of the legs and feet is quickly and abruptly *stopped*

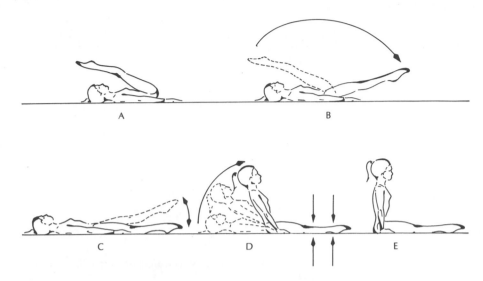

A   B

C   D   E

FIGURE 3.4. An example of how "transfer of momentum" is used to execute a basic "kip action" sequence.

(illustration C). This instantaneous stopping action of the lower body's motion results in a portion of its momentum being transferred into the upper body (illustration D). Consequently, the performer is able to capitalize upon such change of motion and arrive in the desired upright sitting position (illustration E).

Looking closely at this "kip action" sequence provides insight not only in terms of what transfer of momentum actually involves but more importantly in terms of how to maximize its effect. In skills of this nature, the aspiring gymnastic student is often given fragmented coaching suggestions such as "extend vigorously at the hips," or in more mundane terms, "kick harder with your legs and feet." Yet the wise coach becomes well aware that it is not simply a matter of how hard one kicks. *Rather, it is a matter of how "quickly" one stops how hard one kicks!* Herein lies the hidden component to attaining effective momentum transfer for this as well as *all* power-oriented gymnastic skills.

Careful study reveals that even complex movements can be viewed as an integrated series of individual momentum transfers which occur in a specific sequential pattern (kinetic chain)[2] to produce a desired outcome. Figure 3.5 compares a mechanical model with a practical skill model to demonstrate this concept. Just as each successive link in the chain unfolds to allow the momentum of the turning sprocket wheel to ultimately be transferred into the entire assembly (sprocket wheel *plus* chain), so too does the gymnast undergo a similar set of motion transfers in executing a Hecht Dismount from the uneven parallel bars. The initial illustration in example no. 2 represents the action occurring during the backward hip circle (wrap phase)

[2]John W. Northrip, Gene A. Logan, and Wayne C. McKinney, *Biomechanical Analysis of Sport* (Dubuque, Iowa: Wm. C. Brown, 1974), p. 199.

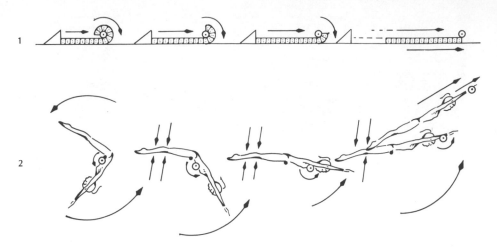

FIGURE 3.5. Progressive momentum transfers occurring in: (1) mechanical model; (2) practical skill model.

of the skill. Notice how the body is deeply piked about the bar with the legs and feet forming a straight-line segment and the arms, head and trunk forming a slightly curved or "hollowed" segment. To attain a maximum quantity of internal swing, the performer literally unwinds from this hollowed upper body shape in a timely sequential fashion such that the actual initiation of hip joint extension serves as the cue to begin rapidly opening the entire upper body. (Note that the turning sprocket wheel has also been inserted into this example to magnify the mechanics of how the upper body progressively unfolds). As each successive internal swinging motion builds upon the immediately preceding motion, a sort of "kinetic chain" is established. Such a coordinated series of momentum transfers allow the performer to summate an optimal amount of force at a particular moment and in a particular direction. In this case, greater "Hecht action" off of the bar would be the end product.

3.2 EXTERNAL SWING

In its most elementary form, the mechanics of external swing are quite similar to that of any circular swinging motion. As depicted in figure 3.6, circular motion of the body speeds up (acceleration) throughout the entire descent phase, with the greatest velocity being attained at the exact bottom of the swing. Just as the continuous downward pull of gravity is responsible for this increase in velocity during the descent, so too is it equally responsible for the corresponding decrease in velocity (deceleration) during the ascent. (Immediately prior to arriving at the apex of the ascent swing, this decrease in velocity becomes evermore apparent. The performer experiences a feeling of relative weightlessness which serves to facilitate execution of the forthcoming movement.)

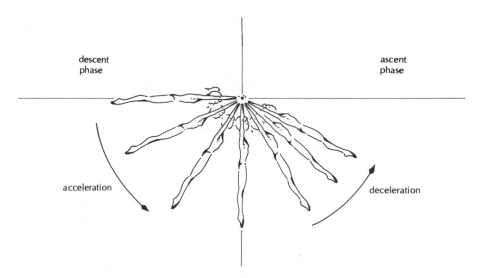

FIGURE 3.6. Basic external swing about the upper rail of the uneven parallel bars.

It must be pointed out, however, that the amount of external swing realized in the ascent phase is always somewhat less than in the descent phase. This is because friction, created mainly by the interaction of the hands circling about the axis of rotation as well as by air resistance, reduces the amount of upswing that otherwise (in a friction-free state) might have been attained. In spite of this relative difference in swing amplitude between the descent and ascent, there exists an important relationship: *The greater the amplitude in the descent phase, the greater the potential for increased amplitude in the resulting ascent phase.* This relationship holds particular implication for all skills characterized by external swing in that much of what happens to maximize skill execution is directly dependent upon the nature of the *descent phase*. To a large extent, the degree of refinement for any swinging skill inevitably reverts back to the amount of swing amplitude that the performer can *effectively achieve and control* in the descent phase. Ideally, *the gymnast should attempt to utilize a maximum controllable amplitude in the descent swing* (of every skill) *so as to have a correspondingly maximum amount of potential amplitude to work with during the ascent phase.*

There are two important mechanical factors which serve to regulate (and ultimately maximize) descent swing amplitude. The first, and perhaps most obvious, variable deals with the *starting height* of the swing. As shown by the comparative illustrations presented in figure 3.7, the performer in the second example initiates the "mount phase" of the glide kip from a region of *higher* location (relative to the bar) than does the performer in the first example. A higher starting position means that the gymnast can cover greater distance (more amplitude) in the descent phase. This is a distinct advantage in that it allows gravity to act upon (accelerate) the body for a longer duration of time. Consequently, a greater quantity of motion can be made available to maximize amplitude in the oncoming ascent phase.

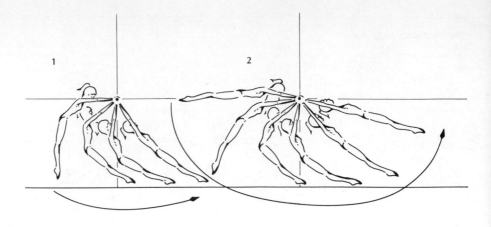

FIGURE 3.7. The effect of "starting height" on external swing amplitude in performing the glide phase of a kip on the uneven parallel bars: (1) low starting height; (2) high starting height.

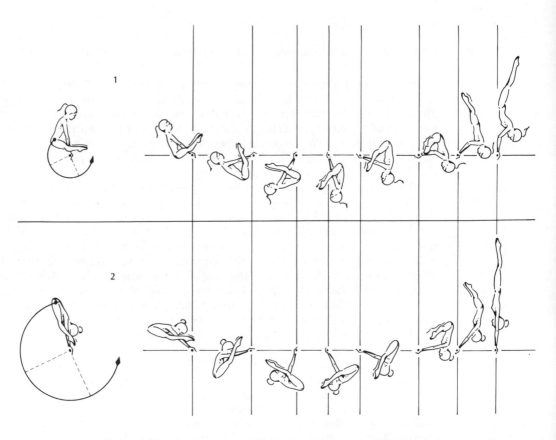

FIGURE 3.8. The effect of radius distance on external swing amplitude in performing a Stalder on the uneven parallel bars: (1) short radius of rotation; (2) long radius of rotation.

A second and equally important consideration for maximizing descent swing amplitude is *distance,* i.e., the distance between the body's mass center (located at or near the performer's waist) and the axis of rotation (bar). This distance, commonly referred to as the swing's *radius of rotation,* should be as great as is mechanically possible throughout the entire descent phase of virtually every skill. Compare, for example, the effect of a long versus short radius of rotation in executing a Stalder on the uneven parallel bars (fig. 3.8). Because the second performer has assumed a fully compressed body shape and is positioned comparatively further away from the bar, the effective radius of rotation is significantly greater than in the first performer. (In fact, if the performer in the second example had wanted to maximize descent swing amplitude to its fullest extent, she could have assumed a fully extended body shape throughout a large portion of the descent phase before executing the actual "Stalder-in-action.") This increased radius distance not only provides for greater descent swing amplitude but also insures a smoother transition into the ascent phase. As can be observed, the end product is a greater quantity of motion being made available to execute the upswing portion of the Stalder effectively.

Whenever the radius distance of a rotating body is *decreased,* its turning velocity is proportionately and simultaneously *increased,* and vice versa. For example, if greater turning velocity (speed of rotation) is desired at a particular point in the swing, the performer need only alter her body shape (within the context of the given skill) such that the radius distance is appropriately shortened. Conversely, by increasing this radius distance, the turning speed is proportionately decreased. Although understanding this aspect of rotary motion is particularly useful in terms of controlling and regulating any external swinging movement, its true effectiveness is inevitably dependent upon the quantity of rotary motion (angular momentum) *already existing* in the swing. *This is why attaining a maximum starting height and positioning the body's mass center as far as possible away from the bar during the descent phase of every swing are critical prerequisites to full utilization of the angular momentum principle.* Consequently it is not simply a matter of knowing when and how much to shorten or lengthen one's radius of rotation. (This aspect is comparatively easy to master.) Rather, it is a matter of understanding how to *first obtain a maximum appropriate quantity of rotary motion!*

3.3 BOTTOMING EFFECT OF THE SWING

The "bottoming effect" refers to the interaction between the performer and her axis of rotation (bar rail) during external swinging movements. Because the uneven parallel bar rail has considerable elastic properties, it tends to bend (deflect) according to the amount and direction of the force applied. As this applied force (deflection) terminates, the rail quickly returns to its original shape (restitution). This bending of the rail, similar to cocking an archer's bow, can be most advantageous, allowing the performer to "store energy" momentarily for the use in the very next movement.

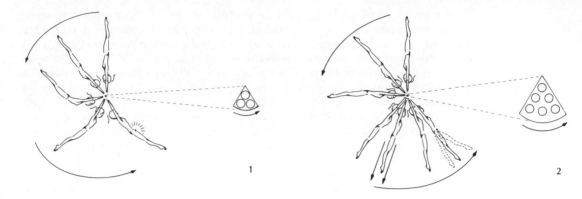

FIGURE 3.9. Comparative effects of two descent phase techniques on rail action in basic long-hand swinging: (1) shallow bottoming effect; (2) deep bottoming effect.

When circling about an external axis, the concurrent *internal* swinging motions of the body determine, to a large extent, the intensity and pattern of rail action. This rail action, in turn, significantly influences the ultimate outcome of the skill. To demonstrate the concept, compare the effects of two different descent phase techniques on rail action in basic long-hang swinging (fig. 3.9). In the first example, the performer has allowed the forces inherent in the descent swing to distort her relaxed body shape to a point such that a large overarch is created. Not only does such a body shape fail to produce a sufficient intensity and duration of rail action throughout the bottom of the swing (see exploded view of rail action), but it also makes proper body alignment and tension most difficult to attain relative to the upcoming movement, i.e., the wrap sequence. By comparison, the performer in the second example has utilized the necessary muscular control to maintain a slightly hollowed, yet elongated, body shape throughout the majority of the descent phase. *Immediately prior* to arriving at the exact bottom of the swing, notice how this slightly hollowed body shape is *released* into a fully extended shape. This "unloading action" causes the rail to be depressed more deeply and for a comparatively longer period of time than

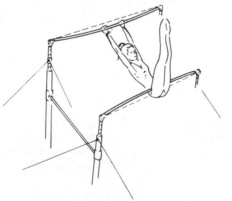

FIGURE 3.10. A fore-shortened view of how proper scooping or wrapping action can effectively deflect (cock) both bar rails.

in the first example. As the legs (uppermost thighs) make contact with and wrap (scoop) around the lower bar, both rails are drawn in toward each other (cocked as in an archer's bow), ready to release their stored energy for the upcoming movement sequence (see fig. 3.10).

To further develop this "bottoming effect" concept, figure 3.11 reveals the continuing role of rail action in executing a sequentially related skill series from the preceding long-hang swing example, i.e., into a wrap and Hecht Dismount. Just as the legs complete their backward "scoop" about the lower bar, the hands simultaneously release the upper bar (illustration A) and the performer immediately begins to unfold rapidly from the fully piked (deeply hollowed) body shape. It is this vigorous, timely opening from a deeply hollowed to a fully extended body shape that drives the hips forcefully against the lower rail, thereby maintaining much of the energy already stored there (illustrations B, C, and D). Notice too how the backward circling motion of the *total body unit* serves to "dynamically stablize"[3] the legs and feet in an approximate horizontal position relative to the ground.

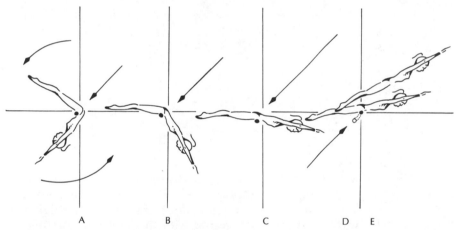

FIGURE 3.11. The role of rail action in facilitating external amplitude in a Hecht Dismount from the uneven parallel bars.

Upon attaining a straight-line shape, the rapid extension motion is instantaneously *stopped,* causing its for-upward momentum to be transferred into the entire body. At that precise moment, the energy stored in the deflected rail is released, providing additional "lift" (hence greater external amplitude) to the skill's airborne phase (illustrations D and E).

It can be safely stated that rail action plays a critical part in virtually every category of external swinging movement. There are, for example, numerous skills and variations that stem from the "uprise phase" of a basic belly whip on the uneven parallel bars. *Yet the degree of success inherent in any of these sequentially related skills invariably reverts back to the quality and quantity of motion initially generated in the uprise phase itself.* Figure 3.12 depicts how a gymnast can employ rail action (deflection-restitution) to provide that additional

[3]Ibid., p. 163.

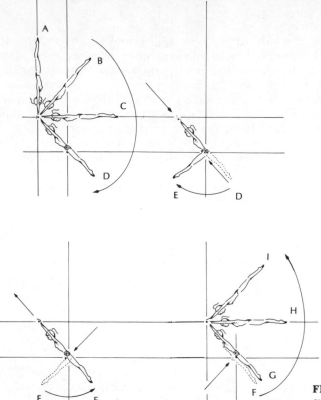

FIGURE 3.12. Effect of rail action in facilitating external amplitude in a belly whip uprise on the uneven parallel bars.

measure of lift so essential to the maximum execution of any oncoming skill. In illustration D, notice that the performer makes contact with the lower rail at a point *just below* the hip joint axis (uppermost thighs). The body's downward momentum, together with the continual circling motion of the legs wrapping about the bar, causes both rails to be pulled in (deflected) toward each other. Rail tension is greatest when the body dynamically attains a fully piked or hollowed shape (illustration E). As the hip joints immediately begin to vigorously extend (kickback action), simultaneously the upper rail also begins to uncock from its previously deflected shape, thereby enhancing this extension action by pulling the entire body unit in its direction. Because of the vigorous hip joint extension (illustrations E and F), deflection in the lower rail is maintained until the body attains its straightline shape. At that precise moment (the instantaneous "stopping" of hip joint extension), the energy stored in the deflected lower rail is forcefully unleashed (restitution), further enhancing the back-upward momentum already present in the total body unit (illustrations F and G). Increased amplitude in the uprise phase becomes the net effect (illustrations G, H, and I). Remember, it is the "degree" of this timely rail action (deflection-restitution) that determines, to a large extent, the "degree" of external amplitude one can expect to achieve from this, as well as any sequentially related, "uprise" skill.

30

3.4 THE TANGENT RELEASE

Force always acts in the precise *straight-line direction* in which it has been applied. Consequently, any resulting body motion tends to travel the same straight-line path and will speed up (accelerate) at a rate proportional to the magnitude of that force. The only factor which can alter this state of affairs is the introduction of one or more additional forces. If, for example, a force is applied in a direction exactly opposite to the already existing motion, the body will begin to slow down (decelerate). The relationship between the magnitude and angle of the force applied determines whether or not a body will move and, if so, at what rate of speed and in which direction.

All external swinging movements are the result of such a series of forces simultaneously interacting with one another, causing the body to undergo a continuous change in direction. The Straddle-Cut Dismount on the uneven parallel bars pictured in figure 3.13 illustrates the nature of this effect. Although gravity is the force which tends to accelerate the performer in a straight-line downward direction, the body's mass center is obviously *not* traveling straight downward. Rather, it is seen as continuously changing direction (circling) relative to its axis of rotation. This is due to the mutual force relationship that exists between the gymnast and the uneven parallel bar rail. Since the body is attached to the apparatus (a *fixed* axis of rotation), it would be impossible for it to travel a straight-line path. However, the tendency to do just that causes the performer to exert a force *away from* (centrifugal or center-fleeing) the bar rail. At the very same time, the rail (being fixed) exerts a force on the performer which is both equal in magnitude and opposite in direction, i.e., *toward* the center of rotation (centripetal or center-seeking). Because these directly opposing forces are of equal magnitude, they would seem to cancel out one another's effect. Yet this is not the case. For the "center-fleeing" force cannot possibly move the apparatus which is firmly attached to the colossal mass of the earth! However, the "center-seeking" force can and does possess sufficient magnitude

FIGURE 3.13. Straddle-Cut Dismount.

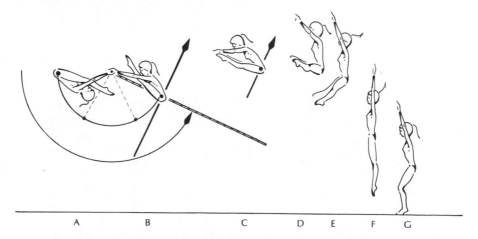

to produce a continuous change in direction for the comparatively lighter mass of the performer. The observed effect of these combined forces is a circular swinging motion of the total body unit about the bar (illustrations A and B).

Yet notice that as soon as the performer "releases" the bar rail, this centrifugal-centripetal force relationship also ceases to exist and the body is projected along a straight-line path at an angle perpendicular to its radius of rotation (illustrations B and C). Once airborne, the body's mass center travels a perfectly regular curved path (illustrations C through G).

Because a performer's mass center *always* exits from any external swinging movement at a precise 90 degree angle to the body radius (*tangent to the swing),* this "tangent-release" principle can be usefully applied to all release grip skills. Whether it is a hand-release skill (such as a kip from the low bar to the high bar) or a body-release skill (such as a Hecht), the desired direction of each airborne phase must be clearly understood so that the appropriate release can be timed accordingly. Or to put it another way, *proper timing of a skill's "release phase" is a critical variable to success in all airborne movements that are sequentially related to external swing.*

4
The Mechanics of Impact

Candice Greene, Acadiana Gymnastic Club, Lafayette, Louisiana.

The term "impact" generally refers to the interaction of one object colliding with another and the effects of such a collision. These objects usually possess some degree of elasticity, a property which causes them to return to their original shape (restitution) once they have been deformed (compression) as a result of collision. All other factors being equal, the "quickness" with which their original shapes are restored determines, to a large extent, the net effect of their interaction.

Although the human body is considered to be quasirigid rather than elastic in nature, many concepts dealing with elastic properties can still be usefully applied. Just as elastic objects (such as vaulting boards and uneven parallel bar rails), upon being compressed, develop a potential energy for immediate use, so too does the human body, with its internal muscular network, possess a similar potential to develop and expend an instantaneous working energy. This is particularly apparent in the impact phases associated with virtually every airborne gymnastic movement. In fact, impacts such as those seen in takeoffs, arm-repulsions, and even landings significantly influence the potential quality of skilled execution. With this in mind, let us take a closer look at the mechanics involved in each of these critical impact phases.

4.1 LEG IMPACT AND TAKEOFF

The effectiveness of the takeoff sets the uppermost limits of what the gymnast can hope to attain during the airborne phase of any skill. It is during this time that the path (trajectory) followed by the performer's center of gravity and the amount of rotary motion (angular momentum) available for skill execution are *irrevocably established*. Since both of these variables are without question of utmost importance to success, we need to consider carefully the nature and function of each as well as to examine their inherent interrelationship to the takeoff.

Trajectory

The particular shape taken by any given trajectory is the direct result of the horizontal and vertical velocities derived from impact. Referring back to the tumbling sequence presented in figure 2.2, for example, we can see that the handspring trajectory has a relatively low, long shape (emphasizing horizontal amplitude) while the shape of the somersault trajectory is proportionately higher and shorter (emphasizing vertical amplitude). This is because a comparatively greater amount of *horizontal* motion was used to execute the backward handspring phase whereas for the somersault phase a comparatively greater amount of *vertical* motion was used.

Although a number of gymnastic movements, such as the postflight phases in vaulting, emphasize the attainment of maximum amplitude in both directions, *vertical amplitude* or "lift" invariably serves as an essential component to success in the majority of airborne skills. The fact that it would be impossible to attain any amount of horizontal amplitude without some vertical lift substantiates this observation. And too, the continuous downward pull of gravity makes the attainment of vertical amplitude noticeably more difficult to achieve than its counterpart, horizontal amplitude. For these reasons lift is generally considered to be the more essential factor of the two and as such deserves particular attention.

To develop the concept, let us look at the techniques used in executing a Layout Dive Forward Roll, particularly in terms of maximizing lift (fig. 4.1). Now the degree to which maximum lift can be realized depends upon both the conditions existing at the precise moment of *impact* as well as what occurs immediately following impact, i.e., the actual *takeoff*.

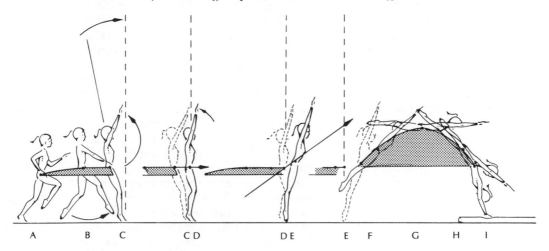

FIGURE 4.1. A conceptual model depicting the mechanics of the hurdle (A, B, and C), the impact (C and D), the takeoff (D and E) and the airborne (E, F, G, H, and I) phases respectively for executing a layout dive forward roll.

The nature of the run and *particularly the hurdle* sets the stage for the conditions at impact. From a practical viewpoint, it is obvious to most coaches that the smaller the amount of downward motion the gymnast experiences as a result of the hurdle, the greater will be the resulting potential to maximize upward vertical lift. What is perhaps not quite so obvious centers on how to accomplish this and why it works. If the hurdle phase can be executed so that the body's mass center (1) continues moving forward very quickly (with maximum controlled horizontal velocity), (2) has a low flight pattern (flat trajectory) and thus (3) remains airborne for a very brief time period, the performer will have little, if any, downward motion to contend with during actual impact. This technique of execution is particularly advantageous in that, rather than having to waste effort arresting unwarranted downward motion, the performer can instead use most, if not all, available vertical force to generate that much needed lift.

During the airborne phase of the hurdle (illustration B) notice how the total body unit rotates backward to a point such that at touchdown an observable backward-leaning body angle relative to the vertical is formed (illustration C). Observe that as the feet make contact with the ground at a point well in front of the body's mass center, the trunk and arms are simultaneously lifting in a for-upward direction. (It appears, though, that many gymnasts, as well as coaches and teachers, are as familiar with leg action at touchdown as they are unfamiliar with trunk and arm actions. Quite often does one observe the aspiring performer, although blocking correctly with the legs, bent over at the hips and shoulders to such a degree that the trunk and arms are leaning in a for-downward direction. Such compensatory techniques tend to reduce the potential effect of the impact as well as to inhibit correct body shape and position once airborne.)

This "blocking action" (angle of input)[1] seen in illustration C is essential to proper execution of the skill because it allows the performer just enough time in which to summate her available forces in a precise vertical direction. Practically speaking, selecting the appropriate amount of body lean (blocking angle) should be determined by the speed and direction of the performer's mass center at touchdown. In other words, the faster, flatter, and shorter the hurdle trajectory, the greater must be the angle of block if maximum lift is to be achieved. The ideal situation, of course, would be to attain a maximum controlled horizontal speed during the hurdle phase and then to block quickly in accordance with that speed.

Notice that the force of impact causes the hip, knee, and ankle joints momentarily to undergo slight flexion (illustrations C and D). Although this would appear to contribute to *downward* motion, such an effect is essentially canceled out because at the very same moment the total body unit is also rocking *for-upward* about the feet which are firmly in contact with the mat.[2] In addition, the simultaneous "stopping action" of the *for-upward* arm throw further offsets any potential downward motion that otherwise might have occurred. As a result, the performer's center of mass travels *horizontally forward* during actual impact (and for-upward during the takeoff).

Throughout this entire movement sequence, it is important to emphasize proper body tension and carriage. Standing as tall as is mechanically possible, particularly during impact, maximizes the height of the performer's

---

[1] Angle of input, often referred to as "blocking" or "blocking action," can be defined as the angle formed by the total body unit (center of mass) relative to the vertical at the exact moment the performer makes contact with the ground and/or apparatus.

[2] James G. Hay, "The Biomechanics of Vaulting" (Paper presented to the United States Gymnastic Federation Coaches' Congress, St. Louis, Mo., November 1973).

mass center at the start and thus adds to the potential vertical distance that can ultimately be achieved from the ground. In addition, greater downward force can be exerted against the ground when the ankle, knee, and hip joints are in a *slightly* flexed, rather than a deeply flexed, position.

Assuming that all of these impact conditions have been favorably met, the amount of lift that the performer can ultimately hope to attain now becomes dependent upon the effectiveness of takeoff itself. More specifically, it depends upon the magnitude of vertical forces which can be exerted against the ground and the length of time during which these forces act.[3] This quantity, commonly known as "vertical impulse," is mathematically expressed as the product of *vertical force* and *time.* With this concept in mind, it would seem reasonable to suggest that a performer attempting to improve vertical lift from the ground should strive to maximize both of these variables. However, such is not the case: Studies specific to jumping activities have repeatedly shown that a shorter takeoff time results in a comparatively greater lift from the ground.

Although at first glance this may appear to be an unsolvable paradox, there exists at least one logical explanation for such a perplexing discovery. Assuming no differences in conditions at impact, suppose that as the time of force application decreased, the magnitude of vertical forces were to increase and at a *proportionately greater rate* than the time decreased. Such a relationship would account for why a greater net "vertical impulse" can be attained with a shorter takeoff time.

Precisely how the human body accomplishes this feat is not fully understood. From the practical point of view, though, it is more important for us to understand (1) that upon impact a *brief* and *very slight* flexion of the legs followed by an *instantaneous* and most forceful extension results in a short takeoff time and (2) a short takeoff time produces greater lift than a longer one (illustrations D, E, and F).

Angular Momentum

In gymnastics angular momentum can be defined as the "quantity" of rotary motion made available for skill execution. Although it can be, and very often is, transferred from one body part to another, the actual initiation of effective rotary motion inevitably originates from the ground (and/or apparatus which is firmly attached to the ground). Depending upon the nature of the skill in question, the performer can employ one or a combination of the following techniques to generate the appropriate quantity of rotary motion:

Rotating One Body Part about Another

There are a number of skills which require that the gymnast initiate rotation without the benefit of any preceding motion. For example, consider the takeoff mechanics presented in figure 4.2 for executing a *standing*

[3]Ibid.

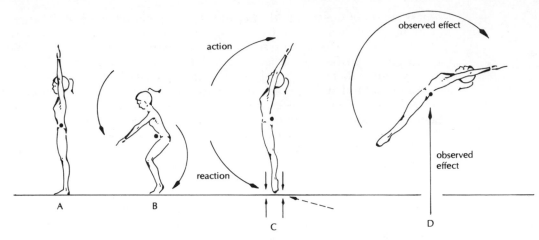

FIGURE 4.2. The mechanics for initiating a standing backward somersault.

backward somersault. Starting from a fully extended standing position (illustration A), the performer briefly assumes a semisquat stance (illustration B), and then immediately and forcefully pushes the legs against the ground while simultaneously extending (throwing) into a slightly arched body shape (illustration C). In addition to providing the necessary lift, the forceful leg drive against the ground establishes a momentarily fixed or anchored base of support about which the freely swinging upper half of the body can rotate. Just prior to becoming airborne, the rapid throwing motion of the upper body is abruptly stopped, causing its backward momentum to be transferred into the total body unit (illustrations C and D).

As previously brought out in chapter 3's section on "Internal Swing," the *speed* and *amplitude* of the throw establishes the quantity of rotary motion available for transfer while the *quickness* with which this throwing action can be *stopped* determines, to a large extent, the net effectiveness of this transfer. The observed effects of these action-reaction inputs against the ground are vertical lift of the total body unit and backward rotation about the performer's center of mass (illustration D).

Direction of Takeoff

Direction of takeoff is another important variable affecting the potential quantity of available rotary motion. As depicted in figure 4.3, if the performer takes off in a direction *opposite to* the intended rotation, i.e., traveling *forward* while attempting to rotate *backward* as in a "gainer" somersault (example no. 1), a portion of the backward rotary motion must be spent accomplishing this change in direction, i.e., forward travel. This is why rotation becomes increasingly more difficult to generate in all gainer-oriented skills. On the other hand, if the takeoff is in the *same* direction as the intended rotation, i.e., traveling *backward* while also attempting to rotate *backward* as in a backward handspring (example no. 2), a portion of the potential vertical lift can be traded for increased rotation.

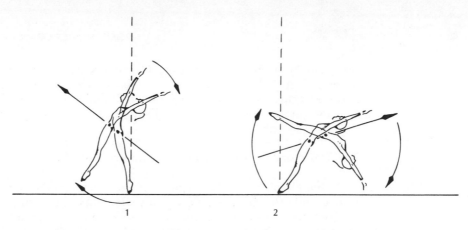

FIGURE 4.3. The effect of takeoff direction on resulting rotary motion: (1) gainer somersault takeoff tends to inhibit rotary motion; (2) backward handspring takeoff tends to facilitate rotary motion.

Because virtually every advanced tumbling and vaulting skill requires an extremely large amount of angular momentum, the position the body's mass center (relative to the vertical) at *actual* takeoff is observed to be leaning (and thus traveling) in the *very same direction* as the intended rotation. When performing multiple twist-somersault skills, for example, the wise gymnast is always willing to "trade off" a small portion of potential vertical lift in order to reap tremendous dividends in rotation.

Converting Horizontal to Rotary Motion

Imagine what would happen to a tennis ball after being vertically dropped from an auto traveling horizontally forward at a *relatively slow rate of speed*. After striking the ground, the ball would not only begin to rebound in a for-upward direction, but also it would possess a given quantity of rotary motion or spin. This "spinning effect" occurs because at impact a portion of the ball's horizontal motion is transferred or converted into rotary motion. If, by comparison, the auto (and thus the ball) were traveling horizontally forward at a *very high rate* of speed, a significantly greater amount of spin would have then been imparted on the ball. Consequently, the amount of *horizontal motion* that an object possesses at impact has a direct bearing on the amount of resulting rotary motion observed in the rebound.

Angular momentum, or the quantity of rotary motion that must be generated to execute advanced vaulting and tumbling skills successfully, is also regulated, to a large extent, by the amount of horizontal motion existing at impact. It is precisely at this moment that the performer's mass center begins to rotate about the feet which are firmly anchored to the ground. All other factors remaining the same, *the greater the realized horizontal velocity during impact, the greater will be the resulting quantity of rotary motion at take-off.*

To further conceptualize this principle, consider the rather large amount of angular momentum that would be required to execute a double somersault from a traditional tumbling sequence. By generating as much horizontal motion as mechanically possible during the round-off and backward handspring phases, a comparatively greater quantity of that much needed backward rotary motion can then be made available to successfully accomplish the double somersault. This is precisely why the trajectories of these lead-in skills, i.e., round-off and backward handspring, should be *low* to the ground, occur over a *brief* time interval, and most important of all, be *very fast* in terms of horizontal velocity.

The Trajectory-Angular Momentum Interrelationship

Although direction and speed of the performer's mass center during impact and takeoff have a significant effect on the potential outcome of any performance, they constitute only part of the total picture. The gymnast must also clearly understand exactly what she is trying to accomplish—the particular mechanical objectives characteristic to the skill's airborne phase. In addition to having an accurate conceptual model of the desired trajectory pattern (lift and travel) and knowing how much angular momentum (rotation) is required, the performer must also be critically aware of the effect that each of these variables has upon the others. For "lift," "travel," and "rotation" are *mutually interdependent* and, as such, cannot truly be separated in the practical sense. *Any change in one necessarily requires some adjustment or change in the others—trading off a portion of one for greater emphasis in another.*

In this light, the following principles are provided not only to demonstrate the close interrelationship of these three variables but also to serve as general guidelines for appropriate skill execution:

1. As "lift" is further and further emphasized, the amount of resulting "travel" progressively decreases while the difficulty in attaining "rotation" progressively increases.
2. As "rotation" is further and further emphasized, the amount of resulting "travel" progressively decreases while the difficulty in attaining "lift" progressively increases.

A clear understanding of the nature and function of each skill's airborne phase is essential to the appropriate utilization of these variables. For example, the performer must know whether the motion emphasis should center on attaining vertical velocity as in a somersault (*lift* with rotation), horizontal velocity as in a backward handspring (*travel* with rotation), or perhaps a combination of all three as in the postflight phases of elite-level vaulting (*lift, travel,* and *rotation*).

Championship skill execution becomes essentially a matter of learning how to strike the most effective balance or proportion of emphasis for each variable. In every case, however, *the wise performer should attempt to maximize the most essential variable(s) to the fullest extent while still retaining just enough takeoff force to accomplish successfully the variable(s) of lesser importance.*

Whatever the requirements or objectives for the skill in question, the *angle of input* (also referred to earlier as blocking) determines, to a large extent, the relative emphasis that can be placed on each of these variables. Compare, for example, the three angles of input presented in figure 4.4 and assume that all other conditions specific to the "lead-in skill" (round-off) remain the

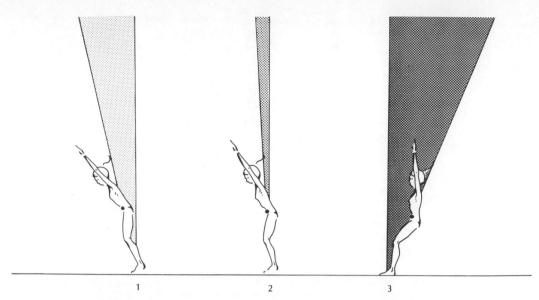

FIGURE 4.4. A comparison of three different angles of input for executing specific airborne skills: (1) emphasizes "lift" as in a backward somersault; (2) emphasizes "rotation" as in a double backward somersault; (3) emphasizes "travel" as in a backward handspring.

same. Because the performer in the first example has a rather noticeable angle of block in a direction *opposite* to the intended motion, the opportunity to emphasize maximum lift at the expense of some rotation and travel is made available, i.e., the single backward somersault. As the blocking angle becomes smaller and smaller approaching zero degrees as seen in example no. 2, the opportunity to generate maximum rotation at the expense of some lift and travel is made available, i.e., the double backward somersault. In the third example, the angle of block is in the *very same direction* as the intended rotation. Consequently, the opportunity to emphasize travel at the expense of some rotation and lift becomes apparent, i.e., the backward handspring. The *angle of input* then can be considered a major source, a causative factor, a controllable variable that significantly influences the "nature of the trade-off" between trajectory and angular momentum.

It is a common belief that, because skills differ in terms of their objectives, different mechanical techniques must therefore be employed. Actually, this should not be the case at all. Unlike many sport activities, most gymnastic movements are both symmetrical in pattern and simplistic in nature. Many aspects of these skills can and should be categorized and taught according to their technical similarities. In fact, *a vast majority of the observed differences exist more in terms of degree and not kind.*

Using the very same skills presented in figure 4.4, figure 4.5 attempts to illustrate this finding by simply rotating the reference planes to a point such that the angles of input (body lean) at touchdown are identical for each example. *Since no change has been made in terms of relative body shape, a striking degree of mechanical similarity becomes quite obvious!* This is but one of innumerable examples that can be cited in support of the premise that basic movement principles have relevant, universal application to gymnastic technique and as such serve to clarify correct technical execution for a broad category of skills.

41

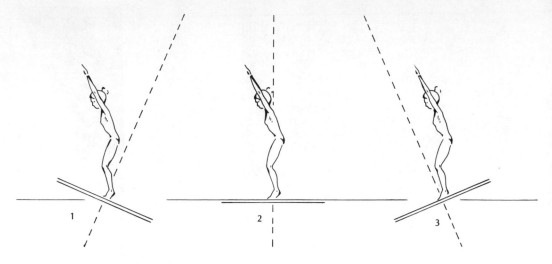

FIGURE 4.5. Rotating the reference planes in order to equalize angles of input reveals that a high degree of mechanical similarity exists among all leg impact skills.

4.2 ARM IMPACT AND REPULSION

Most vaulting and tumbling sequences can be described as a precisely timed series of impacts alternating from feet to hands to feet in a reciprocal fashion. Although the hands, arms, and shoulder girdle serve as the body's prime repulsion (push-off) mechanisms during the inverted support phase of any skill, *the actual principles involved to generate continued lift, travel and rotation are identical to those presented for leg-oriented takeoffs.*

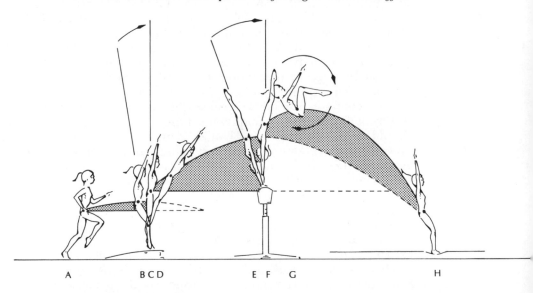

FIGURE 4.6. Critical phases of a handspring front somersault vault: run and hurdle (A and B); impact and takeoff (B and C); preflight (C, D, and E); impact and repulsion (E and F); postflight (F and G); landing (H).

For example, figure 4.6 includes two critical contact phases used in executing a Handspring Forward Somersault Vault, foot contact with the board (takeoff) and then hand contact with the horse (repulsion). Just as the run, hurdle, and leg impact set the stage for the *takeoff*, so too do they, as well as the takeoff, preflight and arm impact, collectively set the stage for the *repulsion*. In light of this "sequential cumulative effect," let us consider the following mechanical similarities:

Lift

Since attaining the appropriate amount of vertical velocity is an important objective of the arm-repulsion phase, the performer should attempt to make hand contact with the horse *as soon as possible* during the ascent phase of the preflight trajectory. For this to be possible, the preflight trajectory must possess the very same characteristics as its preceding hurdle trajectory— *short, flat,* and *very fast.* Such a consideration minimizes the downward motion at impact and allows for a quicker and more forceful "repulsion" from the horse, i.e., increased vertical lift.

Travel

Because of the comparatively large amount of rotary motion required in the skill's postflight phase, i.e., executing a one and one-half forward somersault from hands to feet, the performer is confronted with having to trade off a portion of horizontal velocity for increased rotation *while at the same time* retaining a sufficient quantity (of horizontal motion) to insure an appropriate travel distance away from the horse. And it is only by means of a *short, flat,* and *very fast* hurdle, an instantaneous takeoff, and a *short, flat,* and *very fast* preflight that enough horizontal motion can be made available to accomplish both postflight objectives—increasing rotary potential for the somersault while still retaining sufficient horizontal travel.

Rotation

In addtion to the aforementioned trade-off there are additional factors that can serve to insure that much needed rotation. For example (when using a *short, flat, very fast* hurdle trajectory), if the angle of input is comparatively small, minimizing backward body lean at actual touchdown on the board, the potential forward rotary motion of the takeoff is greatly increased. (This set of affairs also helps to establish a preflight trajectory which is very similar to that of the hurdle trajectory, *short, flat,* and *very fast.*) Consequently, the performer can capitalize upon the forward rotary motion already existing in the preflight phase by exerting a forceful for-downward push against the horse during actual hand contact. This type of "repulsion action" causes the freely swinging lower half of the body to rotate quickly about the momentarily anchored upper half and thus further increases rotary potential in the upcoming postflight phase.

Since vaulting can be conceived of as a "specialized" form of tumbling, the mechanics for both activities are essentially the same. However, vaulting is somewhat unique in that, to execute any given skill sequence, the performer must travel from a region of lower location (floor), to a region of higher location (board), to one of even higher location (horse). This "staircase effect" can be readily observed in figure 4.6 by comparing the hurdle, preflight and postflight trajectories. Just as a person attempting to run up a flight of stairs with great speed would want to make contact with each oncoming step *while the body motion is still rising upward* (from the preceding step), so too should the vaulter attempt to make contact with the *board* as well as the *horse* while the body motion is still in the ascent phase of the respective input trajectories—hurdle trajectory to the board and preflight trajectory to the horse. In this way a greater potential quantity of motion can be made available and thus be appropriately apportioned among lift, travel, and rotation to meet the particular demands of each skill's postflight phase.

Although the arms play an important role during impact and repulsion for any skill having an inverted support phase, their ultimate effectiveness inevitably depends upon the performer's ability to take maximum advantage of concomitant *shoulder girdle action*, i.e., the "lifting effect" on the total body unit as a result of forcefully *elevating* the shoulder girdle either *prior to* or *at* actual contact.[4] Precise timing of this motion is contingent upon the nature of the skill's input trajectory. For example:

1. *If the skill is of such a nature that arm impact cannot be realized until the initial descent phase of the input trajectory (as in a backward handspring), the shoulder girdle should be fully elevated prior to hand contact.* This insures contact with the ground at the earliest possible moment and thus minimizes much of the unwarranted downward motion. The fully elevated shoulder girdle, upon sustaining the existing impact force, momentarily undergoes slight depression and then instantly returns (ballistic kickback action)[5] to full elevation, driving the total body unit vertically into the air.

2. *If the skill is of such a nature that arm impact can be realized during the ascent phase of the input trajectory (as in the Handspring Forward Somersault Vault), the shoulder girdle should be vigorously moving (exploding) into a position of full elevation just as the hands are making contact with the horse.* This timely action provides further lifting impetus to an already rising body, i.e., the "staircase effect."

This lifting effect as a result of vigorous *elevation* should always be accompanied by *another rather subtle shoulder girdle motion*. The exact direction of this motion is dependent upon whether the performer intends to rotate forward or backward as a result of the repulsion phase. In this light, the following

[4]For a more complete description of shoulder girdle motions, refer to chapter 6: "The Common Denominator—The Handstand."

[5]Gene A. Logan and Wayne C. McKinney, *Anatomic Kinesiology* (Dubuque, Iowa: Wm. C. Brown Co., 1977), pp. 72–73.

arm-repulsion guidelines can also be applied to all tumbling-oriented skills regardless of event:

1. *In backward rotating skills.* As the lifting effect of elevation is occurring, *the shoulder girdle should be simultaneously rounding or hollowing forward about the trunk.*[6] This concomitant shoulder girdle action during the repulsion phase serves to *facilitate backward rotary motion* of the total body unit.

2. *In forward rotating skills.* As the lifting effect of elevation is occurring, *the shoulder girdle should simultaneously be flattening or retracting backward about the trunk.* This concomitant shoulder girdle action during the repulsion phase serves to *facilitate forward rotary motion* of the total body unit.

4.3 LEG IMPACT AND LANDING

The basic objective of the landing is to effectively reduce the performer's linear and rotary motions to zero immediately upon contacting the ground. Although this may appear to be a relatively simple task to master, in practice it is often very difficult. This is because the very nature of any landing phase is contingent upon all that has gone before it. Seemingly minor inaccuracies in the earlier phases of the skill can often add up to produce major difficulties in the landing. In fact, consistently poor control in the landing phase of a skill is usually a very good indication that the real problem lies with one or more of its preceding phases, the takeoff phase and/or repulsion phase.

To demonstrate this point, compare the techniques employed in landing a Tsukahara Vault presented in figure 4.7. Because of insufficient height and/or rotation in the postflight phase, the performer in the first example fails to attain a fully extended body shape prior to actual touchdown. Contacting the ground with an already noticeably compressed body shape reduces the potential distance through which the performer's stopping (landing) force can be applied. By comparison, the postflight phase depicted in the second example possesses both sufficient height and rotation. Consequently, the body is able to assume a *fully extended or elongated shape prior to actual touchdown.* In effect, the performer is seen stretching or reaching for the ground in an attempt to make foot contact as early as possible with the mat. Besides significantly improving the leverage advantage in the legs, this increase in distance through which the stopping force can be applied (compare the size of the vertical arrows shown at touchdown for each example) requires less muscular effort on the part of the gymnast. As a result, greater and more effective *control* of the landing phase can be realized.

Just as the angle of input directly influences the characteristics of the

---

[6]For a more complete description of shoulder girdle motions, refer to chapter 6: "The Common Denominator—The Handstand."

FIGURE 4.7. A comparison of two techniques used in executing and landing a Tsukahara Vault: (1) poor technique; (2) good technique.

takeoff, so too does the *angle of touchdown*[7] significantly affect the quality or control of the landing. Selecting the most appropriate landing angle depends, as before, on the nature of the skill and how well it has been executed. Assuming, though, that the movement sequence is properly executed, the following guidelines should prove helpful:

1. If the skill is of such a nature that the body is both *traveling and rotating in the very same direction,* the performer should attempt to counteract this momentum by touching down with the body *leaning in the exact opposite direction.* (See example no. 1 in fig. 4.8.) The actual amount of this body lean or angle of touchdown is directly related to the combined quantity of horizontal and rotary motions existing in the skill's airborne phase: Greater quantities of horizontal and rotary motions present in the airborne phase require a correspondingly greater angle of touchdown in the landing phase.
2. If the skill is of such a nature that the body is *traveling in one direction* while *rotating in the exact opposite direction,* little or no body lean at touchdown is necessary. (See example no. 2 in fig. 4.8.) This is because these directly opposing motions tend, for the most part, to cancel out one another. Consequently, a more upright body position can be attained at touchdown.

Landings are essentially the reciprocal of takeoffs. From a conceptual viewpoint, they are what the backward roll is to the forward roll. The very same techniques are employed. Only the sequence is reversed! The implication here is to view skills as much as possible according to their *technical similarities.* In this way, new and/or seemingly complex movement patterns become little more than a reapplication of already mastered skill sequences.

---

[7]Angle of touchdown refers to the angle formed by the body's center of gravity relative to the vertical at the exact moment the performer makes landing contact with the ground.

46

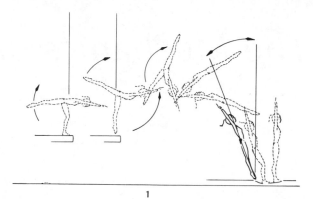

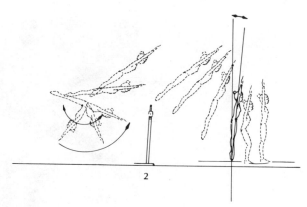

FIGURE 4.8. Two examples of touchdown angles for improving landing control: (1) Forward Aerial Dismount from the balance beam; (2) Hecht Dismount from the uneven parallel bars.

5
The Mechanics of Rotation

Diane Ellingson, University of Utah, Salt Lake City, Utah. Photo by Paul Jackson.

In most airborne gymnastic skills, one or a combination of rotary motions can be observed which occur about one or a combination of the following three traditional axes of rotation depicted in figure 5.1: no. 1, rotation about the body's *lateral axis* as in forward and backward somersaulting skills; no. 2, rotation about the body's *anterior-posterior axis* as in sideward somersaulting skills; and no. 3, rotation about the body's *longitudinal axis* as in twisting skills. These three axial lines are always at right angles to and intersect with one another at a conceptual point known as the body's center of mass (center of gravity).

Certain airborne skills are characterized *solely* by a *somersaulting* component, for example, the Hecht Backward Somersault Dismount from the uneven parallel bars (fig. 9.29), while others are characterized *solely* by a *twisting* component, i.e., the Tour Jeté on the balance beam (fig. 8.12). These uniaxial rotations may appear comparatively easy to understand as well as to control. However, when *combined* (somersaulting with twisting) within the context of a single skill, as in a Full Twisting Backward Somersault in Floor Exercise (fig. 7.42), the situation undoubtedly becomes a bit more complex. In this light, let us first examine the rotational mechanics specific to *somersaulting* and then specific to *twisting* before attempting to combine these concepts under the single heading of Biaxial Rotation.

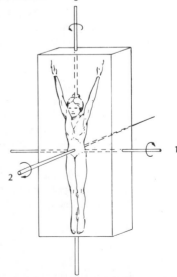

FIGURE 5.1. The three traditional axes about which the body can rotate: (1) lateral axis; (2) anterior-posterior axis; (3) longitudinal axis.

49

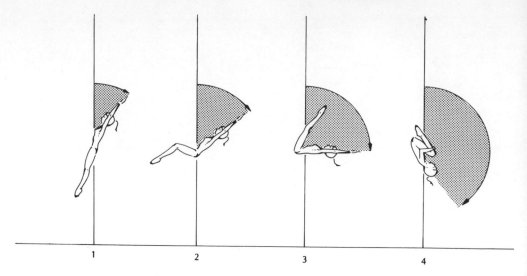

FIGURE 5.2. The effect of body shape upon ease of rotation: (1) fully extended shape; (2) pucked shape; (3) piked shape; (4) tucked shape.

5.1 SOMERSAULT ROTATION

In the preceding chapter it was discovered that the shape of the airborne trajectory as well as the angular momentum a body possesses are both determined at takeoff.[1] Since even the best performers are capable of remaining airborne only for a very brief period of time, it would be reasonable to state from a practical viewpoint that:

All effective somersaulting rotation must be initiated from the ground (or the apparatus which is firmly attached to the ground).

Once initiated, somersaulting rotation continues to occur throughout the entire airborne phase of the trajectory.

With trajectory and angular momentum already established at takeoff, *the only aspect of the skill which the performer can control to some extent is the rate of rotation.* This is accomplished by changing or altering the shape of the body once airborne. As revealed in figure 5.2, the *ease* with which a body can rotate is directly related to its *shape.* Because of its comparatively shorter radius, the "pucked" body shape (no. 2) has proportionately lesser reluctance to rotate than does the fully extended body shape. If the body were further compressed into a piked, or better yet "fully tucked," shape, the tendency to rotate would be significantly increased. This measure of control available to the performer during the airborne phase of any somersaulting skill can be expressed in terms of the following relationships:

Progressively shortening the turning radius of an airborne body—going from a fully extended to a fully tucked body shape—serves to increase proportionately its rate of rotation.

[1] For a more complete discussion on how to regulate trajectory and angular momentum, refer to chapter 4: "The Mechanics of Impact."

Conversely, progressively lengthening the turning radius proportionately decreases a body's rate of rotation.

The *timing* as well as the *quickness* with which a performer alters body shape also have a direct bearing on the resulting degree of somersault rotation that can be realized during the airborne phase of any skill. In executing a double backward somersault, for example, the sooner and the faster a performer can change from the fully extended to a fully tucked body shape once airborne, the earlier and quicker will the required somersault rotation be completed. These considerations help the performer complete a majority of the somersault rotation during the apex of the airborne trajectory. (See the principle of peaking discussed in chapter 2.)

It must be remembered, however, that in terms of the "quantity" of rotary motion, nothing appreciably can be gained or lost once airborne. Rather it is basically a matter of *trading off* radius length for increased rotational rate (or vice versa) according to the dictates of the skill. This concept of "robbing Peter to pay Paul," so to speak, further emphasizes the critical importance of the takeoff. For:

Neither the amount, timing, nor quickness of shortening the body's turning radius can adequately increase the performer's rotational rate without already having generated a sufficient quantity of rotary motion (angular momentum) prior to becoming airborne.

5.2 TWISTING ROTATION

Twisting can be described as rotation about the longitudinal axis of the body. Because it is "rotational" in nature, the principles involved are essentially the same as those presented for somersaulting. Looking at the basic Jump Full Twist depicted in figure 5.3 demonstrates this concept. In initiating the actual jump (illustrations A and B), notice how the legs and feet push against the ground *(action)* in a downward-clockwise direction. (See top view of illustration B.) During the very same moment, the ground pushes against the performer's body *(simultaneous reaction)* with a force that is both equal in magnitude and opposite in direction, i.e., an upward-counterclockwise direction. Obviously, the amount of force that the gymnast exerts against the ground is not nearly sufficient to move the tremendous weight of the earth! However, the earth's reaction force possesses sufficient magnitude to produce motion in the performer's body. The "observed effects" of these action-reaction forces are *lift* and *rotation* (about the performer's long axis) in a direction exactly opposite to the force exerted by the performer (illustrations C, D, and E).

This example also provides insight into a number of important guidelines that can be applied to most twisting skills that are initiated from the ground (or any fixed base of support). Notice that:

1. Except for the feet which are firmly anchored to the ground during the initiation or push phase (illustrations A and B), all parts of the body collectively move in the intended direction of the twist.

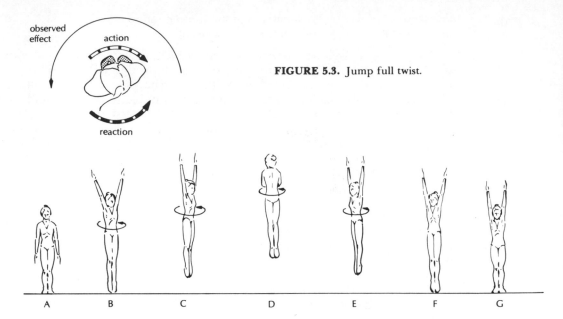

FIGURE 5.3. Jump full twist.

2. In order to render the illusion of initiating the twist after becoming airborne, observe how the arms, upon being thrown overhead, are also spread slightly in a lateral direction (illustrations A and B).

3. Although scarcely discernible, the twist is actually initiated as the total body unit is extending into a straight-line shape (illustrations A and B).

4. Upon becoming airborne (illustrations B and C), the performer is fully and completely extended with the twisting rotation occurring throughout the long axis of the straight-line body shape.

5. Upon obtaining full and complete body extension, the arms are quickly swung in the direction of the twist, pulled inward, and placed symmetrically across the chest. This timely decrease in the body's turning radius serves to increase its rate of twist (illustrations C and D).

6. As far as possible throughout the entire airborne phase, all parts of the body rotate about the performer's long axis in the same direction, through the same angle, and in the same amount of time. In other words, the twist is *uniform,* encompassing as much of the total body unit as possible (illustrations C, D, and E).

7. In order to render the illusion of terminating and/or completing the twist while still airborne, observe how the arms, upon being returned overhead, are again spread slightly in a lateral direction (illustrations E and F).

8. Raising the arms above the head in a lateral direction serves to increase the body's turning radius. This timely change in shape decreases the body's twisting rate, thus facilitating a more "squared" and controlled landing (illustrations F and G).

5.3 BIAXIAL ROTATION

The term "biaxial rotation" refers to any combination of somersaulting and twisting occurring simultaneously within the context of a given skill. To be successful, an appropriate balance must be struck between these two rotary components. However, it must be remembered that *somersaulting is generally considered the more difficult rotation to achieve* and as such should always receive priority emphasis. There are at least three reasonable justifications which support this premise: (1) Because of the approximate rectangular shape of the fully extended human body (fig. 5.1), it takes a significantly greater effort to generate rotation about either the lateral or anterior-posterior axes (somersaulting) than about the longitudinal axis (twisting); (2) Many advanced skills (particularly those characterized by twisting into and/or out of double somersaults) require that the gymnast, after becoming airborne, "borrow" or convert a portion of the somersault rotation for twist initiation; (3) It should be obvious that, regardless of the twisting requirements, a sufficient quantity of somersault rotation must first be initiated from the ground (or apparatus) so as to insure a potentially safe landing.

Although the underlying mechanical principles remain the same, (one or a combination of) the following three basic techniques can be used for initiating a twist rotation while somersaulting: On-Ground Twist Initiation; Body Extension Twist Initiation; and Unequal Radius Twist Initiation. Depending upon the objectives and conditions characteristic to the given skill, there are inherent advantages as well as disadvantages specific to each technique. With this in mind, let us carefully examine the nature and function of each.

On-Ground Twist Initiation

While *all effective somersault rotation must be initiated from the ground* (or apparatus), *twist rotations do not necessarily have to be ground-initiated.* However, in using this particular technique, the actual initiation of the twist does occur prior to becoming airborne. In fact, the "twisting" observed in most single somersault skills is usually initiated from the ground and in much the same fashion as was presented for the basic Jump Full Twist (fig. 5.3).

Compare, for example, the techniques used for initiating, executing, and completing a Backward Somersault with a Full Twist, a Double Full Twist and a Triple Full Twist respectively (fig. 5.4). Notice that observed positions and body shape changes are, for the most part, identical throughout the entire movement sequence in each of these skills. A review of the section on Twisting Rotation will reveal that the eight basic guidelines presented have been strictly adhered to in every case.

Because the airborne phases of both the double full and triple full twisting backward somersaults require comparatively greater quantities of twisting momentum, the observed amount of "on-ground twist initiation" must necessarily be proportionately greater. (This is accomplished *during takeoff* by quickly raising the arms above the head using a slightly more lateral position, i.e., wider arm-set, while at the same time more forcefully rotating the total body unit about its longitudinal axis.) In addition, increasing the

53

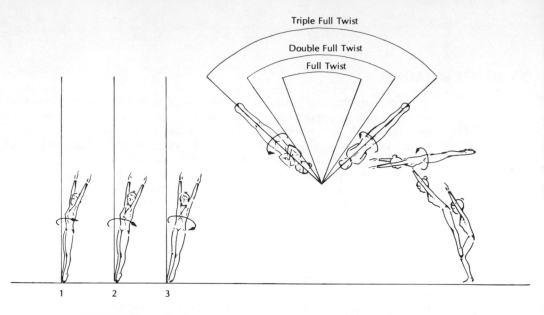

FIGURE 5.4. A comparison of the takeoff and wrap phases of a twisting backward somersault: (1) full; (2) double full; (3) triple full.

number of twist rotations requires that the actual *"wrap phase"* be executed a bit *sooner* (once airborne) and be maintained for a comparatively *longer duration of time.* It must be emphasized, however, that *these supposed differences are essentially a matter of degree and not kind.*

There are several *advantages* specific to initiating twist rotation from the ground and among these are:

1. Because the ground (and/or apparatus—both inherently *stable* bases of support) serves as the point of initiation, this technique holds the *greatest potential for generating a maximum quantity of twisting rotation.* Consequently, it is generally considered to be the most effective technique for initiating twist rotations in single somersault skills and *particularly in multiple twisting single somersault skills.*

2. Since the actual "wrap phase" serves to decrease simultaneously the body's turning radius about its longitudinal and lateral axes, the *potential* for executing a majority of both the somersaulting and the twisting rotations within the smallest portion of the trajectory's apex becomes readily apparent. *Appropriately timed,* this technique renders the illusion that the entire twist has been initiated, executed, and completed exclusively during the airborne phase of the skill, i.e., "peaking" the skill.

3. The bilateral position of the arms during the wrap phase of the skill serves to maintain body shape symmetry as well as to render the illusion of having attained greater height (vertical lift) from the ground.

On-Ground Twist Initiation also imposes some functional limitations and *disadvantages.* Among these are:

54

1. This technique is not appropriate for that category of double somer-saulting skills requiring that the *twist not be initiated* (much less exe-cuted) *until the performer* has fully completed the first somersault and *is entering into the second somersault,* as in the Back In–Full Out (Backward Somersault In and a Full Twisting Backward Somersault Out).

2. There is a tendency to overinitiate the twist by extending into an unduly arched (rather than a straight-line) body shape at takeoff with the upper body twisted about the lower body to such a point that the symmetry, as well as the efficiency, of the movement is lost. Re-member, twist initiation falls into that category of movements which employ *highly unobvious changes in body shape.* (See the principle of closure presented in chapter 2.)

3. Because all rotating bodies seek the axis of least resistance, there is a natural tendency (particularly in single somersault skills having multi-ple twist rotations) for a straight-line body shape to somersault slightly off of top dead center. In other words, rather than the somersault rotating through a plane of motion that is directly perpendicular to the ground, there is a slight but observable cant or tilt to the rotation. Many gymnasts refer to this phenomenon as "pancaking" the somersault.

Body Extension Twist Initiation

Contrary to the belief of many teachers and coaches, *twisting rotation can be,* and very often is, *initiated after the performer becomes airborne.* As depicted in the postflight phase of the Yamashita Full Twist Vault (fig. 5.5), the actual potential *to initiate effective twisting* is made possible by vigorously extending one-half of the body about the other half during a time in which the total body unit possesses a large quantity of somersault rotation. This rapid extension motion creates a sort of internal *gyroscopic effect* similar to that of a rotating bicycle wheel (illustration C). The performer has a "dynamically" stable base (in the somersaulting plane) from which a twist rotation can be initiated. Although hardly discernible, notice that the *twist* through the longitudinal axis of the upper body *is initiated off of the dynamically stable lower body* and that it occurs *slightly prior to attaining complete hip joint extension.*

As the total body unit forms a straight-line shape, its twisting radius decreases and the resulting rate of twist rotation correspondingly increases (illustrations C, D, and E).

It should be pointed out that airborne twisting can also be initiated *without* the benefit of any already existing somersault rotation. A basic Swivel Hips on the Trampoline is a classical example. Since this movement sequence has *no* somersaulting component, the execution of the twist phase is accom-plished exclusively by extending the hips while initiating the twist off of the final aspect of this extension motion—seat drop to full body extension with one-half twist and returning to a seat drop. However, such instances are quite rare in the Olympic All-Around Events for Women. In fact, the vast majority of airborne gymnastic skills are characterized by considerable

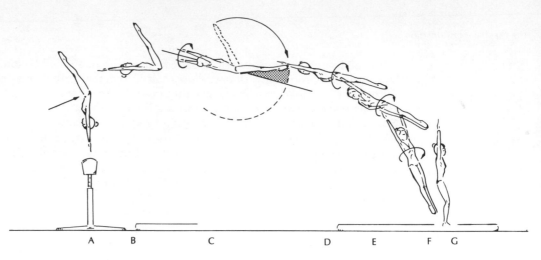

FIGURE 5.5. An example of the body extension twist technique used in executing a Yamashita full twist vault.

somersault rotation. This is particularly advantageous in that, *without suffi-cient somersault rotation to capitalize upon, the Body Extension Technique would, at best, be limited in capability to initiating one full twist* (360 degrees).

Advantages specific to the Body Extension Technique include:

1. Because the impetus for twist initiation for most skills is derived from two sources, i.e., the already existing somersault rotation and the body's internal swing rotation, this makes it particularly appropriate for *double somersaulting skills with the twist requirements confined to, and only to, the second somersault.* Typical examples would include the Backward Somersault In–Full Twisting Backward Somersault Out and the Backward Somersault In–Double Full Twisting Backward Somersault Out.

2. In addition, this technique can readily be *combined with the On-Ground Technique* for executing double somersaulting skills having *twist re-quirements in both somersaults.* More specifically, the On-Ground Tech-nique is used exclusively to initiate the twist component of the first somersault and the Body Extension Technique is then employed dur-ing the beginning of the second somersault to provide additional impetus for the successful completion of the skill's twist requirements. A Full Twisting Backward Somersault In–Full Twisting Backward Somersault Out is a typical example.

3. *When used exclusively,* this technique affords the performer the *option to initiate* (as well as to terminate) *the twist at any time* during the skill's airborne phase.

4. The actual *twist* can be *initiated by extending out of any compressed body shape*—tucked, piked, or pucked, *and can be executed in either a pucked or an extended body shape.*

Some of the *disadvantages* or trade-offs inherent in the Body Extension Technique are:

56

1. *Without sufficient somersault rotation,* it is virtually ineffective as a twist initiation technique for those skills requiring multiple twist rotations (greater than 360 degrees). This realization further substantiates the critical importance of the take-off.
2. Twisting with a pucked body shape results in a roll (or comparatively slower) type of twist action. However, this disadvantage is somewhat offset in that the performer can obtain visual contact with the ground earlier and for a longer duration of time.
3. Twisting with a fully extended body shape results in comparatively later (and thus shorter in duration) eye contact with the ground. Yet the realized twisting action is much quicker, i.e., peaking the twist.

The Backward Somersault In–Full Twisting Backward Somersault Out depicted in figure 5.6 attempts to acquire the best of both worlds—early and then continuous eye-ground contact while still being able to "peak" the full twist. Notice that, because the performer initially extends only to a pucked rather than a fully extended body shape (illustrations C, D, and E), the actual opening out of the tucked body shape can be early enough to maintain the already established visual contact with the ground (illustrations C and D). As the full twist is being initiated as well as executed, notice how the performer's head, although in alignment with the trunk, is always positioned so that *continual eye contact with the ground* can be maintained. Because the initial aspect (the first 90 degrees) of the twist is executed in a pucked body shape, it gives the appearance of being comparatively slow (illustrations E and F). However, as the legs and feet approach top dead center, they are vigorously extended (illustrations F and G). By increasing the body's somersaulting radius while simultaneously decreasing its twisting radius, this timely exten-

FIGURE 5.6. Backward somersault in–full twisting backward somersault out.

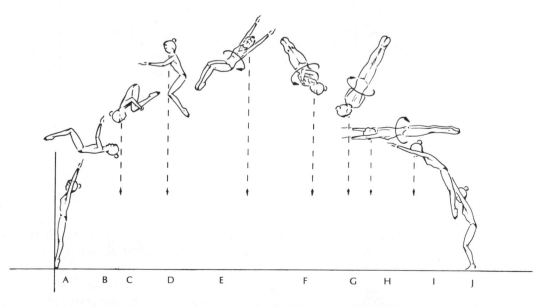

sion action allows the performer the opportunity to execute a majority of the remaining twist (270 degrees) within the smallest percentage of the second somersault's trajectory (illustrations F, G, and H). Consequently, in addition to early and then continuous eye-ground contact, the actual twist has been effectively "peaked."

Unequal Radius Twist Initiation

Another technique sometimes employed to initiate a twist rotation after the performer becomes airborne is the Unequal Radius Technique. Essentially, the gymnast borrows a small portion of the already existing somersault rotation and converts it into twisting rotation. As depicted in figure 5.7, this is accomplished by *altering the shape on one side of the somersaulting body so that an unequal radius of rotation is established.* Because only the right half of the somersaulting body's radius is shortened, it has a natural tendency to rotate faster than the left half. Yet since both halves are attached to one another, this is, of course, not possible. Consequently, this unequal tendency, or better said, this "unbalanced impetus" for increasing somersault rotation seeks the axis of least resistance—the body's longitudinal or twisting axis. As a result, a portion of the somersault rotation is converted into twisting rotation.

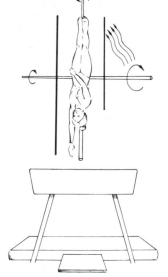

FIGURE 5.7. An example of the unequal twist initiation technique used in executing a handspring full twist vault.

The actual *direction of twist is determined by the relationship between direction of the somersault and which side of the body's radius is shortened.* The interaction between these two variables can be expressed according to the following principles:

1. If the *right side* of the body is shortened while executing a *forward somersaulting skill,* the direction of the resulting twist will be *to the performer's left.*
2. If the *right side* of the body is shortened while executing a *backward somersaulting skill,* the direction of the resulting *twist* will be *to the performer's right.*
3. If the *left side* of the body is shortened while executing a *forward somersaulting skill,* the direction of the resulting *twist* will be *to the performer's right.*
4. If the *left side* of the body is shortened while executing a *backward somersaulting skill,* the direction of the resulting *twist,* will be *to the performer's left.*

For example, in the above illustration (fig. 5.7), the gymnast (upon completing the "repulsion phase" of a handspring vault) is *somersaulting forward* and has *shortened* the turning *radius* on the *right side* of the body. Notice that the resulting *direction of the twist is,* in fact, to the performer's *left.* These four basic principles readily apply to all twisting skills which employ the Unequal Radius Technique.

Advantages specific to the Unequal Radius Technique include:

1. *When used either in conjunction with the On-Ground Technique or with the Body Extension Technique, it serves as a useful supplement* for that category of biaxial skills having minimal rotational requirements, i.e., single somersaults with no more than a one-half twist and half somersaults (such as dive rolls and postflight phases of handspring vaults) with no more than a full twist.
2. *When used exclusively,* this technique affords the performer the *option to initiate* (as well as to terminate) *the twist at any time* during the skill's airborne phase.
3. Since one arm remains overhead throughout the entire twisting phase, a *comparatively greater measure of control* is maintained *within the somersault component* of the skill. Such a characteristic helps to insure more favorable landing conditions.

There are several *disadvantages* or limitations to the Unequal Radius Technique and among these are:

1. *Without sufficient somersault rotation, it is virtually ineffective as a twist initiation technique for any skill.*
2. When used alone, it has limited practical value. Compared to the other two techniques, the *potential quantity of twist rotation that can be initiated is quite small* (360 degrees or less).
3. Since this technique renders a *very slow twist action,* it cannot be effectively "peaked."
4. Certain twisting movements, such as those seen in the preflight phase of most advanced vaulting skills, require that both hands make instan-

taneous contact with the apparatus *as soon as possible* after takeoff. (An example is the full twisting handspring "onto" the vaulting horse.) Because the full twist must be initiated, executed, and completed in such a brief period of time, it would be impractical (and perhaps even dangerous) to rely exclusively on the Unequal Radius Technique. *More often that not,* in these instances, *it must be used in conjunction with the On-Ground or the Body Extension Technique.*

The question often arises as to *which direction of twist should be chosen for executing which types of skills.* This appears to be a rather perplexing problem especially when individual differences of the gymnasts are taken into account. Although there may be some rather unique exceptions, it is generally a good idea to *learn how to twist in the very same direction* (be it to the left or to the right) *for both forward and backward somersaulting skills.* Such an approach insures greater transfer of learning as well as conceptual clarity to most twisting skills.

One time-tested and generally accepted procedure for determining a performer's natural or preferred twisting direction is to have her attempt the basic Jump Full Twist (fig. 5.3). *Once discovered, all twist-oriented airborne skills should be learned according to the gymnast's preferred twisting direction.*

Although not an airborne skill, the round-off in tumbling could be considered a possible exception to the rule. If feasible, it should be *executed opposite to* the performer's *established airborne twisting direction.* In so doing, a greater variety of biaxial skills can be executed "into" and "out of" the round-off.

6
The Common Denominator—
The Handstand

Kelly Curtis, Acadiana Gymnastic Club, Lafayette, Louisiana.

The very symbol of the sport, the handstand, is indeed one of the most important fundamental skills in gymnastics. Although it is often viewed only as an individual skill, the handstand is repeatedly seen on every event throughout every exercise in virtually every movement sequence. In fact, it serves as the basic foundation upon which the more advanced skills are built. Because of its universal application, the handstand must be fully understood and mastered by all aspiring gymnasts.

Traditionally, the handstand was conceived as a skill in which the gymnast merely assumed an inverted balanced position on the hands. Little attention was given to proper alignment of body shape. As seen in the first example of figure 6.1, it generally consisted of a two-segment arrangement with the arms forming the straight-line segment and the legs, trunk, and head jointly comprising the curved-line segment. For many years this type of body shape was steadfastly advocated by teachers and coaches alike. Holding the head up and arching the back were not only in keeping with supposedly proper technique but also were considered key teaching points for controlling one's balance.

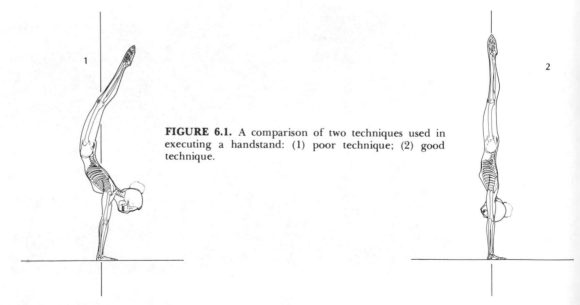

FIGURE 6.1. A comparison of two techniques used in executing a handstand: (1) poor technique; (2) good technique.

Aesthetically speaking, it cannot be denied that the natural flow of this curved-line segment about the straight-line segment holds an interesting appeal. Too, the arched back and the decreased shoulder angle can at least be partially justified from a functional viewpoint in that these shapes help to improve stability by positioning the total body mass slightly closer to the ground.

While these concepts are valid in and of themselves, they fail to pinpoint the ultimate objective of the handstand. It is not simply a question of attaining successful balance, rather it is a question of the *way* in which successful balance is attained. Besides having an aesthetic appeal, the body shape must directly relate to maximum technical execution in the broadest possible category of gymnastic skills. Such a realization inevitably leads the gymnast to search for a handstand technique that is truly the common denominator of gymnastic movement.

In this light, a second example is presented as a conceptual model for correct technique in performing a handstand. Notice that the entire body is very stretched, very straight, and very long. In fact, a straight line can be drawn through the body from hands to feet. The basic idea here is to align each of the body parts one on top of the other so that the performer's weight is positioned directly through the midline of the body and directly over the hands or base of support. Although this straight-line body position appears rather simple and straightforward to understand, success in the actual performance requires a great deal of practice with particular attention given to the proper alignment of each body part. However, once the technique is mastered, considerably less effort will be required to maintain such a position.

Experience has shown that effective learning of the handstand is best realized using a step-by-step approach. First and foremost, it is essential that the performer be physically able to assume a straight-line body position. This is often referred to as "body shape," the posture of the position so to speak. The second and final step in the learning sequence requires placing this aligned body shape or posture "on-balance." *Practice attaining a correctly aligned body shape first and then work on learning to balance.*

An excellent, proven method for practicing this one-segment body shape while not as yet having to deal with the balance phase is to hang from the high rail of the uneven parallel bars so that the body can be fully stretched without the feet being able to touch the ground. Besides having the opportunity to concentrate solely on correct body shape, this *Bar-Hang Method* shown in figure 6.2 also requires that many of the very same muscles be used in the very same way to line up each of the body parts just as in the actual handstand itself. In addition, the constant pull of gravity helps stretch and guide the total body to the desired straight-line shape.

Although performers generally find it quite easy to maintain straight arms, straight legs, and pointed toes, a close look at the "Bar Hang" method reveals that the following additional key areas require particular attention in terms of mastering the straight-line shape for the total body:

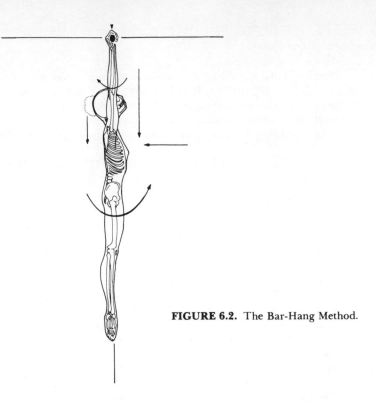

FIGURE 6.2. The Bar-Hang Method.

Arm-Trunk Angle Must Be Straight.

Performers often experience difficulty in raising the arms completely and directly over the trunk, which results in something less than a straight-line body shape. Rotating or turning the arms slightly inward (see the direction of the arrow in the illustration) helps to line up the arms in relation to the trunk. Success in this area also helps to align the head correctly, directly between the arms.

Head-Trunk Angle Must Be Straight.

Another common tendency of many performers is to arch the head backward at the neck rather than maintaining it in a neutral position (directly between the arms). A slight upward tilt of the head is suggested to help maintain visual contact between the hands without breaking the straight-line shape.

Shoulder Girdle Must Be Fully Elevated.

In order to attain a completely stretched position with the greatest distance possible between the hands and the feet, it is necessary to fully elevate the shoulder girdle. This raising of the shoulders as high as possible toward the ears is accomplished by pushing the total body as far as possible away from the bar (without actually letting go). Done properly, it feels as if the head and neck sink in between the shoulders. (Observe the illustrations in fig. 6.3 for a pictorial description of this action. Notice that elevating the shoulder girdle provides an additional length or stretch to the body.)

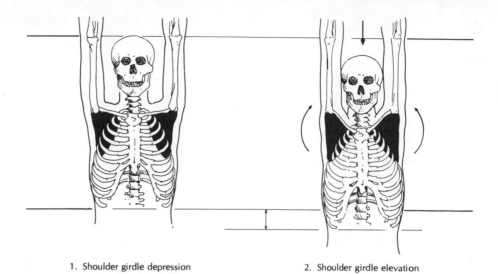

1. Shoulder girdle depression   2. Shoulder girdle elevation

FIGURE 6.3. A comparison of shoulder girdle positions: (1) poor technique; (2) good technique.

Hip or Pelvic Girdle Must Be Straight.

Because there is usually a slight curvature or arch in the lower back, the pelvic girdle must be rotated under (see direction of arrows in fig. 6.2). This is accomplished by contracting the stomach (abdominal) muscles so that the lower half of the body falls in line with the upper half. This action, often called posterior pelvic girdle rotation, not only helps to create a stretched, straight posture, but also it stabilizes the center of the body—a most important factor in virtually every advanced skill.

Although learning correct body shape for a handstand requires a great deal of practice with special emphasis on the above four areas, keep in mind that *mastery of this phase makes the second phase, placing the body on balance,* much easier to learn.

At this point, we need to look at the illustrations presented in figure 6.4 for an understanding of how to maintain correct body shape while proceeding from an upright standing position to the handstand balance position. Notice that, except for the support leg, the straight-line body shape is maintained throughout the entire movement sequence. The flexing or bending about the hip joint of the support leg is the only observable body shape change. In the first illustration, the performer starts with arms held high over the head and proceeds through a front scale (illustration 2) to a needle scale position (illustration 3). At this point, the body weight is shifted onto and over the hands so that the support leg can be raised overhead to line up with the lead leg (illustration 4). As the legs come together forming a straight-line shape of the total body, the performer's entire weight is now centered directly between the hands (illustration 5). This handstand position has the exact same body shape as seen in the Bar-Hang method presented in figure 6.2 except, of course, that the total body unit has been turned upside down.

1   2   3   4   5

FIGURE 6.4. A Step-Up to a Handstand.

Careful attention to straight-line body shape while proceeding to the handstand will help provide much greater consistency and carry over into many other gymnastic movements. Learning such basic skills as hand-springs, walkovers, cartwheels, and round-offs, to mention just a few, will depend upon the performer's ability to properly step up (kick) to a correct handstand position. So it makes sense to take the time and effort to master this technique in its entirety.

The final phase in the learning sequence, *balance*, is basically a matter of maintaining the weight of the body directly over and between the hands. Figure 6.5 shows a top view of the performer's hand placement on the floor. It is interesting to observe that this hand placement provides a rectangular base of support. This means that, because a rectangular base is compara-tively wide from side to side and narrow from front to back, the greatest difficulty in controlling balance will be in the forward and backward direc-tions. There is usually little or no difficulty in controlling balance in the side-to-side directions. With this basic concept in mind, we must focus our attention on learning to control even the slightest tendency of the body to

FIGURE 6.5. Top view of correct hand placement for executing a handstand.

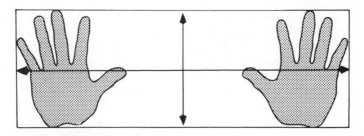

sway in the forward and backward directions while balancing in a handstand position.

Balancing on the hands is essentially the same as balancing on the feet. To demonstrate the point, consider the front scale position presented in illustration 2 of figure 6.4. If the performer were to "hold" this front scale position on balance, what would be used to control and maintain the weight of the body over the support foot? Even the very first attempt will reveal that in order to balance effectively, *the ankle joint on the support leg side is the single most important "control center" for balance.* The muscles about this ankle are constantly working to check and countercheck the body weight so that balance is maintained over the support foot. The very same principle can be applied to balancing on the hands. Since handstand balancing requires that the hands serve as the base of support, the *wrist joints then become the major "control centers" which constantly work to maintain the body on balance!*

Figure 6.6 compares two common techniques used in balancing a handstand. The first type seen in no. 1 is generally referred to as *counterbalancing* and requires the use of the *wrists, shoulders, back* and *hips* to control large body sway motions. This gross balancing technique is often observed in the beginning stages of learning. However, as the performer gains greater command of the act of balancing, body sway motions become less and less apparent. The second and more desirable technique is called *on-line balancing* and requires only the use of the *wrists* to control the fine or small body sway motions. Notice that the total body unit remains frozen in its straight-line shape and only the wrists are used to maintain balance. *On-line balancing should be the desired technique to master for all gymnastic performers.*

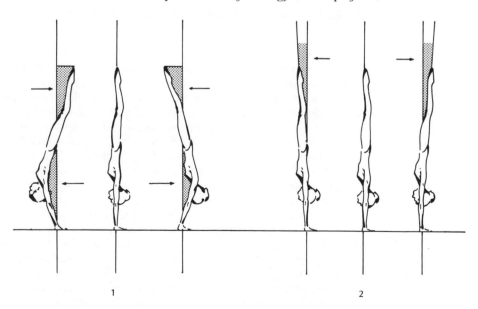

FIGURE 6.6. A comparison of two techniques used in balancing a handstand: (1) Counter-Balancing; (2) On-Line Balancing.

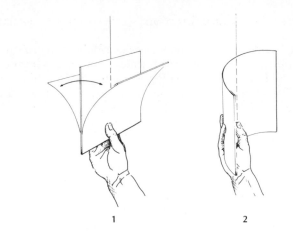

FIGURE 6.7. The effect of a flat versus a hollowed shape on strength: (1) weak shape; (2) strong shape.

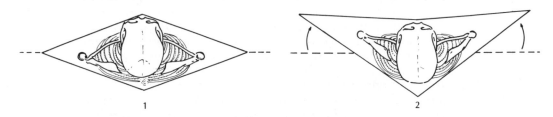

FIGURE 6.8. The effect of a flat versus a hollowed shoulder girdle shape on handstand stability: (1) weak shape; (2) strong shape.

"Hollowing" the shoulder girdle is a rather important and quite effective technique used to further stabilize the gymnast's body for on-line balancing. The underlying concept is similar to the example presented in figure 6.7. Whenever a *flat* sheet of paper is held upright, it has a tendency to collapse or fold over in either a forward or backward direction (no. 1). By slightly hollowing or rounding the paper about its long axis, it becomes structurally more sound (no. 2). Just as this slightly "hollowed" arrangement improves the paper's capability to retain its shape, a slightly hollowed shoulder girdle enhances the gymnast's capability to maintain a straight-line body shape.

Figure 6.8 demonstrates how this paper-shape comparison can be applied to attain greater functional stability in the upper body. In the first example, notice that the performer's shoulder girdle is in position similar to the flat sheet of paper presented in figure 6.7. Such a thin-line shape undoubtedly places the gymnast at a disadvantage in terms of stabilizing the upper body (arm-trunk) region. By moving the shoulder girdle forward about the trunk to a point where a hollowed shape is formed (no. 2), improved stability in the upper body becomes readily apparent. This technique enhances not only on-line balancing for the handstand but also for the large majority of related gymnastic skills.

An effective method for training and strengthening all the muscles involved in maintaining both *correct body shape* and *on-line balancing* is presented in figure 6.9. Essentially, it consists of having a helper or spotter tilt and hold the performer's body off-balance in both the forward and backward directions. While being tilted, the performer's task is to attempt to maintain the straight-line body shape. Remember that the farther the performer's body is tilted away from a balanced position, the more difficult it becomes to maintain correct body shape. This smply means that, during the initial training sessions, allow the performer's body to tilt only to the extent that the straight-line body shape can be maintained. As the performer's muscles become better trained and strengthened to withstand the added pressure, progressively greater degrees of the *Body Tilt Method* can be practiced. In the final analysis, the performer should be able to maintain correct body shape while being tilted from a handstand balance position to a lying position on the floor in both the forward and backward directions!

Here are some of the more important points to remember in learning to perform a handstand correctly:

1. Practice correct body shape *first* and then work on learning to balance.
2. The *Bar-Hang Method* is an excellent method for learning to assume a very stretched, very straight, and very long posture.
3. Maintain the straight-line body shape position while learning to kick to the handstand.
4. The basic objective in the act of balancing is to maintain the weight of the body directly over and between the hands.
5. Although learning to counterbalance is an important first step, remember that the ultimate technique is *On-Line Balancing*. Use of the wrists is the key.

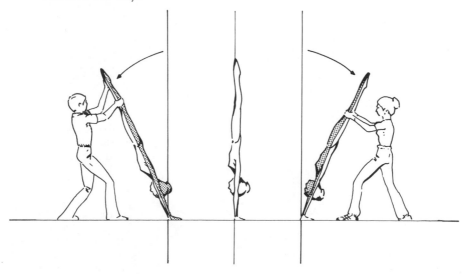

FIGURE 6.9. The Body Tilt Method.

6. Practice the *Body Tilt Method* often to train and strengthen the muscles involved in maintaining correct body shape.

Since a very large majority of gymnastic skills involve, at some time or another, weight bearing on the hands (as well as swinging from the hands) it is a good idea to fully understand and master correct body shape. The handstand is indeed the common denominator in the process of gymnastic growth. Work hard to develop a good one.

7
Analysis of Core Floor Exercise Skills

Kelly Curtis, Acadiana Gymnastic Club, Lafayette, Louisiana.

FORWARD MOVING SKILLS

7.1 Tucked Forward Roll

A. The skill is begun from a standing position with the arms held directly overhead. Notice that this straight-line body shape is fully and completely extended.

A-B. The performer bends over (deep pike) at the hips until the hands make contact with the mat. The head is ducked forward, and the body is lowered onto the upper back by bending slightly at the shoulder and elbow joints. As the hips move in front of the shoulders, the entire upper body begins to form a curved or hollowed shape. This helps to insure a smooth rolling action.

B-C. The hips extend to a point such that the *entire body unit* now forms a slightly curved one-segment shape. Such an extension at the hip joints increases momentum in the roll.

C-D. Because this slightly curved body shape ultimately facilitates "peaking" the upswing phase of the skill, it should be maintained for as long as possible. At the *very last moment,* however, the hip joints flex, causing the entire upper body to begin its rise off the mat. The knee joints simultaneously flex, causing the feet to be positioned underneath the oncoming body weight.

D-E. Using foot contact as the final vertical reference point for support, notice that the already accrued momentum of the actual "roll phase" allows the performer to begin standing immediately, i.e., at the start of the upswing phase of the skill. Observe that the upper body unit (arms, head, and trunk) now assumes a straight-line shape and maintains a slight backward leaning position relative to the hips. Forward momentum, rather than forward body lean, is an important factor to successful execution.

E-F. The skill is completed such that all body segments line up both with one another and with the upper vertical at the exact same time.

F. The final position of the skill is identical to its starting position.

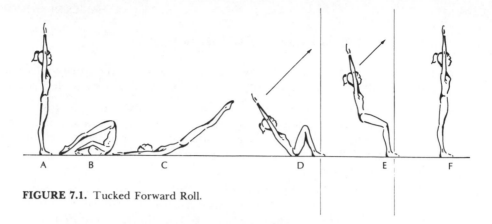

FIGURE 7.1. Tucked Forward Roll.

7.2 Piked Forward Roll—Straddled Stand

A-B-C. These movements are identical in nature to the illustrations and descriptions presented for the Tucked Forward Roll (7.1 A,B, and C).

C-D. Again, the slightly curved or hollowed body shape is maintained until the last possible moment of the roll phase. Just prior to making leg contact with the mat, the hip joints flex, causing the upper body to begin its rise off the mat. At the very same time, the feet are spread very wide to allow the existing momentum in the roll to begin rocking the performer onto a straddled stand. Remember that the wider one's feet are spread, the less effort will be required to lift the body onto the final straddled balance position.

D-E-F. Throughout the upswing phase, observe that the upper body unit (arms, head, and trunk) again assumes a straight-line shape and maintains a slight backward lean relative to the hips.

F-G. The skill is completed such that all body segments line up both with one another and with the upper vertical reference at the exact same time.

G. The attainment of a straight-line, straddle balance position represents final completion of the skill.

FIGURE 7.2. Piked Forward Roll–Straddled Stand.

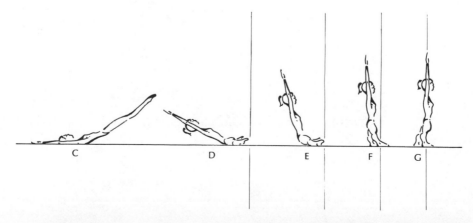

7.3 Piked Forward Roll—Straight Leg Stand

A-B-C. These movements are identical in nature to the illustrations and descriptions presented for the Tucked Forward Roll (7.1 A,B, and C).

C-D. From this slightly hollowed body shape, the hip joints begin to flex vigorously, causing the upper body to rotate quickly about the lower body. Just as the legs and feet contact the mat, so too do the hands make contact with and press against the mat at a point directly to the sides of the knee joint region.

D-E. Notice how the use of full and complete hip joint flexion provides the performer a better opportunity to maximize the hand push against the mat. This action, together with the momentum already accrued in the roll phase, causes the body to begin its straight-leg rise to a stand.

E-F. In order to "peak" the skill appropriately, the performer must open up her hip joint angle *very early* in the upswing phase. This action of early hip joint extension can *only* be accomplished by obtaining a sufficient amount of forward momentum in the roll phase.

F-G-H. The hips continue to extend such that the upper body and the lower body line up both with one another and with the upper vertical reference at the exact same time.

H. The attainment of a standing position with the arms held directly overhead represents final completion of the skill. Notice that this straight-line body shape is fully and completely extended.

FIGURE 7.3. Piked Forward Roll–Straight Leg Stand.

7.4 Step-up Handstand—Forward Roll

A. The skill is begun from a standing position with the arms held directly overhead. Again this straight-line body shape is fully and completely extended.

A-B-C. Essentially, the performer begins from a stand, proceeds through a front scale, and arrives at a needle scale. This movement is accomplished solely by flexing the hip joint of the support leg to a point such that the hands are able to make contact with and press against the mat. Notice that no change has occurred in the straight-line body shape formed by the lead leg, trunk, head, and arms.

C-D. At this point the entire body weight shifts onto the hands. In order to raise the trail leg, the performer's straight-line body shape actually leans slightly beyond perpendicular.

D-E. As the trail leg rises to line up with the lead leg, the total body unit simultaneously shifts back onto a perpendicular balanced position.

E-F-G. By substantially reducing finger pressure against the mat, the entire body unit begins to fall in a forward direction. As the performer undergoes this initial descent phase from the handstand, the entire body unit begins to assume a slightly hollowed shape. The elbows remain locked (straight) while the hands maintain a forward pressing tension against the mat. This latter action ensures greater control throughout the descent.

G-H. Constant muscular tension throughout the entire body (particularly in the shoulder region) helps to prevent the natural tendency to collapse or fold in at one's jointed and/or weaker points. Just prior to the upper shoulders making contact with the mat, the head is ducked in a forward direction.

H. In terms of body shape and motion direction, this illustration is identical to that presented in the Tucked Forward Roll (7.1 C). As a result, the performer is now in a position to execute any of the sequentially related skills.

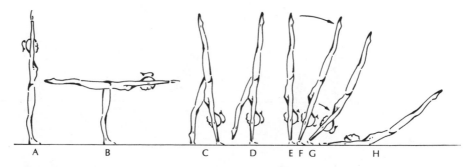

FIGURE 7.4. Step-up Handstand–Forward Roll.

7.5 Front Limber

A-B-C-D-E. The movements are identical in nature to the illustrations and descriptions presented for the Step-up Handstand–Forward Roll (7.4A through E).

E-F-G. By momentarily reducing finger pressure against the mat, the total body unit has an increased tendency to fall in a forward direction. As soon as this tendency to fall off-balance is felt by the performer, the hands begin to push against the mat also in a forward direction. Although the legs and feet continue to rotate forward, this action causes the shoulders to shift backward to a point slightly behind the hands (base of support). The idea here is to maintain the body's mass center directly over its base of support until just before the feet make contact with the mat. Notice that the deep curve formed by the fully arched body shape is equally distributed throughout the shoulder, back, and hip regions. It must be pointed out that the greater the degree of *total* body arch attained by the performer, the closer the feet can be placed next to the hands. And the closer this hand–foot relationship becomes, the easier and smoother will be the resulting transfer of body weight from hands to feet.

G-H-I. As the feet make contact with the mat, the body weight begins to shift forward. Observe how the deep curve formed by the fully arched body shape is initially skewed to the left (over the hands), then is perfectly regular (over both the hands and feet), and finally becomes skewed to the right (over the feet).

I-J. The hips rock onto and actually beyond the new base of support (feet) so that the trailing upper body can begin its rise off the mat.

J. The attainment of a fully extended standing position with the arms held directly overhead represents final completion of the skill.

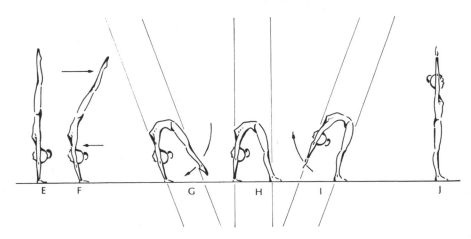

FIGURE 7.5. Front Limber.

7.6 Forward Walkover

A-B-C. The movements are identical in nature to the illustrations and descriptions presented for the Step-up Handstand–Forward Roll (7.4 A,B, and C).

C-D-E. As the lead leg continues to rotate about its hip joint axis, the total body weight begins to shift onto the hands. Once a full split relationship in the legs is attained, the entire lower body unit begins to rock forward about the upper body. Notice that the performer is passing through a split-legged handstand position.

E-F-G-H. The basic mechanics for this aspect of the skill are essentially the same as those presented for the Front Limber (7.5 F, G, H, and I). In the Forward Walkover, however, the performer must maintain as wide a leg-split as possible throughout the entire sequence. Also, the transfer of body weight occurs from the hands and onto a *single* leg. Consequently, to ensure a smooth, controlled weight transfer, the placing of the lead leg as close as is mechanically possible to the hands *prior* to the actual transfer must be emphasized.

H-I-J. The hips rock onto and actually beyond the new base of support (foot) so that the trailing upper body can begin its rise off the mat. The trail leg should be held as high as possible throughout the stand-up phase of the skill.

J. The attainment of a fully extended standing position with the arms held directly overhead represents final completion of the skill.

FIGURE 7.6. Forward Walkover.

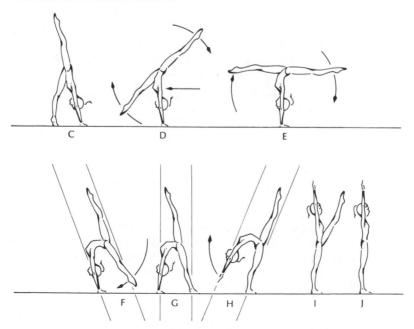

7.7 Bounding Forward Handspring

A. The "Jap-Spring" pictured in this illustration is one of several possible preparatory techniques that can be used to initiate a variety of tumbling skills. This technique, consisting basically of springing for-upward into the air with a slightly arched, forward leaning body position, can be executed either from a standing jump, a step-walk, or a run.

A-B-C. As the performer steps out from the Jap-Spring, the body quickly rotates forward about the hip joint of the support leg. Notice that the hands make contact with the mat at a point such that the slightly hollowed body shape forms a *sizable angle* with the vertical reference line. This angle of input, often referred to as "blocking," is necessary to attaining appropriate rebound action. Upon hand contact with the mat, the support leg forcefully extends at the knee joint, causing increased forward rotation in the total body. Remember that the shoulder girdle is in a position of full elevation at this time.

C-D-E. The impact of the body's momentum against the mat forces the shoulder girdle to be *momentarily* depressed. As the support leg is vigorously extended and then abruptly stopped to line up with the lead leg, the momentarily depressed shoulder girdle quickly returns to its originally elevated position. It is this instantaneous "kickback action" (repulsion) of the shoulder girdle that lifts the body through a handstand and into the air. In addition, notice the very discreet changes occurring in the shape of the total body: from slightly hollowed, through a direct straight-line vertical, and into a slight arch. Although these timely fluctuations in body shape are essential to the dynamics of the movement, they should be as minute and unobvious as possible.

E-F. Remember that the amplitude realized in the airborne phase is always the direct result of the preceding repulsion phase. Once airborne, however, the performer's center of mass follows its established perfectly regular curved path (parabolic trajectory). As the body continues rotating forward about its mass center, it begins to realign into a straight-line shape.

F-G-H. In preparation for landing, the performer maintains complete body extension until just prior to making contact with the ground. The arms remain directly overhead and in line with the trunk while the legs are stretching or reaching for the mat. Because this technique provides the gymnast with the largest possible distance through which to apply a stopping force, greater and more effective control in the landing phase can be realized. Notice that only the hip, knee, and ankle joints flex to absorb the impact.

At touchdown, observe that the total body unit forms a noticeable backward leaning angle with the vertical. This allows the performer to "check" the forward motion of the skill. (If, however, the objective were to immediately execute some sequentially related follow-up skill, the performer would attempt to touchdown in a comparatively more upright body position.)

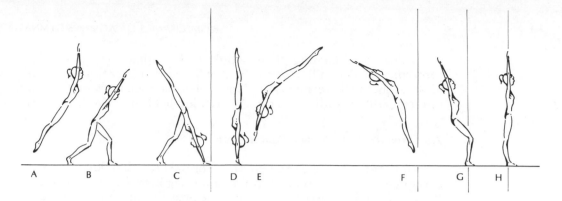

FIGURE 7.7. Bounding Forward Handspring.

H. The attainment of a fully extended standing position with the arms held directly overhead represents final completion of the skill.

7.8 Bounding Forward Handspring—Step-out

A-B-C. These movements are identical in nature to the illustrations and descriptions presented for the Bounding Forward Handspring (7.7 A, B, and C).

C-D-E. Although the support leg vigorously extends at the knee joint to enhance the body's forward rotation, its hip joint remains fully flexed so that the performer can attain as wide a split-legged step-out as possible. Except for the fact that the split-legged relationship is steadfastly maintained, the repulsion and airborne phases of this skill are identical in nature to the descriptions presented for the Bounding Forward Handspring (7.7 C, D, E, and F).

E-F. In preparation for landing, the performer maintains complete body extension with the trail leg held as high as possible overhead. The arms remain directly overhead and in line with the trunk while the lead leg stretches downward for the mat. Only the hip, knee, and ankle joints of the landing leg flex to absorb the impact.

FIGURE 7.8. Bounding Forward Handspring–Step-out.

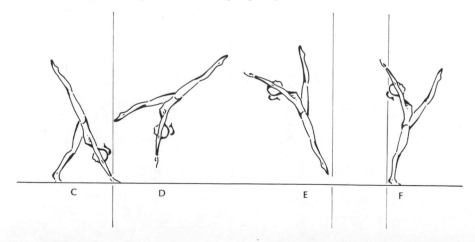

F. The actual landing phase should be such that the performer, upon contacting the mat, still retains sufficient forward momentum to execute any of the sequentially related skills. Notice that the total body unit is in a fully upright position with the arms and trail leg held high overhead.

7.9 Forward Handspring—Punch Jump

A-B-C-D-E. These movements are, for the most part, identical in nature to the descriptions presented for the Bounding Forward Handspring (7.7 A, B, C, D, E, and F). However, because the objective of these two skills are *not* exactly the same, certain critical differences in mechanics do exist. Notice that the hands make contact with the mat at a point such that the slightly hollowed body shape forms a *relatively small angle* with the vertical reference line. With all other factors being equal, the smaller the blocking angle in the input phase, the greater will be the resulting quantity of forward rotation during the airborne phase. This increased forward rotation places the gymnast in a more upright position for the oncoming "punch phase."

E-F-G.   In preparation for the punch phase, the performer is completely extended with the upper body slightly trailing the lower body. The arms remain directly overhead and in line with the trunk while the legs are stretching for the mat. Notice that the hip, knee, and ankle joints flex only slightly to absorb the landing impact and then *immediately* extend again to ensure an effective rebound action. The total time lapse for the punch phase should be very brief indeed.

G. The attainment of maximum vertical lift with the gymnast in a slightly hollowed body shape represents the final completion of the skill. Selection of the appropriate amount of forward rotary motion depends upon which of the sequentially related skills is to follow the punch phase. For example, somersaulting skills and variations require a greater quantity of forward rotary motion than do dive rolling skills and variations.

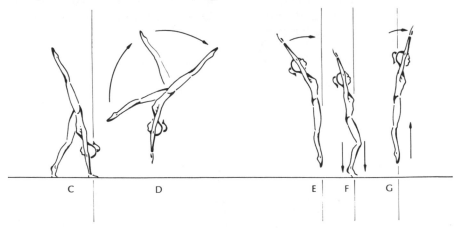

FIGURE 7.9. Forward Handspring–Punch Jump.

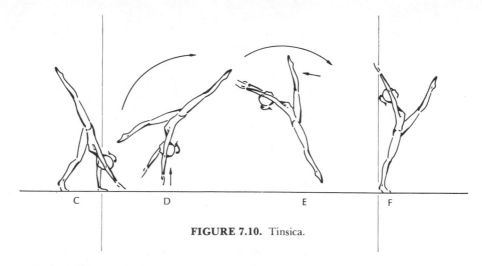

FIGURE 7.10. Tinsica.

7.10 Tinsica

A-B-C-D-E-F. Except for the initial hand placement on the mat during the input phase, these movements are identical in nature to the illustrations and descriptions presented for the Bounding Forward Handspring–Step-out (7.8 A, B, C, D, E, and F). Notice that the *trail arm* (second in the hand placement sequence) is the one responsible for maintaining alignment with the head, trunk, and lead leg. Although positioned well in front of the support leg, the shoulder joint of the *lead arm* forms a slightly decreased angle with the trunk. The rhythmical step-step action of the hands occurs in rapid sequence so that maximum vertical rebound can be attained.

The amount of block (angle of input) of the total body unit varies according to the skill's objective. In this example, the objective is to execute a high, bounding movement pattern which accentuates the step-out phase. Consequently, the slightly hollowed body shape makes hand contact with the mat such that a *sizable angle* is formed with the vertical. This angle of input is similar to the one presented for the Bounding Forward Handspring (7.7 C). Often, however, the *objective changes* in that the Tinsica, like the Forward Handspring–Punch Jump (7.9 C), becomes a transitional movement which is used to set up some sequentially related airborne skill (e.g., Tinsica-Tigna). Because a greater quantity of forward rotation is needed in these cases, their angles of input are comparatively smaller. The amount of block, therefore, must be commensurate with the ultimate objective of the skill.

7.11 Forward Headkip

A. Although this skill can be initiated from a variety of "lead-in skills," the Jap-Spring entry is presented because it lends a high degree of symmetry to the changes that occur in terms of both body shape and movement level: Notice that the performer goes from a region of high location with a fully extended body shape (A), through a region of low location with a fully closed body shape (B-C), and returns again into a region of high location with a fully extended body shape (D-E).

81

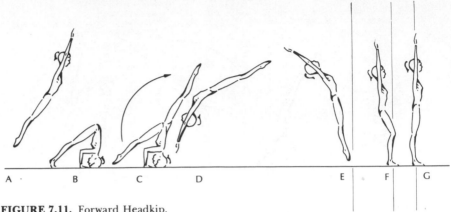

FIGURE 7.11. Forward Headkip.

A-B. As the feet contact the mat, the total body unit is in a forward leaning direction. This off-balance landing enhances the performer's forward horizontal motion—prerequisite to maximum execution of the skill. By flexing at the hips, the upper body is quickly lowered onto the hands to a point such that the head just touches the mat. Although a majority of this for-downward motion is absorbed by the arms and shoulders, the actual hand-head placement on the mat is quite similar in position to that of a basic headstand. The forceful push of the legs against the mat in a for-downward direction serves to further increase the forward rotary motion of the body.

B-C. As the body's mass center instantly rotates for-upward onto the top of its new base of support (the triangular area formed by the hands and head), the hip joints begin to extend vigorously.

C-D. Just prior to the legs attaining a straight-line relationship with the trunk, this rapid extension motion in the hips is instantaneously stopped, causing its momentum to be transferred into the entire body. This "stopping action" of the legs serves as the cue to begin a forceful hand push-off. Notice that this hand push-off occurs throughout the performer's entire range of motion. Remember, the quickness with which the gymnast can complete the required movements of this repulsion phase greatly influences the extent of amplitude that can be realized in the airborne phase.

D-E. Once airborne, the performer's center of mass follows a perfectly regular curved path (parabolic trajectory). As the body continues rotating forward about its mass center, it begins to realign into a straight line shape.

E-F-G. These movements are identical in nature to the illustrations and descriptions presented for the Bounding Forward Handspring (7.7 F, G, and H).

G. The attainment of a fully extended standing position with the arms held directly overhead represents final completion of the skill.

Whenever the Forward Headkip serves as a "lead-in movement" to some sequentially related forward airborne skill, it is characterized by the very same mechanics as those presented for the "punch phase" of the Forward Handspring–Punch Jump (7.9 E, F, and G).

7.12 Layout Dive Forward Roll

A. A very fast, accelerating, and yet controlled run is an essential pre-requisite to maximum execution of the skill. Although standing tall, with the head and trunk held upright, the total body unit has a slight forward lean.

A-B. During the airborne phase of the hurdle, the body actually begins to rotate in a *backward* direction. At the very same time, the arms are lifted directly overhead, and the legs are extended, brought together, and placed well out in front of the body. The hurdle should be *short* in duration, *low* to the ground and *quick* in terms of forward horizontal speed (velocity).

B-C. As the feet make contact with the mat, notice that the total body unit is leaning backward, forming a sizable angle with the vertical. Because the performer is already traveling quite fast in a forward direction, this angle of input (blocking) places the body in a more advantageous position for attaining maximum vertical lift at takeoff. Notice also that the impact of the body's momentum causes *slight* and very *brief* flexion at the ankle, knee and hip joints. These joints instantaneously begin to extend forcefully (kickback action) as the performer approaches the vertical.

C-D. The initiation of *maximum* vertical lift, appropriate forward rotation with a fully extended body shape are desirable characteristics of the takeoff. (Remember, *vertical height* is a more important objective from the aesthetic viewpoint than is horizontal distance).

D-E-F-G-H. Once airborne, although the mass center follows a perfectly regular curved path, the performer's body undergoes slight changes in shape: slightly hollowed (D), straight-line (E), slightly arched (F), straight-line (G), and slightly hollowed (H). Although these timely fluctuations in body shape are important to the dynamics of the movement, they should be as minute and as unobvious as possible.

G-H. In preparation for the roll phase, the performer assumes a slightly hollowed, yet fully extended body shape with the arms stretching or reaching for the mat. Because this technique provides the gymnast with the largest possible distance through which to absorb the downward momentum of the body, greater and more effective control in the roll phase can be realized. At touchdown, the arms begin to flex slightly to lessen the intensity of the oncoming roll-out.

FIGURE 7.12. Layout Dive Forward Roll.

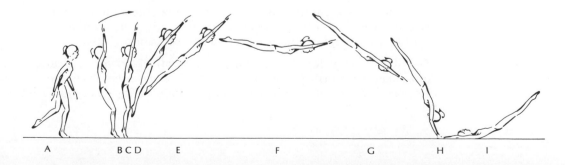

A   B C D   E   F   G   H   I

H-I. Constant muscular tension throughout the entire body (particularly in the shoulder region) helps prevent the natural tendency to collapse or fold in at one's jointed and/or weaker points. Just prior to the upper shoulders making contact with the mat, the head is ducked in a forward direction. Notice that the slightly hollowed shape of the total body unit is maintained.

I. In terms of body shape and motion direction, this illustration is identical to that presented in the Tucked Forward Roll (7.1 C). As a result, the performer is now in a position to execute any of the sequentially related skills.

7.13 Diving Forward Walkover

A. A very fast, accelerating, and yet controlled run is an essential prerequisite to maximum execution of the skill. Notice that, although standing tall, with the head and trunk held upright, the total body unit has a slight forward lean.

A-B. As the performer jumps for-upward into the Jap-Spring, the arms raise for-upward and continue to circle in a counterclockwise direction.

B-C-D. This rapid arm swing pattern continues throughout the entire step-out phase and must be timed such that the arms form a slightly decreased angle with the trunk *just as* the push leg (left leg) makes contact with the mat. Although the upper body undergoes forward rotation about both hip joints, observe that the push leg is planted well in front of the body to ensure an effective "blocking" action for the oncoming dive phase.

D-E. Notice that the impact of the performer's momentum causes *slight* and *very brief* flexion at the ankle, knee, and hip joints. As the body rocks for-upward about its push leg, these joints *instantaneously* begin to extend *forcefully* (kickback action). At the very same time, the rapid counterclockwise motion of the arms is abruptly stopped at a point such that they form a straight-line relationship with the trunk. Except for the push leg, the entire body unit then begins to assume an arched shape.

E-F. The initiation of maximum vertical lift, appropriate forward rotation, and a deeply arched body shape with fully split legs are desirable characteristics of the takeoff.

F-G. Notice that, as the hands contact the mat, the total body unit forms a noticeable angle with the vertical. This "blocking" angle enhances the rebound action of the shoulder girdle in the repulsion phase.

G-H-I-J. Except for the resulting comparatively lower vertical lift, the repulsion and airborne phases of this skill are nearly identical to the descriptions presented for the Bounding Forward Handspring–Step-out (7.8 D, E, and F).

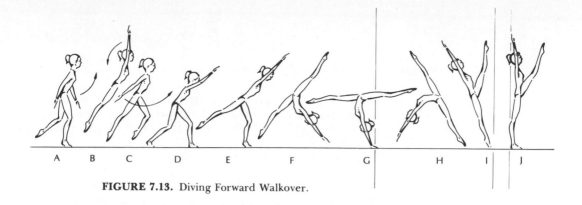

FIGURE 7.13. Diving Forward Walkover.

7.14 Tucked Forward Somersault

A-B-C. These movements are identical in nature to the illustrations and descriptions presented for the Layout Dive Forward Roll (7.12 A, B, and C) except that in the somersault the performer must initiate a slightly greater amount of forward rotary motion. This can be accomplished by slightly decreasing the blocking angle at touchdown as well as executing a more forceful for-upward *upper body throw* at takeoff.

C-D. The initiation of *maximum* vertical lift and appropriate forward rotation with a fully extended body shape are desirable characteristics of the takeoff. (Remember, *vertical* height is a more important objective from the aesthetic viewpoint than is horizontal distance).

D-E-F-G-H. Once airborne, although the mass center follows a perfectly regular curved path, the performer's body undergoes *very obvious* and *specifically timed* changes in shape: from fully opened or extended just after takeoff, to fully closed or tucked at the peak of the airborne trajectory, and returning to full extension immediately prior to landing.

H-I-J. The landing phase is identical in nature to the illustrations and descriptions presented for the Bounding Forward Handspring (7.7 F, G, and H).

J. The attainment of a fully extended standing position with the arms held directly overhead represents final completion of the skill.

FIGURE 7.14. Tucked Forward Somersault.

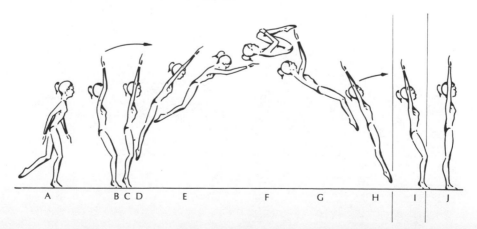

7.15 Forward Handspring—Dive Forward Roll

This skill sequence is actually a combination of the illustrations and descriptions presented for the Forward Handspring—Punch Jump (7.9 A through 7.9 F) and the Layout Dive Forward Roll (7.12 C through 7.12 I).

7.16 Forward Handspring—Tucked Forward Somersault

This skill sequence is actually a combination of the illustrations and descriptions presented for the Forward Handspring—Punch Jump (7.9 A through 7.9 F) and the Tucked Forward Somersault (7.14 C through 7.14 J).

7.17 Forward Aerial Walkover

No. 1 (Underswing Arm-Lift Technique)

A. A very fast, accelerating, and yet controlled run facilitates maximum execution of the skill. Although standing tall, with the head and trunk held upright, the total body unit has a slight forward lean.

A-B. As the performer jumps for-upward into the Jap-Spring, the arms raise for-upward and continue to circle in a counterclockwise direction.

B-C-D-E. This rapid arm swing pattern continues in its counterclockwise direction throughout the entire step-out phase and must be timed such that

FIGURE 7.17. Forward Aerial Walkover.

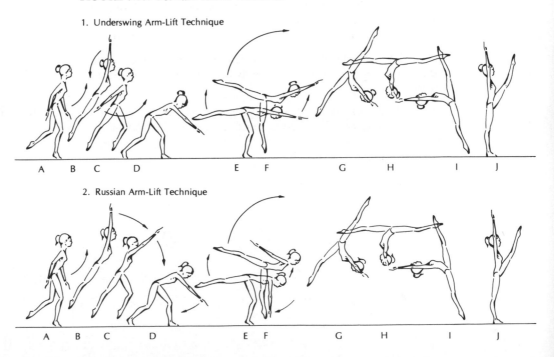

1. Underswing Arm-Lift Technique

A   B   C   D   E   F   G   H   I   J

2. Russian Arm-Lift Technique

A   B   C   D   E   F   G   H   I   J

the arms form a slightly decreased angle with the trunk just as the final support leg begins its vigorous push-off from the mat. Although the upper body undergoes *considerable* forward rotation about both hip joints, observe that the final support leg is planted well in front of the total body unit to ensure an effective "blocking" action for the oncoming takeoff phase.

The impact of the performer's momentum causes *slight* and *very brief* flexion at knee and ankle joints of the final support leg. Notice that the slightly hollowed body shape, formed by the lead leg, trunk, head, and arms, is positioned perpendicular to and directly over its momentary base of support.

E-F. During takeoff, the knee and ankle joints of the support leg *instantaneously* begin to extend forcefully (kickback action). At the very same moment, the slightly hollowed body shape also begins its forceful extension to a point such that the lead leg, trunk, head, and arms now form an arched body shape. Because the body already possesses a sufficient amount of forward rotary motion, these actions primarily serve to provide the gymnast with the necessary vertical lift to execute the airborne phase of the skill.

The initiation of maximum vertical lift, appropriate forward rotation, and an arched body shape with fully split legs are desirable characteristics of the takeoff.

F-G-H-I. Once airborne notice that, although the mass center follows a perfectly regular curved path, the performer's body undergoes *very slight* and *specifically timed* changes in shape: In rising to the top of the airborne phase, the arms are brought from directly overhead to a lateral position perpendicular to the trunk. This timely shortening of the body's turning radius allows the greatest percentage of forward rotary motion to occur during the exact "peak" of the airborne trajectory.

I-J. As the performer prepares for landing, the arms return to their original overhead position while the legs maintain their fully split relationship. Notice how the lead leg stretches downward for the mat. At actual touchdown, only the ankle, knee, and hip joint of the lead leg undergo slight flexion to absorb the impact.

J. The attainment of a fully extended standing position with a controlled amount of forward motion is a desirable characteristic of the landing. Notice that the arms remain directly overhead with the hip joint of the trail leg maintaining its fully flexed step-out position.

No. 2. (Russian Arm-Lift Technique)

Except for the obvious change in circular direction (clockwise) of the arm throw, the mechanics and timing of the various body movements are identical to the illustrations and descriptions presented for the "underswing arm-lift technique". Notice that this change in direction is initiated at the exact apex of the Jap-Spring phase, accelerated throughout the step-out phase, and is quickly and abruptly terminated at the precise moment of takeoff.

7.18 Tucked Backward Roll

A. The skill is begun from a standing position with the arms held directly overhead. Notice that this straight-line body shape is fully and completely extended.

A-B-C. By pressing downward with the balls of the feet, the total body unit begins to rock backward. A quick, yet controlled flexion of the hip and knee joints lowers the body onto the buttocks. The arms remain directly overhead. There should be *no* forward body lean.

C-D. As the body weight is being transferred onto the buttocks, the hip joints extend slightly to enhance the backward momentum of the roll. The knee joints then immediately and completely extend so that the entire body unit now assumes a slightly hollowed shape. This helps to ensure a smooth rolling action.

D-E. As the performer rolls onto the upper back, the arms bend so that the hands (fingers forward) can contact and push against the mat at head level. The hips undergo full flexion (deeply piked) and the head is ducked forward.

E-F. Notice that the arms begin to fully extend (lifting the entire body) *as soon as* the hands make contact with the mat. Appropriate timing of the arm push not only eliminates pressure on the head and neck, but also it allows the feet to be placed more closely to the hands. This latter aspect greatly facilitates "peaking" the stand-up phase of the skill.

For the sake of aesthetic appeal, it should be emphasized that the knee joints remain extended and locked *until* the feet make contact with the mat. At this point, the already accrued momentum of the actual roll phase, the vigorous push-off action of the hands, and the timely flexion of the knee joints collectively enhance the performer's potential to execute the entire stand-up phase on the upswing side (peaking) of the vertical reference line.

F-G. As the hip and knee joints continue to extend into a standing position, observe that the upper body unit (arms, head, and trunk) is now

FIGURE 7.18. Tucked Backward Roll.

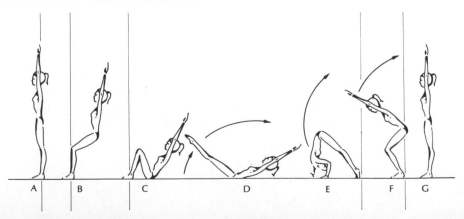

assuming a straight-line shape. The skill is completed such that all body segments line up with one another and with the upper vertical at the exact same time.

G. The final position of the skill is identical to its starting position.

7.19 Piked Backward Roll—Straddled Stand

A. The skill is begun from a standing position with the arms held directly overhead. Notice that this straight-line body shape is fully and completely extended.

A-B-C. By pressing downward with the balls of the feet and flexing at the hip joints, the body begins to fold in forward while moving in a backward direction. Notice that the performer attains full and complete hip joint flexion so that hand contact (fingers forward) with the mat can occur *early* in the descent phase. The actual hand placement should be well behind the feet. These actions help to ensure a smooth weight transfer throughout the entire descent.

C-D. Once weight is felt on the hands, the hip joints begin a controlled extension so as to lower the total body unit onto the backs of the legs and buttocks. While the arms are being repositioned directly overhead, this hip joint extension continues to a point such that a slightly hollowed body shape is formed.

D-E. As the performer rolls onto the upper back, the arms bend so that the hands can contact and push against the mat at head level. The head itself is being ducked forward. At the very same time, the hips undergo full flexion while the legs are being widely straddled.

E-F-G. Except for the facts that the knees remain fully extended and the legs are widely straddled, this phase of the skill is identical in nature to the descriptions presented for the Tucked Backward Roll (7.18 E, F, and G).

G. The final position of the skill is identical to the starting position except, of course, the legs are widely straddled.

FIGURE 7.19. Piked Backward Roll–Straddled Stand.

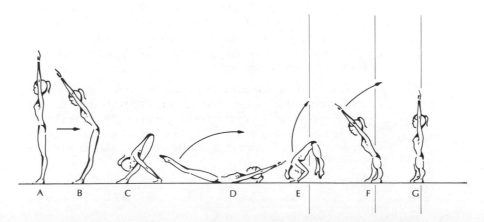

A   B   C   D   E   F   G

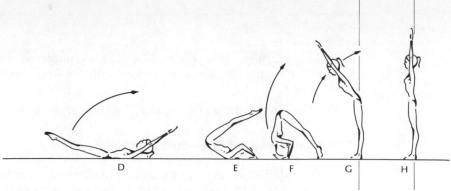

FIGURE 7.20. Piked Backward Roll–Piked Stand.

7.20 Piked Backward Roll—Piked Stand

A-B-C-D. These movements are identical in nature to the descriptions and illustrations presented for the Piked Backward Roll–Straddled Stand (7.19 A, B, C, and D).

D-E-F-G-H. Except for the knees remaining completely extended throughout the entire skill, these movements are identical in nature to the descriptions and illustrations presented for the Tucked Backward Roll (7.18 D, E, F, and G).

7.21 Backward Roll Extension—Handstand

A-B-C-D. These movements are identical in nature to the descriptions and illustrations presented for the Piked Backward Roll–Straddled Stand (7.19 A, B, C, and D).

C-D. Because the final objective of the skill requires that the body be *lifted* with *straight arms* into a handstand position, a comparatively large amount of backward rolling momentum is desirable. This is accomplished just as the body weight is transferred onto the buttocks. A forceful extension of the hip joints quickly rotates the upper body in a backward direction. Just as the total body unit begins to form a slightly hollowed shape, the rapid hip joint extension is instantaneously and abruptly *stopped*. This "stopping action" of the upper body causes its backward rotating momentum to be transferred into the total body.

D-E. As the performer rolls onto the upper back, the extended arms are placed directly overhead with the hands turned slightly inward. Notice that the entire arm-hand unit makes contact with the mat at the exact same time. Although the head is being ducked forward, the total body unit maintains its slightly hollowed shape.

E-F. The actual arm-hand contact serves as the cue to begin a forceful and continuous for-downward push against the mat. *Constant muscular tension* throughout the entire body (particularly in the shoulder region) helps to prevent the natural tendency to collapse or fold in at one's jointed and/or weaker points. Notice that the head maintains its alignment with the trunk.

90

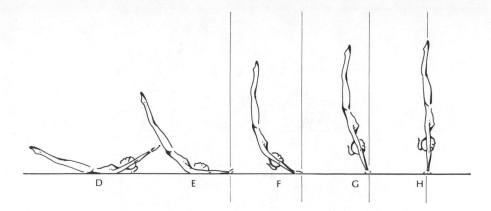

FIGURE 7.21. Backward Roll Extension–Handstand.

F-G-H. Using the hand contact as the final vertical reference point for support, as well as the comparatively large amount of backward rolling momentum previously attained in the actual "roll phase," the performer begins extending out of the slightly hollowed body shape very early in the upswing phase of the skill. At no time should any part of the body transcend the upper vertical until the actual handstand has been attained. Ideally, the skill is completed such that all body segments line up with one another and with the upper vertical at the exact same time.

H. The attainment of a fully extended handstand position represents final completion of the skill. (It is interesting to note that this skill's mechanics are identical to those presented for the "roll-out phase" of the Step-up Handstand–Forward Roll (7.4). Yet the order of sequence is exactly reversed).

7.22 Valdez

A. The skill is initiated from an upright sitting position. The hip and knee joints of the push leg (left leg as illustrated) are flexed to a point such that the push foot can be placed directly alongside the knee of the extended kick leg. Note that the initial support hand (left hand as illustrated) is not only placed relatively close to the hips but also is fully rotated in an outward direction. The extended "throw" arm is parallel to the extended kick leg, and the shoulders are square to one another and to the hips.

A-B. By vigorously pushing downward with the flexed leg while simultaneously driving the extended lead leg upward, the total body unit begins to rise off the ground and to rotate directly backward about the shoulder joint of the support arm. In order to avoid the natural tendency of leaning backward during the actual "throw," a continuous and steadfast back-downward push of the support hand should be emphasized. And finally, notice that during the initiation of the throw, as well as throughout the entire movement sequence, there is no turn or twist about the long axis of the body.

B-C-D. Note that the flexed leg continues its vigorous downward push until it attains a position of full extension. The extended lead leg also

91

FIGURE 7.22. Valdez.

continues its rise while the "throw" arm simultaneously reaches upward and then backward for the mat. Except for the extended lead leg, the total body unit assumes a deeply arched shape. And finally, notice the fully split position of the legs.

D-E. It is important to emphasize that both legs become airborne *prior* to the hand of the "throw" arm making contact with the mat. As soon as this contact is made, however, the total body weight should shift slightly to the "throw" arm side so that the initial support hand (left hand as illustrated) can be more easily realigned to assume the standard "fingers-forward" handstand position.

E-F-G. The actual "throw" phase should provide sufficient backward momentum to allow the total body unit to assume a straight-line shape on the upswing side of the vertical. (Although the performer could have chosen to arrive either in a fully split-legged or a legs together handstand position, the accompanying illustrations depict the latter.)

G-H-I. To ensure a smooth, controlled weight transfer, notice how the hip joint of the step-down leg (left leg as illustrated) undergoes full and complete flexion so as to allow the oncoming support foot to be placed reasonably close to the hands.

I-J-K. Essentially, the performer steps down into a near needle scale, proceeds through a front scale, and arrives at a fully extended standing position. The completion of this movement is accomplished solely by extending the hip joint of the support leg to a point such that the entire body unit assumes a straight-line shape. During this time, however, notice that no change has occurred in the straight-line shape already formed by the trail leg, trunk, head, and arms.

92

K. The attainment of a fully extended standing position with the arms held directly overhead represents final completion of the skill.

7.23 Back Limber

A. The skill is begun from a standing position with the arms held directly overhead. Notice that this straight-line body shape is fully and completely extended.

A-B-C. As the upper body unit (arms, head, and trunk) begin to arch over in a backward direction, notice that the lower body unit (hips and legs) shifts slightly forward. This counterbalanced distribution of body weight allows the performer's mass center to remain directly over its base of support until the hands make contact with the mat. Notice that the deep curve formed by the fully arched body shape is equally distributed throughout the shoulder, back, and hip regions. It must be emphasized that the greater the degree of total body arch attained by the performer, the closer the hands can be placed next to the feet. And the closer this hand-foot relationship becomes, the easier and smoother will be the resulting transfer of body weight from feet to hands.

C-D-E. Just as the hands begin to contact the mat, the body weight starts to shift backward. Observe how the deep curve formed by the fully arched body shape is initially skewed to the left (over the feet), then is perfectly regular (over both feet and hands), and finally becomes skewed to the right (over the hands).

E-F-G. The shoulders rock onto and actually beyond the new base of support (hands) so that the trailing lower body can begin its rise off the mat.

G. The attainment of a fully extended handstand position represents final completion of the skill. (It is interesting to note that this skill's mechanics are identical to those presented for the Front Limber (7.5). Yet the order of sequence is exactly reversed.)

FIGURE 7.23. Back Limber.

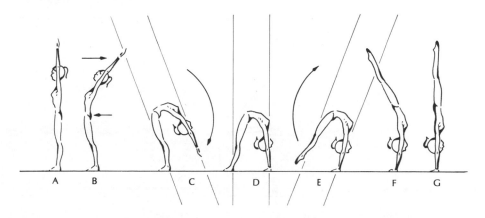

7.24 Backward Walkover

A. The skill is begun from a standing position with the arms held directly overhead. Notice that this straight-line body shape is fully and completely extended.

A-B-C-D-E-F-G. The basic mechanics for these movements are essentially the same as those presented for the Back Limber (7.23 A through G) except, of course, that the performer must execute and *maintain* as *wide* a *leg split* as possible. In the initiation of the actual "walkover phase," the gymnast is required to control the movement with a *single* support leg. Consequently, the use of constant muscular tension throughout the entire support leg (especially at the hip joint) should be emphasized.

G-H. To ensure a smooth, controlled weight transfer, notice how the hip joint of the lead leg is fully flexed so as to allow the lead foot to be placed reasonably close to the hands.

H-I-J. Essentially, the performer steps down into a near needle scale, proceeds through a front scale, and arrives at a fully extended standing position. During this time, however, notice that no change has occurred in the straight-line shape already formed by the trail leg, trunk, head, and arms.

FIGURE 7.24. Backward Walkover.

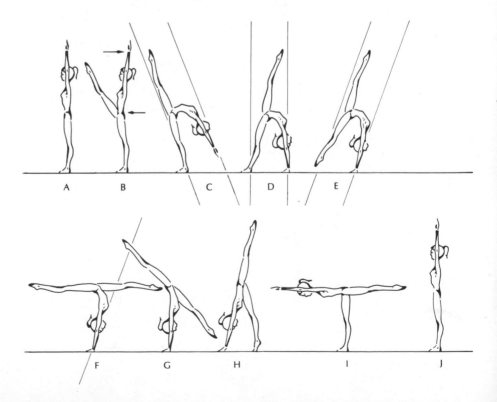

J. The final position of this skill is identical to its starting position. It is interesting to note that this skill's mechanics are the same as those presented for the Forward Walkover (7.6). Yet the order of sequence is exactly reversed.

7.25 Backward Roll Extension—Snap-Down

A-B-C-D. These movements are identical in nature to the descriptions and illustrations presented for the Piked Backward Roll–Straddled Stand (7.19 A through D).

D-E-F-G-H-I. These movements are identical in nature to the descriptions and illustrations presented for the Backward Roll Extension–Handstand (7.21 D through H) except, of course, that the backward rolling momentum carries the performer *through* a straight-line and *into* a slightly arched body shape. Notice, however, that this action occurs just as the total body unit becomes directly perpendicular to the ground. Another exception is the position of the shoulder girdle. Rather than in its normal position of full elevation, the girdle should be completely *depressed* at this moment so that a more effective push-off can ultimately be realized.

I-J. The actual arrival of the performer into this slightly arched body shape serves as the cue to *immediately* begin the "snap-down" phase. At that precise moment, the shoulder girdle is vigorously elevated causing the extended arms to push forcefully against the mat. The total body unit quickly assumes a hollowed shape. Notice that the performer uses only as much "hollow" in body shape as is necessary to arrive in the desired upright punching position. These actions, appropriately executed, help to provide the necessary lift, travel, and backward rotary motion for an effective snap-down.

J-K. Just as the feet make contact with the mat, the total body unit is in a very slight forward leaning position. Because the gymnast is already *rotating* in a *backward* direction, this angle of input (blocking) places the body in a more advantageous position for attaining *maximum vertical lift* at takeoff, necessary to follow-up skills such as somersaults and dive rolls. Often, however, the objective at takeoff is to attain a *large quantity of backward*

FIGURE 7.25. Backward Roll Extension–Snap-down.

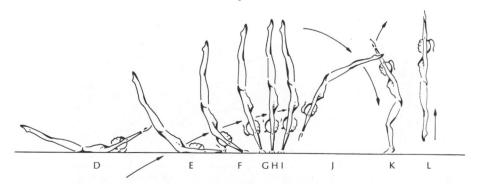

D   E   F   GHI   J   K   L

horizontal motion, a prerequisite to proper execution of backward hand-springs. In this case, the performer must produce a comparatively greater amount of backward rotary motion during the snap-down phase so that the total body unit can land in a slight backward leaning position.

K-L. Although the impact of the body's momentum causes *slight* and *very brief* flexion at the hip, knee, and ankle joints, these joints *instantaneously* begin to extend forcefully or push against the mat.

L. For somersaulting and dive roll skills, the initiation of *maximum vertical lift,* appropriate backward rotation, and a fully extended body shape are desirable characteristics at takeoff. For backward handsprings, the initiation of *maximum backward horizontal motion,* appropriate backward rotation, and a fully extended body shape are the desirable characteristics.

7.26 Standing Backward Handspring

A. The skill is begun from a standing position with the arms held directly overhead. Notice that this straight-line body shape is fully and completely extended.

A-B. By pressing downward with the balls of the feet, the total body unit begins to rock in a backward direction. Notice that at the very same moment the performer also begins to assume a hollowed shape.

B-C. As the body continues to rock off-balance, the hip, knee, and ankle joints undergo *partial* and *very brief* flexion. Carefully study the hollowed shape formed by the upper body and its position relative to the lower body. Essentially, the total body unit, although hollowed, is now falling backward.

C-D. By vigorously extending *first* the hips and *then* the lower back, upper back, and shoulders in a rapid, sequential fashion, the upper body begins to rotate quickly backward about the lower body while forming the desired slightly arched shape. At the very same time, the forceful extension of the legs against the mat drives the total body unit in a back-upward direction. (Remember, *rotational speed* and *horizontal distance* are more important objectives for backward handspring takeoffs than is vertical height).

FIGURE 7.26. Standing Backward Handspring.

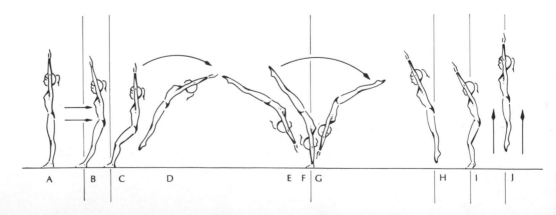

D-E. Once airborne, the performer's center of mass follows its established, perfectly regular, curved path. Although rotating quickly in a backward direction, notice that the actual trajectory is long and low to the ground. The slightly arched body shape should be maintained throughout the entire airborne phase.

E-F. Upon touchdown, the shoulder girdle should be fully elevated. In addition, notice that the shoulders are directly over the hands at contact while the slightly arched body shape forms a sizable angle with the vertical reference line. This angle of input (blocking) is a prerequisite to attaining appropriate rebound action.

F-G. The impact of the body's momentum against the mat forces the shoulder girdle to be *momentarily* depressed. As the total body unit quickly begins to assume a slightly hollowed shape, the momentarily depressed shoulder girdle immediately returns to its originally elevated position. It is this instantaneous "kickback action" (repulsion) of the shoulder girdle that lifts the body through a handstand and into the air. Notice also that the performer uses only as much "hollow" in body shape as is necessary to arrive in the desired upright punching position.

G-H-I-J. These movements are identical in nature to the descriptions and illustrations presented for the Backward Roll Extension–Snap-down (7.25 J, K and L).

7.27 Backward Handspring Series

Successive Backward Handsprings can be initiated from a variety of "lead-in" skills: Backward Roll Extension–Snap-down, Standing Backward Handspring, Round-off, or from a number of backward somersaulting variations. Yet, regardless of type, the *actual landing phase* of any "lead-in" skill is characterized by the *very same transitional mechanics into* the Backward Handspring Series. With this in mind, let us assume that a Standing Backward Handspring is chosen as the "lead-in" skill to the Backward Handspring Series and begin the analysis with the snap-down phase.

F-G-H. These movements are for the most part, identical in nature to the illustrations and descriptions presented for the snap-down phase of the

FIGURE 7.27. Backward Handspring Series.

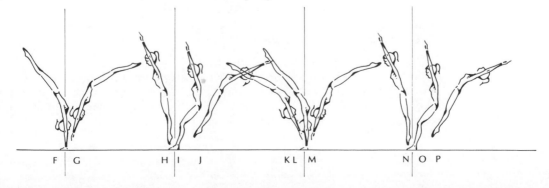

Standing Backward Handspring (7.26 F, G, and H). However, because the Standing Backward Handspring is now being employed as a "lead-in" skill for additional backward handsprings, a comparatively greater amount of backward rotary motion must be accrued during the snap-down phase. This will allow the performer to land in a fashion such that the *total body unit,* although standing upright, forms a noticeable angle with the vertical reference line in a *backward-leaning direction.*

H-I. Just as the feet make contact with the mat, the total body unit is in a backward leaning position. Because the gymnast is already *rotating* in a backward direction, this angle of input (blocking), places the body in a more advantageous position for attaining maximum backward *horizontal motion,* a prerequisite for smooth transition into the oncoming backward handspring.

I-J. The hip, knee, and ankle joints flex slightly to absorb the impact at touchdown and *immediately* and *forcefully* extend to ensure an effective rebound action. At the very same time, the total body unit forms the desired slightly arched shape.

J-K. Except for possessing a comparatively greater amount of backward rotary motion, these movements are identical in nature to the descriptions and illustrations presented for the Standing Backward Handspring (7.26 D and E).

K-L-M-N-O-P. These movements merely repeat the very same Backward Handspring sequence just presented (7.27 F through J).

7.28 Standing Tucked Backward Somersault

A. The skill is begun from a standing position with the arms held directly overhead. Notice that this straight line body shape is fully and completely extended.

A-B. In preparation for the jump, the arms are lowered while the ankle, knee, and hip joints undergo *partial* and very brief flexion. Although the performer has assumed an open-tucked position, notice that the total body unit remains "on-balance."

B-C. By *immediately* and *forcefully* extending the legs while at the same time throwing the arms and then the entire upper body in an upward-backward direction, the gymnast is lifted *vertically* off the ground while *rotating* in a backward direction. The initiation of maximum vertical lift and appropriate backward rotation with a fully extended body shape are desirable characteristics of the takeoff.

C-D-E-F-G. Once airborne notice that, although the mass center travels a directly *vertical* path, the performer's rotating body undergoes *very obvious* and *specifically timed* changes in shape: from fully opened or extended at takeoff, to fully closed or tucked at the peak of the airborne phase, and returning to full extension immediately prior to landing.

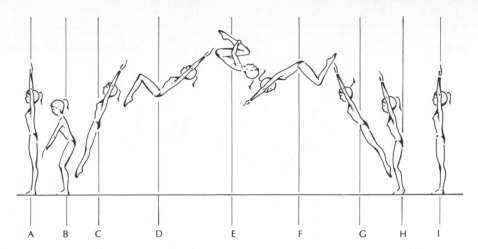

FIGURE 7.28. Standing Tucked Backward Somersault.

G-H-I. In preparation for landing, the performer maintains complete body extension until just prior to making contact with the ground. The arms remain directly overhead and in line with the trunk while the legs are stretching or reaching for the mat. Because this technique provides the gymnast with the largest possible distance through which to apply a stopping force, greater and more effective control in the landing phase can be realized. Notice that only the ankle, knee, and hip joints flex to absorb the impact.

Observe that at touchdown the total body unit forms a very slight forward leaning angle with the vertical. Because this allows the performer to "check" the backward motion, additional landing control can be realized.

I. The final position is identical to its starting position.

7.29 Backward Handspring Series—Tucked Backward Somersault

F-G-H-I-J-K-L. These movements are identical in nature to the illustrations and descriptions presented for the Backward Handspring Series (7.27 F through L).

L-M-N. The impact of the body's momentum against the mat forces the shoulder girdle to be *momentarily* depressed. As the total body unit quickly begins to assume a slightly hollowed shape, the momentarily depressed shoulder girdle immediately returns to its originally elevated position. It is this instantaneous "kickback action" (repulsion) of the shoulder girdle that lifts the body through a handstand and into the air. These actions, appropriately executed, help to provide the necessary lift, backward horizontal motion, and backward rotary motion for an effective snap-down.

N-O. Just as the feet make contact with the mat, the total body unit is in an observable *forward leaning position*. Because the gymnast is already *rotating* in a *backward* direction, this angle of input (blocking) places the body in a more advantageous position for attaining maximum *vertical lift* at takeoff, a prerequisite to proper execution of the oncoming Tucked Backward Somersault.

99

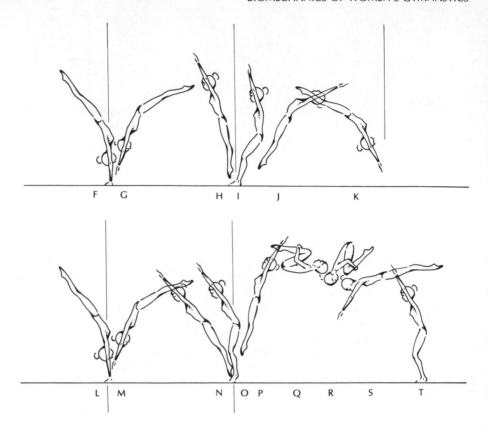

FIGURE 7.29. Backward Handspring Series–Tucked Backward Somersault.

O-P.   Although the impact of the body's momentum causes *slight* and *very brief* flexion at the ankle, knee, and hip joints, these joints *instantaneously* begin to *extend forcefully* or push against the mat. Because of the already accrued backward momentum, the performer should attempt to extend *only* to a point such that the total body unit forms a straight-line shape. Undue body arch in the takeoff phase negatively affects both mechanical efficiency and aesthetic appeal.

The initiation of maximum vertical lift and appropriate backward rotation with a fully extended body shape are desirable characteristics of the takeoff. (Remember, *vertical* height is a more important objective from the aesthetic viewpoint than is horizontal distance.)

P-Q-R-S.   Once airborne, although the mass center follows a perfectly regular curved path, the performer's body undergoes *very obvious* and *specifically timed* changes in shape: from fully opened or extended at takeoff, to fully closed or tucked at the peak of the airborne trajectory, and returning to full extension immediately prior to landing.

S-T. The landing phase is identical in nature to the illustrations and descriptions presented for the Standing Tucked Backward Somersault (7.28 G, H, and I).

SIDEWARD MOVING SKILLS

7.30 Cartwheel

A. The skill is begun from a sideward standing position with the arms held directly overhead. Notice that this straight-line body shape is fully and completely extended.

A-B-C. Essentially, the performer begins from a stand, proceeds through a side scale, and continues rotating sideways about the hip joint of the support leg until the lead hand makes contact with the mat. Notice that no change has occurred in the straight-line body shape formed by the lead leg, trunk, head, and arms. In order to ensure a smooth weight transfer, the lead hand should be placed as close as possible to the support foot without, of course, interrupting the straight-line body shape.

C-D. As the body weight is being transferred onto the lead arm, the lead leg begins to rotate sideways about its hip joint. Notice that this action serves to place the legs in a fully straddled-split position just as the performer passes through the handstand.

D-E-F-G. The second half of the skill is actually a mirror image of the first half. In order to ensure a smooth weight transfer back onto the feet, notice how the lead leg is placed as close as possible to the support hand without, of course, interrupting the remaining straight-line body shape.

G. The final position of the skill is identical to its starting position.

FIGURE 7.30. Cartwheel.

FIGURE 7.31. Lead Arm Cartwheel.

7.31 Lead Arm Cartwheel and 7.32 Trail Arm Cartwheel

Both of these skills are identical in nature to the illustrations and descriptions presented for the Cartwheel (7.30) except that only the lead arm or the trail arm (as the case may be) is used during the inverted support phase. Also during this phase, notice that the nonsupport arm is positioned such that the symmetry of the movement is at least not affected or at best enhanced. Once the performer steps down from the inverted support position, the nonsupport arm is realigned directly overhead.

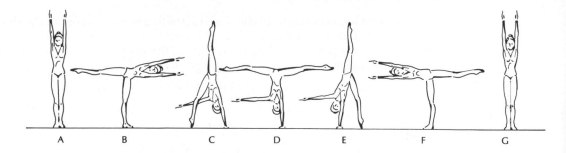

FIGURE 7.32. Trail Arm Cartwheel.

7.33 Dive Cartwheel

A-B-C. These movements are identical in nature to the descriptions and illustrations presented for the Diving Forward Walkover (7.13 A, B, and C).

C-D. The rapid counterclockwise arm swing pattern continues throughout the entire step-out phase and must be timed such that the arms form a slightly decreased angle with the trunk *just as* the final support leg (left leg) makes contact with the mat. Although the slightly hollowed shape formed by the lead leg, trunk, head, and arms undergoes considerable forward rotation about the hip joint of the final support leg, observe that the support

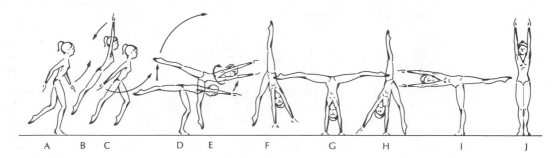

FIGURE 7.33. Dive Cartwheel.

leg itself is planted well in front of the body so as to ensure an effective "blocking" action for the oncoming dive phase.

D-E. The impact of the performer's momentum causes *slight* and *very brief* flexion at the ankle, knee, and hip joints. As the body rocks for-upward about its support leg, these joints *instantaneously* begin to *forcefully* extend (kickback action) driving the body up-forward into the air. At the very same time, the rapid counterclockwise motion of the arms is abruptly stopped at a point such that a straight-line body shape is formed by the lead leg, trunk, head and arms. Although the one-quarter turn is initiated as the body passes through the aforementioned slightly hollowed shape, the actual execution of the twist occurs as the body assumes a straight-line shape. It is important to emphasize that the body should turn (twist) as a *single* unit.

The initiation of maximum vertical lift, appropriate sideward rotation, and a straight-line body shape with widely split legs are desirable characteristics of the takeoff.

E-F-G. Once airborne notice that, although the mass center follows a perfectly regular curved path, and although the body is rotating sideward about its mass center, the actual body shapes assumed by the performer are the very same as those presented for the Cartwheel (7.30 B, C, and D).

G-H-I-J. Except for possessing a slightly greater amount of sideward rotation, these movements are identical in nature to the illustrations and descriptions presented for the Cartwheel (7.30 D through G).

7.34 Aerial Cartwheel

No. 1 (Underswing Arm-Lift Technique)

The mechanics of this skill are, for the most part, identical in nature to the illustrations and descriptions presented for the Dive Cartwheel (7.33). However, because the objectives of these two skills are not exactly the same, certain critical differences in mechanics do exist. In the Aerial Cartwheel, a significantly greater amount of sideward rotary motion at takeoff is required. Provided a maximum amount of vertical lift is still attained, this

1. Underswing Arm-Lift Technique

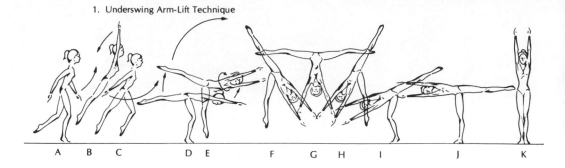

2. Russian Arm-Lift Technique

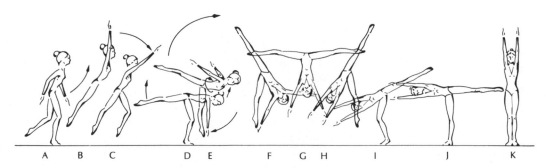

FIGURE 7.34. Aerial Cartwheel.

increased sideward rotary motion enables the performer to complete the *entire* cartwheel while airborne. Attempting to place the lead leg underneath the body *as soon as possible* prior to landing should be emphasized.

No. 2 (Russian Arm-Lift Technique)

Except for the obvious change in direction (clockwise) of the arm throw, the mechanics and timing of the various body movements are identical to the illustrations and descriptions presented for the "underswing arm-lift technique." Notice that this change in direction is initiated at the exact apex of the Jap-Spring phase, accelerates throughout the step-out phase, and is quickly and abruptly terminated at the precise moment of takeoff.

ANALYSIS OF THE ROUND-OFF

Because it serves as the major "lead-in" skill to a majority of backward tumbling sequences, the importance of mastering the Round-Off cannot be overemphasized. At a glance, accurate execution of this skill may appear comparatively easy to achieve. Yet experience has shown the contrary. In fact, most elite level teachers and coaches agree that the Round-Off is both difficult to master

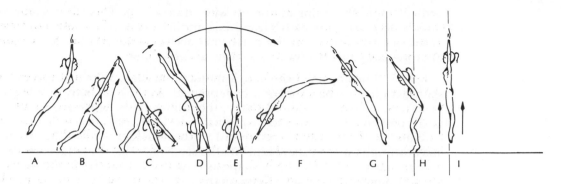

FIGURE 7.35. Round-Off (punch jump).

and absolutely essential to future gymnastic success. In this light, careful study, appropriate practice, and the achievement of a reasonable level of specific task mastery are necessary before attempting a Round-Off in combination with any of the sequentially related "follow-up" skills.

7.35 Round-Off (Punch Jump)

A. The "Jap-Spring" pictured in this illustration is one of several possible preparatory techniques that can be used to initiate a variety of tumbling skills. This technique, consisting basically of springing for-upward into the air with a slightly arched, forward leaning body position, can be executed either from a standing jump, a step-walk, or a run.

A-B-C. As the performer steps out from the Jap-Spring, the body quickly rotates *directly forward* about the hip joint of the support leg. This *directly forward input action* is critical to the final outcome of the skill because it ensures that the body's momentum will continue in a *straight-line path* down the mat rather than deviate in some undesirable lateral direction. At the very same time, a one-half turn (outward twist) is *initiated* about the long axis of the straight-line body shape formed by the lead leg, trunk, head, and arms. It is important to emphasize that this entire body shape should turn (twist) as a *single unit*.

Although the hands contact the mat in sequential fashion, notice that they are placed well in front of, yet directly in line with, the inside of the support foot. In addition to further ensuring that the body's momentum does not deviate in some lateral direction, this strategic hand placement allows the performer sufficient time to complete the entire one-half twist *before* the body arrives at the vertical reference line. Such an angle of input, often referred to as "blocking," is necesssary to attaining appropriate rebound action in the oncoming snap-down phase. (Remember, the shoulder girdle is in a position of full elevation.)

C-D-E. As the hands contact the mat, notice that the slightly flexed support leg forcefully extends (causing increased rotation in the total body) and then quickly begins to line up with the lead leg. This latter action of rapidly decreasing the body's (long axis) radius serves to facilitate *completion* of the one-half turn *before* the performer arrives at the vertical. Notice that the total body unit is now in a slightly arched shape.

E-F-G. The impact of the body's momentum against the mat forces the shoulder girdle to be momentarily depressed. As the total body unit begins to assume a slightly hollowed shape, the momentarily depressed shoulder girdle immediately returns to its originally elevated position. It is this instantaneous "kickback action" (repulsion) of the shoulder girdle that lifts the body through the handstand and into the air. Notice that the performer uses only as much "hollow" in body shape as is necessary to arrive in the desired upright punching position. (Keeping the airborne trajectory comparatively flat and/or low to the ground while attempting to maximize both horizontal travel and backward rotation are desirable characteristics of the snap-down.)

G-H-I. Just as the feet make contact with the mat, the total body unit is in an observable *forward leaning position*. Because the gymnast is already *rotating* in a *backward* direction, this angle of input (blocking) places the body in a more advantageous position for attaining maximum *vertical lift* at takeoff, necessary to any of the sequentially related backward somersault and dive roll variations.

I. The initiation of maximum vertical lift and appropriate backward rotation with a fully extended body shape are desirable characteristics of the takeoff. (Remember, vertical height is a more important objective from the aesthetic viewpoint than is horizontal distance.)

7.36 Round-off (Snap-through)

The mechanics of this skill are, for the most part, identical in nature to the illustrations and descriptions presented for the Round-off (Punch Jump) (7.35). However, because the objectives of these two skills are not exactly the same, certain critical differences in mechanics do exist. Since the Round-off (Snap-through) usually serves as a "lead-in" skill to Backward Handsprings (7.27), its objective is to attain a large quantity of backward horizontal motion

FIGURE 7.36. Round-Off (snap-through).

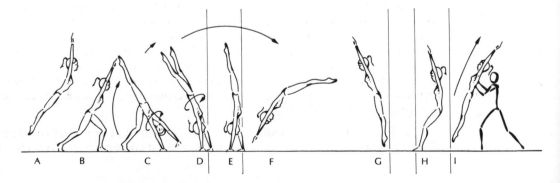

A   B   C   D   E   F   G   H   I

at takeoff. Consequently, the performer must produce a comparatively greater amount of backward rotary motion during the snap-down phase so that the total body unit can touch down in a slight *backward leaning position*.

SELECTED BACKWARD TUMBLING SEQUENCES

7.37 Piked Backward Somersault

L-M-N-O-P. These illustrations depict the traditional snap-down and "punch jump" phases commonly employed to execute any of the sequentially related backward somersault and dive roll variations. It is usually initiated from a Round-off or a Backward Handspring. Yet regardless of the initial input skill, the mechanics of the actual snap-down are, for the most part, identical in nature to the illustrations and descriptions presented for the Backward Handspring Series–Tucked Backward Somersault (7.29 L, M, N, O, and P). In order to complete the Piked Backward Somersault successfully, a slightly greater amount of backward rotary motion during the airborne phase is required. To accomplish this, the performer must execute the actual punch phase of the take-off with a slightly more upright body position.

P-Q-R-S-T-U-V-W. These movements are, for the most part, identical in nature to the illustrations and descriptions presented for the Backward Handspring Series–Tucked Backward Somersault (7.29 P, Q, R, S, and T). However, because the objectives of these two skills are not exactly the same, certain critical differences in mechanics do exist. Notice that, during the airborne phase of the Piked Backward Somersault, the performer's body undergoes changes in shape *solely* because of *hip joint action*. The knee joints remain completely extended throughout the entire somersault. These changes in body shape are both *very obvious* and *specifically timed:* from fully opened or extended at takeoff, to fully closed or *piked* at the peak of the airborne trajectory, and returning to full extension immediately prior to landing.

FIGURE 7.37. Piked Backward Somersault.

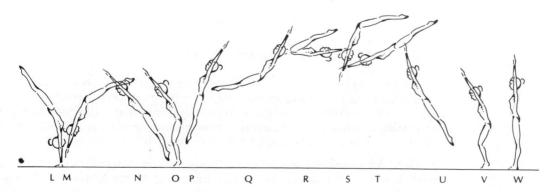

L M   N   O P   Q   R   S   T   U   V   W

7.38 Layout Backward Somersault

O-P-Q-R-S-T-U-V-W. These movements are, for the most part, identical in nature to the illustrations and descriptions presented for the Backward Handspring Series–Tucked Backward Somersault (7.29 O through T). However, because the objectives of these two skills are not exactly the same, certain critical differences in mechanics do exist. In order to complete the Layout Backward Somersault successfully, a comparatively greater amount of backward rotary motion during the airborne phase is required. To accomplish this, the performer must execute the actual punch phase of the takeoff with a *slightly more* upright body position.

Notice that, during the airborne phase of the Layout Backward Somersault, the performer's body undergoes changes in shape *solely* because of *shoulder joint action.* The hip and knee joints remain completely extended throughout the entire somersault. These changes in body shape are both *very obvious and specifically timed.* At takeoff, the total body unit is fully opened or extended with arms held directly overhead. As the performer rises to the peak of the airborne trajectory, notice how the arms are progressively lowered and ultimately positioned next to the sides of the body. During the descent phase, the arms return to their original overhead position.

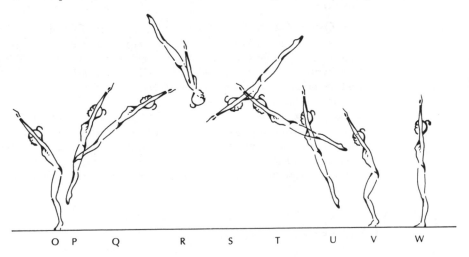

O   P   Q   R   S   T   U   V   W

FIGURE 7.38. Layout Backward Somersault.

7.39 One-Half Twisting Backward Dive Roll

O. Just as the feet make contact with the mat, the total body unit is in an observable *forward leaning position.* Because the gymnast is already *rotating* in a *backward* direction, this angle of input (blocking) places the body in a more advantageous position for attaining maximum *vertical lift* at takeoff, a necessity to the proper execution of the oncoming dive phase.

O-P. Although the impact of the body momentum causes *slight* and *very brief* flexion at the ankle, knee, and hip joints, these joints *instantaneously*

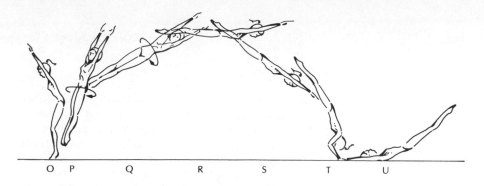

O P Q R S T U

FIGURE 7.39. One-Half Twisting Backward Dive Roll.

begin to *extend forcefully* or push against the mat. Because of the already accrued backward momentum, the performer should attempt to extend *only* to a point such that the total body unit forms a straight-line shape. Undue body arch in the takeoff phase negatively affects both mechanical efficiency and aesthetic appeal.

The actual one-half turn (twist) is initiated during the takeoff phase. As far as possible, the twist should occur uniformly throughout the long axis of the straight-line body shape. In effect, the total body is seen twisting as a *single unit.*

The initiation of maximum vertical lift, appropriate backward rotation, and appropriate twist initiation with a fully extended body shape are desirable characteristics of the take-off. (Remember, *vertical* height is a more important objective from the aesthetic viewpoint than is horizontal distance.)

P-Q-R-S. Once airborne, although the mass center follows a perfectly regular curved path, the performer's body begins to rotate backwards while also twisting about its long axis. By slightly spreading the arms laterally just prior to arriving at the peak of the airborne trajectory, the natural tendency to continue twisting throughout the descent phase is held in check.

S-T. In preparation for the roll phase, the performer assumes a slightly hollowed, yet fully extended body shape with the arms stretching or reaching for the mat. Because this technique provides the gymnast with the largest possible distance through which to absorb the downward momentum of the body, greater and more effective control of the roll phase can be realized. At touchdown, the arms flex slightly to lessen the intensity of the oncoming roll out.

T-U. Constant muscular tension throughout the entire body (particularly in the shoulder region) helps prevent the natural tendency to collapse or fold in at one's jointed and/or weaker points. Just prior to the upper shoulders making contact with the mat, the head is ducked in a forward direction. Notice that the slightly hollowed shape of the total body unit is maintained.

U. In terms of body shape and motion direction, this illustration is identical to that presented in the tucked Forward Roll (7.1 C). As a result, the performer is now in a position to execute any of the sequentially related skills.

7.40 Arabian Somersault

O-P. The mechanics of this skill are, for the most part, identical in nature to the illustrations and descriptions presented for the One-Half Twisting Backward Dive Roll (7.39 O and P). However, because the objectives of these two skills are not exactly the same, certain critical differences in mechanics do exist. In order to complete the Arabian Somersault successfully, a comparatively greater amount of backward rotary motion during the airborne phase is required. To accomplish this, the performer must execute the actual punch phase of the takeoff with a *slightly more* upright body position.

P-Q-R-S-T-U. Once airborne, although the mass center follows a perfectly regular curved path, the performer's body begins to rotate backwards while also turning about its long axis. In addition, the shape of the body undergoes *very obvious* and *specifically timed* changes: from fully extended during the ascent, to fully closed or piked (maximum hip joint flexion) at the peak of the airborne trajectory, and returning to full extension immediately prior to landing.

U-V-W. In preparation for landing, the performer maintains complete body extension until just prior to making contact with the ground. The arms remain directly overhead and in line with the trunk while the legs are stretching or reaching for the mat. Because this technique provides the gymnast with the largest possible distance through which to apply a stopping force, greater and more effective control of the landing phase can be realized. Notice that only the ankle, knee, and hip joints flex to absorb the impact.

Observe that at touchdown the total body unit forms a noticeable backward leaning angle with the vertical. This allows the performer to "check" the forward rotary motion of the skill. (If, however, the objective were to execute immediately some sequentially related follow-up skill, the performer would attempt to touch down in a comparatively more upright body position.)

W. The attainment of a fully extending standing position with arms held directly overhead represents final completion of the skill.

FIGURE 7.40. Arabian Somersault.

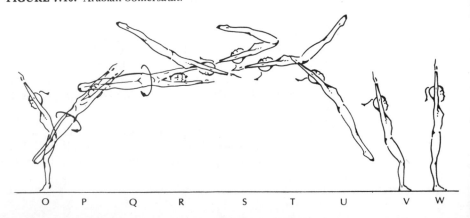

O   P   Q   R   S   T   U   V   W

7.41 Layout Backward Somersault One-Half Twist

O-P. These movements are, for the most part, identical in nature to the illustrations and descriptions presented for the Layout Backward Somersault (7.38 O and P). However, because the objectives of these two skills are not the same, certain critical differences in mechanics do exist. In order to facilitate execution of a one-half twist during the layout backward somersault an additional rotary component about the long axis of the body must be introduced. Although very slight and hardly perceptible, this one-half turn (twist) is actually initiated during the takeoff phase. As far as possible, the twist should occur *uniformly* throughout the long axis of the straight-line body shape. In effect, the total body is seen twisting as a single unit.

The initiation of maximum vertical lift, appropriate backward rotation, and appropriate twist initiation with a fully extended body shape are desirable characteristics of the takeoff. (Remember, vertical height is a more important objective from the aesthetic viewpoint than is horizontal distance.)

P-Q-R-S-T. Notice that during the airborne phase of the skill, the performer's body undergoes changes in shape *solely* because of a *single* shoulder joint action. This change in body shape is both *very obvious* and *specifically timed*. Although a very slight twist has been initiated at takeoff, the total body shape is fully opened or extended with arms held directly overhead. As the performer rises to the peak of the airborne trajectory, notice how the (left) arm is progressively lowered and ultimately positioned next to the side of the body. This shortening of the radius on the left side of the body facilitates twisting in that direction. During the descent phase, the left arm returns to its original overhead position.

FIGURE 7.41. Layout Backward Somersault One-Half Twist.

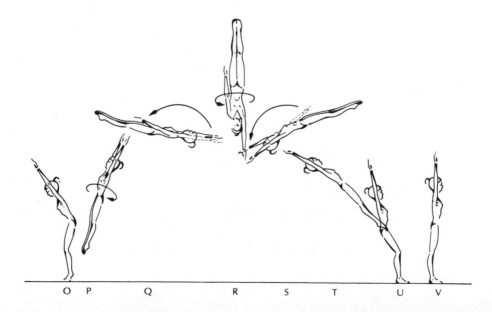

O　P　　　Q　　　　R　　S　　T　　　U　　V

T-U-V. These movements are identical in nature to the illustrations and descriptions presented for the Arabian Somersault (7.40 U, V, and W). Remember that the touchdown angle of the body in reference to the ground is dependent upon whether the objective is to "stick" the landing or proceed into some sequentially related skill.

7.42 Full Twisting Backward Somersault

O-P. These movements are, for the most part, identical in nature to the illustrations and descriptions presented for the Layout Backward Somersault (7.38 O and P). However, because the objectives of these two skills are not exactly the same, certain critical differences in mechanics do exist. In order to facilitate execution of a full twist during the backward somersault, an additional rotary component about the long axis of the body must be introduced at takeoff. Notice that the arms, although still maintained overhead, have been slightly *spread* in a *lateral* direction. Because this comparatively wider body shape increases the performer's twisting radius, the actual rate or speed of the twist is relatively slow and in fact scarcely observable during the takeoff phase. Notice that, as far as possible, the twist occurs *uniformly* throughout the long axis of the straight-line body shape. In effect, the total body is seen twisting as a single unit.

The initiation of maximum vertical lift, appropriate backward rotation, and appropriate twist initiation with a fully extended body shape are desirable characteristics of the takeoff. (Remember, *vertical* height is a more important objective from the aesthetic viewpoint than is horizontal distance.)

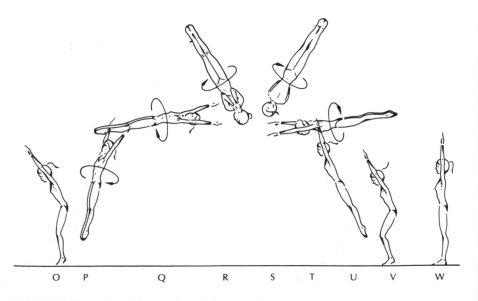

O   P   Q   R   S   T   U   V   W

FIGURE 7.42. Full Twisting Backward Somersault.

P-Q-R-S-T. Notice that, during the airborne phase of the skill, the performer undergoes *very obvious* and *specifically timed* changes in body shape solely because of bilateral arm action. Although the actual twist has been initiated at takeoff, the total body shape is fully opened or extended with arms held *laterally* overhead. As the performer rises to the apex of the airborne trajectory, notice how both arms are quickly pulled inward and positioned next to the front sides of the body. (The fully flexed elbows allow the arms to be placed symmetrically across the chest.) This repositioning of the arms serves to shorten the body's radius of rotation about both its long and lateral axes simultaneously. Consequently, the greatest percentage of both the somersault and the twist can be realized during the "peak" of the airborne trajectory. During the descent phase, the arms return to an overhead lateral position.

T-U-V-W. In preparation for landing, the performer maintains complete body extension until just prior to making contact with the mat. The arms are positioned directly overhead and in line with the trunk while the legs are stretching or reaching for the mat. Because this technique provides the gymnast with the largest possible distance through which to apply a stopping force, greater and more effective control of the landing phase can be realized. Notice that only the ankle, knee, and hip joints flex to absorb the impact.

Observe that at touchdown, the total body unit forms a noticeable forward leaning angle with the vertical. This allows the performer to "check" the backward rotary motion of the skill.

W. The attainment of a fully extended standing position with arms held directly overhead represents final completion of the skill.

8
Analysis of Core Balance Beam Skills

Cathy Olsen, University of Utah, Salt Lake City, Utah. Photo by Paul Jackson.

MOUNTS

8.1 Front Support to Straddled Seat Mount

A. The skill is begun from an erect, yet slightly forward leaning, standing position (use of a vaulting board is optional). The hands are placed approximately shoulder width apart on the top of the beam. The elbow joints are fully extended and remain so throughout the entire sequence.

A-B. By slightly flexing and then forcefully extending the ankle, knee, and hip joints, the total body unit begins to rise for-upward. To facilitate this motion, the performer simultaneously presses downward with the hands against the beam. Immediately prior to arriving in a front support position, the body weight is directed slightly to the side (left arm in this case) of the oncoming leg flank movement (left leg as illustrated).

B-C. This slight shift in body weight toward the (left) side allows the lead (left) leg to circle more easily about and straddle the pivot (left) arm. Notice how the lead leg is lifted and then maintains a horizontal position relative to the ground throughout the remainder of the skill.

C-D. The other (right) arm is quickly repositioned so as to form a symmetrical and balanced alignment with the initial pivot (left) arm. This action provides a more solid support-base about which the total body unit can continue pivoting (90 degree turn to the right).

FIGURE 8.1. Front Support to Straddled Seat Mount.

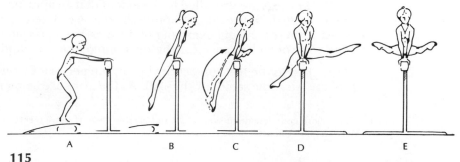

A   B   C   D   E

115

D-E. During this time, the trail (right) leg is being raised to a point such that a straddled seat (straddled "L" support) position is attained.

E. A straddled "L" position with the entire body weight being supported by the hands represents final completion of the skill. Notice that both legs are held horizontal to the ground and that the frontal aspect of the total body is in direct alignment with the longitudinal aspect of the beam.

8.2 Straddle Mount

Although this skill can be initiated from a stand with the hands already in place on top of the beam (refer to illustration A in figure 8.1), a more advanced conceptual model would include attaining a measure of preflight amplitude similar to that seen in vaulting.[1]

A. Using a *fast, low,* and *short* hurdle, the performer contacts the board such that the total body unit is in an upright, yet slightly backward leaning, position relative to the vertical. As the ankle, knee, and hip joints undergo a slight and very brief flexion, the arms are vigorously being thrown in a for-upward direction.

A-B. The instantaneous and forceful extension of the legs against the board "lifts" the body into the air. The horizontal velocity derived from the hurdle phase provides the necessary forward rotation seen in the actual airborne phase. Notice that the performer extends to a point such that a slightly hollowed body shape is formed. Every attempt should be made to *reach for* and make hand contact with the beam as soon as possible. Note that the shoulder girdle is in a fully elevated position.

As the gymnast makes hand contact with the beam, the total body unit must still be rising in a for-upward direction. It is this continued for-upward motion that provides the type of dynamic stability so essential to the proper execution of the very next movement.

B-C. As the legs begin to straddle, the hips continue to rise for-upward so that the body's mass center can be positioned directly over its base of support (hands). Proper straddling action requires that the legs be spread laterally *prior* to flexing at the hip joints. Constant muscular tension throughout the entire body, particularly in the shoulder region, provides the control necessary to lower the body and thus guide the feet onto the top of the beam.

C-D. The legs are straddled to the extent that an approximate 90 degree angle is formed. Notice that, although the feet are placed squarely on top of the beam, there is a slight overhang of the toes. Such gripping action insures added control and balance for the oncoming straddle stand.

D-E. Just as the feet contact the beam, the performer initiates the stand up phase (straddle stand) of the skill. As the arms are being raised laterally

---

[1]For a more complete discussion of the impact and takeoff phases, refer to Chapter 4: "The Mechanics of Impact."

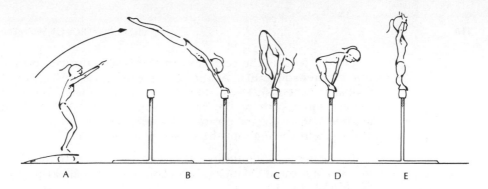

FIGURE 8.2. Straddle Mount.

overhead, the total body unit begins to extend such that the legs rotate forward about the ankles while the upper body simultaneously rotates backward about the hips. These reciprocal motions maintain the body weight directly over the new base of support (feet). Notice that all body segments line up both with one another and with the vertical at the exact same time.

E. The attainment of a straight-line, straddled balanced position represents final completion of the skill.

8.3 Squat Mount

A-B. These movements are identical in nature to the illustrations and descriptions presented for the Straddle Mount, (8.2 A and B).

B-C. As the legs begin to tuck (squat), the hips continue to rise for-upward so that the body's mass center can be positioned directly over its base of support (hands). Proper tucking action requires that the hip joints flex as fully and completely as is mechanically possible *prior* to knee joint flexion. Constant muscular tension throughout the entire body, particularly in the shoulder region, provides the necessary control to lower the body and thus guide the feet onto the top of the beam.

C-D. Notice that *only* the *balls* of the feet make contact with the surface of the beam. Maintaining support of the body weight in this manner is most important because it allows the performer greater ease and freedom to pivot in either direction.

FIGURE 8.3. Squat Mount.

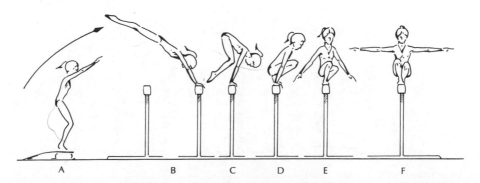

D-E-F. Just as the feet contact the beam, the performer initiates the one-quarter squat turn. As the arms are being raised laterally, the total body unit simultaneously begins to pivot in the intended direction of motion (90 degree squat turn to the right as illustrated). Although the performer assumes a squat-legged position, notice that the trunk and head remain erect and upright throughout the entire pivot motion.

F. Facing the longitudinal aspect of the beam with the body held upright in a strided, squat balance (arms positioned laterally) represents final completion of the skill.

8.4 Squat-through Mount

A-B. These movements are identical in nature to the illustrations and descriptions presented for the Straddle Mount, (8.2 A and B).

B-C. As the legs begin to tuck (squat), the hips continue to rise for-upward so that the body's mass center can be positioned directly over its base of support (hands). In addition, this continued raising of the hips allows for a greater potential clearance in the upcoming "squat-through" phase. Proper squat-through action not only requires that the hip joints flex fully and completely *prior* to knee joint flexion but also that both motions occur as *instantaneously* as possible. Constant muscular tension throughout the entire body, particularly in the shoulder region, provides the control necessary to lower the body and thus guide the legs through the arms en route to a rear support position.

C-D. During the actual squat-through phase, the upper back must be rounded or hollowed so as to provide that added measure of clearance for the legs and feet. This timely hollowing of the back is absolutely essential to successful execution of the skill.

D-E. Notice that, as soon as the feet pass over the surface of the beam, the knee joints and then the hip joints immediately extend to a point such that a slightly arched body shape is formed. Although the backs of the upper legs rest on the beam, the entire body weight should be supported by the arms.

E. A rear support position with a slightly arched body shape represents final completion of the skill.

FIGURE 8.4. Squat-Through Mount.

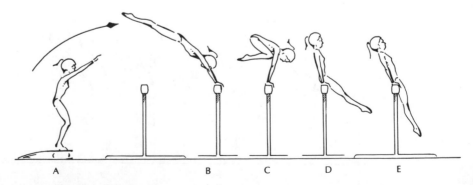

A   B   C   D   E

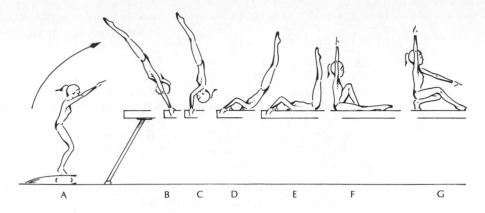

FIGURE 8.5. Forward Roll Mount.

8.5 Forward Roll Mount

A-B. Except for the fact that the performer mounts from the longitudinal aspect of the beam, these movements are identical in nature to the illustrations and descriptions presented for the Straddle Mount, (8.2 A and B).

B-C. As the performer continues to rotate for-upward about the base of support (hands), there is an increased hollowing in the shape of the total body. In addition, observe how the arms begin to flex slowly to ensure a smooth transition into the oncoming roll phase. "Sighting" the beam prior to ducking the head forward is also helpful in that the performer can attain a more accurate assessment of relative body position.

C-D. Constant muscular tension throughout the entire body, particularly in the shoulder region, helps prevent the natural tendency to collapse or fold in at one's jointed and/or weaker points. The objective is to lower *gently* the rolling body onto the upper back.

D-E. To ensure further control and accurate body alignment, notice how the performer maintains hand contact with the beam for as long as possible. In addition, smooth rolling action requires that the vertebrae in the back unfold in a progressive fashion onto the beam's surface.

E-F. The momentum of the roll helps the performer attain an upright sitting position. However, just prior to arriving in this position, observe how the knee of one leg flexes (left leg as illustrated) so that its foot can serve as the new base of support for the oncoming body weight. Notice that the entire upper body now assumes and maintains a straight-line shape.

F-G. As the performer rises to a single leg squat pose, the nonsupport leg, with its knee partially flexed, is rotated slightly outward so that the lateral aspect of the foot can be positioned well in front of the body on the beam's surface. This strategic placement of the nonsupport leg not only lends an aesthetic appeal to the skill but also provides for additional balancing stability.

G. The attainment of a single leg squat pose represents final completion of the skill.

8.6 Step-on Mount

This mount sequence can be performed either as shown (diagonal approach) or from the end of the beam (longitudinal approach).

A. A fast, accelerating, and yet controlled run is essential to maximum execution of the skill. Notice that the performer assumes and maintains an erect body carriage throughout the entire sequence.

A-B. The actual step onto the board is essentially a one-legged hurdle. The airborne phase of the hurdle should be *short* in duration, *low* to the ground, and *quick* in forward horizontal velocity. During this time the arms are being repositioned behind the trunk in preparation for their oncoming for-upward throw.

B-C. As the foot of the push leg (right leg as illustrated) makes contact with the board, the total body unit is leaning backward, forming a sizable angle with the vertical. Because the performer is already traveling forward, this angle of input (blocking) places the body in a more advantageous takeoff position for attaining maximum vertical lift.

Notice that the impact of the body's momentum causes *slight* and *very brief* flexion at the ankle, knee, and hip joints of the push leg. These joints instantaneously begin to extend forcefully (kickback action) as the performer approaches the vertical. During the very same moment, the flexed lead leg (left leg as illustrated) as well as both arms are being vigorously thrown in a for-upward direction. Except for the flexed lead leg, the total body unit should be fully extended at takeoff.

C-D. It is important to emphasize attaining maximum vertical lift. In this way, the foot of the flexed lead leg can *make contact with the beam's surface while the performer's body is still on its upward rise.* Such a consideration facilitates a smooth, effortless, and yet controlled transition onto the apparatus.

D-E. As soon as the foot of the lead leg contacts the beam, the performer should *immediately* proceed (flow) into the very next sequentially related

FIGURE 8.6. Step-On Mount.

A   B   C   D   E

movement. In this case, it is a graceful pose, momentarily held. Regardless of type, the chosen pose or movement skill should complement the nature and objective of the mount.

E. Any pose, momentarily held, that enhances the aesthetic appeal of the performer's body shape can represent final completion of the skill.

8.7 Handstand Mount

A. Using a *fast, low,* and *short* hurdle, the performer contacts the board in an upright body position. Notice that, as the legs undergo slight and very brief flexion, the arms are vigorously reaching forward for the end surface of the beam.

A-B. As the instantaneous and forceful extension of the legs against the board begins to "lift" the body for-upward into the air, the hands make almost immediate contact with and steadfastly push against the surface of the beam. In this way, the entire mount sequence can be initiated, executed, and completed on the upswing (peaking) side of the vertical.

Notice that the hip joints undergo full and complete flexion *prior* to straddling the legs laterally. (However, once this straddling action begins, it should continue until the legs are spread apart as far as is mechanically possible.) During this time, the entire upper body assumes a slightly hollowed shape.

B-C-D-E-F. The for-upward motion derived from the takeoff phase is now being supplemented by the for-downward push of the hands against the beam. These actions allow the performer to progressively "unfold" the existing body shape (seen in illustration B) into the desired straight-line handstand position.

F. The attainment of a fully extended handstand position represents final completion of the skill.

FIGURE 8.7. Handstand Mount.

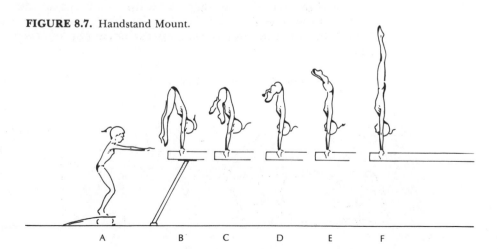

8.8 Front Aerial Mount (Russian Lift)

A. A very fast, accelerating, and yet controlled approach facilitates maximum execution of the skill. As the performer jumps for-upward into the Jap-Spring, notice that the slightly arched body shape has a slight forward lean.

A-B. As the body begins its descent from the apex of the Jap-Spring, the arms also begin to rotate for-downward (clockwise as illustrated). The actual step-out is initiated *just prior* to the sequential foot contact (right foot then left foot as illustrated) with the board.

B-C-D. The rapid arm swing pattern continues in its clockwise direction throughout the entire step-out phase and must be timed so that the arms can ultimately attain a "locked" position *well behind* the performer's body (shoulder joint hyperextension) *just as* the takeoff leg begins its vigorous push-off from the board. Although the upper body undergoes *considerable* forward rotation about both hip joints, observe that the push leg is planted well in front of the total body unit so as to ensure an effective "blocking" action for the oncoming takeoff phase.

The impact of the performer's momentum against the board causes *slight* and *very brief* flexion at the knee and ankle joints of the push leg. Notice that the slightly hollowed body shape, formed by the lead leg, trunk, and head (illustration D), is positioned perpendicular to and *almost* directly over its momentary base of support.

D-E. During takeoff, the knee and ankle joints of the push leg *instantaneously* begin to extend forcefully (kickback action). At the very same moment, the slightly hollowed body shape also begins its forceful extension to a point such that the lead leg, trunk, and head collectively form a slightly arched body shape. Because the body already possesses a sufficient amount of forward rotary motion, these actions primarily serve to provide the gymnast with the vertical lift necessary to execute the airborne phase of the skill.

The initiation of maximum vertical lift, appropriate forward rotation, and a slightly arched body shape with fully split legs are desirable characteristics of the takeoff. In addition, notice that the arms are positioned well behind the trunk in preparation for the oncoming hand contact with the beam.

FIGURE 8.8. Front Aerial Mount (Russian Lift).

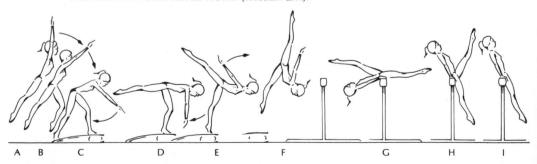

A   B   C   D   E   F   G   H   I

E-F-G. Notice that the body, once airborne, begins to rotate forward about its mass center. Although attaining maximum vertical lift is desirable, the actual path taken by the performer's mass center should be such that hand contact with the beam can be achieved *on the upswing side* of the airborne trajectory. In so doing, the performer's oncoming body weight can be "lowered" more effectively onto the beam.

G-H-I. The rotary motion of the airborne phase allows the body to continue circling forward about its new base of support (both hands as well as the buttock of the lead leg). Notice how the hip joint of the trail leg remains fully flexed until the performer arrives in an upright rear support position.

I. A rear support position with a slightly arched body shape represents final completion of the skill.

LOCOMOTOR SKILLS

8.9 Walking

A through J. The necessity for mastering and continually refining beam walking technique cannot be overemphasized. Not only is it *the* essential lead-up skill to virtually all of the more advanced locomotor skills, but also there is virtually no other movement in balance beam that so accurately exposes both the ability and aesthetic appeal of the performer. In this light, let us consider a basic beam-walking pattern, keeping in mind the following guidelines:

Posture.

An upright, erect body carriage should be maintained at all times. Notice that the head is held high, the shoulder girdle pressed downward (depressed), the arms positioned laterally, the stomach (abdominals) pulled in, and the hips tucked under (posterior pelvic girdle rotation).

FIGURE 8.9. Walking.

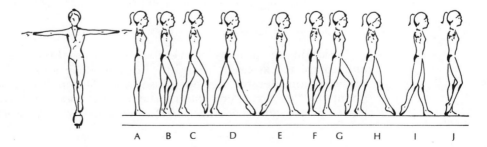

A   B   C   D   E   F   G   H   I   J

Balance.

Every attempt should be made to localize balance at "ankle-level." (See On-Line Balancing Technique discussed in chapter 6.). To assist in body awareness and balance, the performer should maintain constant visual contact with the end of the beam and/or an imaginary extension of the beam.

Movement Technique.

The stride-length of the walk should be appropriate to the size of the gymnast. Each step should precede the performer's oncoming body weight. Notice how each stepping leg is rotated slightly outward at the hip joint with the entire movement being led by the pointed foot. Up-and-down motions as well as side-to-side shiftings should be minimized, or, better yet, eliminated. There should be a consistent, rhythmical tempo to the walking pattern.

Aesthetic Considerations.

Walking the beam should be conceptualized as graceful posture in fluid motion. It should "flow" like a wave in water. There should be a controlled, yet aggressive sureness to the movement.

Method.

Practice walking the beam in both a forward and backward direction. As greater sureness and control are gained, increase the tempo. Walking is the lead-up skill to running.

8.10 Running

A through I. Running on the beam is essentially an exaggerated extension of walking. Although the suggested guidelines presented in figure 8.9 (Walking) can, for the most part, be applied to this skill, certain key differences do exist and among these are:

Posture.

There should be a slight, yet observable forward lean throughout the entire sequence.

Balance.

Balancing suggestions for running are the same as those for walking.

Movement Technique.

Notice that the support leg in each stride pushes through a position of full and complete extension while the hip and knee joints of the swing leg undergo considerable flexion (illustrations D and H). In an attempt to maintain a "level" running pattern, the recovery foot in each stride should be placed directly underneath the performer's body weight (illustrations E and

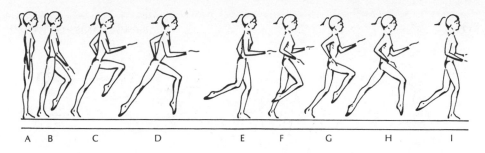

A   B   C   D   E   F   G   H   I

FIGURE 8.10. Running.

I). Finally, notice that the elbow joints remain flexed approximately 90 degrees throughout the entire sequence. This allows the arms to keep pace more easily with the reciprocal running tempo of the legs and thus helps to avoid the tendency of rolling the trunk from left to right.

Aesthetic Considerations.

Just as in walking, running on the beam should be conceptualized as graceful posture in fluid motion. It should "flow" like a wave in water. Again, there should be a controlled, yet aggressive sureness to the movement.

Method.

Master correct walking mechanics first. Develop a reasonable level of sureness and control before gradually increasing stride rate. Practice running for accuracy at ground level *first* before attempting this skill on the beam.

8.11 Leaping (Split Leap)

Leaping generally refers to the execution of any nonsomersaulting aerial skill using both a single-leg takeoff as well as a single-leg landing. Although there are innumerable body shapes that the performer can assume while airborne, the underlying mechanics in virtually all leaping skills are the same. For this reason, the basic Split Leap readily qualifies as a representative example for analysis.

A. A fast, accelerating, and yet controlled approach is essential to maximum execution of the skill.

A-B-C. As the foot of the push leg (right leg as illustrated) makes contact with the beam, the total body unit is leaning backward, forming a sizable angle with the vertical. Because the performer is already traveling forward, this angle of input (blocking) places the body in a more advantageous takeoff position for attaining maximum vertical lift.

C-D-E. Notice that the impact of the body's momentum causes *slight* and *very brief* flexion at the ankle, knee, and hip joints of the push leg. These joints instantaneously begin to extend forcefully (kickback action) and in fact reach full and complete extension as the performer arrives at the vertical.

125

FIGURE 8.11. Leaping (Split Leap).

During this time, the flexed lead leg (left leg as illustrated) as well as both arms are being vigorously thrown in a for-upward direction.

E-F. Although the body travels horizontally forward, it is important to emphasize attaining maximum vertical lift. In this way, the performer will have sufficient time to fully execute the "split phase" of the leap and to land with grace and control. Notice that as the knee of the lead leg extends forward so too does the hip joint of the already straightened push leg begin to hyperextend backward. The performer's head and trunk should remain erect and upright throughout the entire leap.

F-G-H. Once airborne, although the mass center follows a perfectly regular curved path, the performer's body undergoes *very obvious* and *specifically* timed changes in shape: from partially split legs at takeoff, to fully split legs at the peak of the trajectory, and returning to partially split legs immediately prior to landing.

It is interesting to observe that the *lead* leg maintains a horizontal relationship with the beam throughout the entire *ascent* phase and that the *trail* leg maintains this horizontal relationship throughout the entire *descent* phase. Only at the peak of the trajectory do both legs attain such a relationship with the beam.

H-I. In preparation for landing, the performer maintains complete body extension until just prior to making contact with the beam. The arms are being raised laterally overhead to line up with the trunk while the lead leg is stretching or reaching for-downward for the beam. Because this technique provides the gymnast with the largest possible distance through which to apply a stopping force, greater and more effective control in the landing phase can be realized. Notice that only the ankle, knee, and hip joints of the lead leg flex to absorb the impact.

Observe that at touchdown the total body unit is positioned slightly behind the lead (support) leg. Since this allows the performer to "check" the forward motion of the skill, greater effective control of the landing can be realized.

I. Landing in an upright arabesque position with the trail leg held parallel to the beam represents final completion of the skill.

8.12 Leaping (Tour Jeté)

Many leaping skills, in addition to employing single-leg takeoffs and landings, also require some type of airborne turn (twist) about the body's longitudinal axis. The Tour Jeté is a typical example.

A. A fast, accelerating, and yet controlled approach is essential to maximum execution of the skill. Notice that both arms are positioned behind the trunk in preparation for their oncoming for-upward throw.

A-B. As the foot of the push leg (left leg as illustrated) makes contact with the beam's surface, the total body unit is leaning backward, forming a sizable angle with the vertical. Because the performer is already traveling forward, this angle of input (blocking) places the body in a more advantageous takeoff position for attaining maximum vertical lift.

Notice that the impact of the body's momentum causes *slight* and *very brief* flexion of the ankle, knee, and hip joints of the push leg. These joints instantaneously begin to extend forcefully (kickback action) as the performer approaches the vertical. During the very same moment, the extended swing leg (right leg as illustrated) as well as both arms are being vigorously thrown in a for-upward direction.

B-C. Although very slight, the one-half turn (twist) is actually initiated during the takeoff phase. Notice that the twist occurs *uniformly* throughout the long axis of the straight-line body shape formed by the push leg, trunk, head, and arms.

C-D. Although the body travels horizontally forward, it is important to emphasize attaining maximum vertical lift. In this way, the performer will have sufficient time to fully execute both the "one-half turn" and "switch-kick" phases, and then to land with grace and control. The performer's head and trunk should remain erect and upright throughout the entire leap.

D-E. Notice how the legs, en route to the fully split position, are quickly brought together, forming a straight-line shape of the total body unit. This action of momentarily shortening the body's (long axis) radius of rotation increases the speed of the twist and thus allows the performer to complete the *one-half turn* on the *upswing side* of the airborne trajectory.

FIGURE 8.12. Leaping (Tour Jeté).

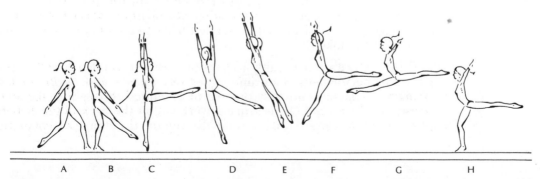

E-F-G. As the legs continue rising to a full split position, notice that the arms are being progressively lowered (laterally backward) to just above shoulder level. These changes in shape greatly increase the body's (long axis) radius of rotation. Any further twisting is for the most part canceled out. Remember that the *full split* position of the legs should be attained *just as the body reaches the peak of the airborne trajectory.*

G-H. In preparation for landing, the performer maintains complete body extension until just prior to making contact with the beam. The arms are being returned laterally overhead to line up with the trunk while the landing leg (right leg as illustrated) is stretching or reaching back-downward for the beam. Because this technique provides the gymnast with the largest possible distance through which to apply a stopping force, greater and more effective control in the landing phase can be realized. Notice that only the ankle, knee, and hip joints of the landing leg flex to absorb the impact. The trail leg (left leg as illustrated) should maintain a horizontal relationship with the beam throughout the entire descent.

H. Landing in an upright arabesque position with the trail leg held parallel to the beam represents final completion of the skill.

8.13 Jumping (Squat Jump)

Jumping generally refers to the execution of any nonsomersaulting aerial skill using a double-leg takeoff and either a single- or double-leg landing. Although there are innumerable body shapes that the performer can assume while airborne, the underlying mechanics in virtually all jumping skills are the same. For this reason, the basic squat jump qualifies as a representative example for analysis.

A. The skill is begun from a standing position with the arms held directly overhead. Although the feet are slightly strided, notice that this straight-line body shape is fully and completely extended.

A-B. In preparation for the jump, the arms circle backward (counterclockwise as illustrated) while the ankle, knee, and hip joints undergo *partial* and *very brief* flexion. Although the performer has assumed an open-tucked position, notice that the total body unit remains "on-balance."

B-C. By immediately and forcefully extending the legs while at the same time throwing the arms in an upward direction, the performer is lifted *vertically* off the ground. The initiation of maximum vertical lift and *zero* horizontal motion with a fully extended body shape are desirable characteristics of the takeoff.

C-D-E. Once airborne, although the mass center travels a directly vertical path, the performer's body undergoes *very obvious* and *specifically timed* changes in shape: from fully opened or extended throughout the ascent phase, to fully tucked (arms remain overhead) at the peak of the airborne phase, and returning to full extension throughout the entire descent phase.

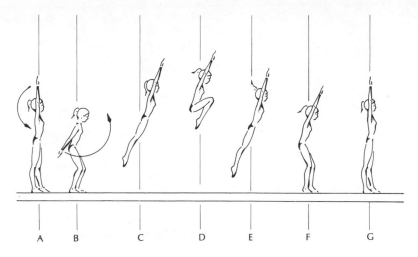

FIGURE 8.13. Squat Jump.

E-F-G. In preparation for landing, the performer maintains complete body extension until just prior to making contact with the beam. The arms remain directly overhead and in line with the trunk while the legs are stretching or reaching for the beam. Because this technique provides the gymnast with the largest possible distance through which to apply a stopping force, greater and more effective control in the landing phase can be realized. Notice that only the hip, knee, and ankle joints flex to absorb the impact.

G. The final position is identical to the starting position.

8.14 Pirouette (Double Pirouette)

The term "pirouette" commonly refers to turning about the longitudinal axis of the body using either the hands (handstand) or the feet (upright position) as the base of support. In the balance beam event, this type of movement is generally executed from a single-leg upright standing position. The amount of turn varies according to the specific objective of the skill. Some pirouettes occur through as little as 45 degrees while others rotate through as much as 720 degrees (2 full revolutions). During this time, a variety of body shapes can be assumed that should serve to enhance the performer's aesthetic appeal as well as to control the actual rate of the turn. The double pirouette is a typical example.

A. The skill can be initiated from a forward lunge position with the arms held perpendicular to one another and parallel to the beam's surface.

A-B. By pushing off with the trail foot (left foot as illustrated) while *simultaneously* extending the hip, knee, and ankle joints of the front leg (right leg as illustrated), the performer's body weight begins to rise for-upward. It is during this time that the pirouette is actually initiated. The idea here is to extend the total body unit upward and into the twist. The trail or swing leg

129

FIGURE 8.14. Pirouette (Double Pirouette).

(left leg as illustrated) is being lifted laterally while the performer begins to turn about the long axis formed by the extending support leg, trunk, and head.

B-C. Notice that *only* the ball of the support foot is in contact with the beam's surface. In addition to further lifting the total body unit, this beam-foot relationship considerably reduces the surface friction of the turn and consequently should be maintained throughout the entire pirouette. The elbows of both arms begin to undergo flexion.

C-D-E-F-G-H-I. As the arms are brought in and across the chest, the knee of the laterally held swing leg flexes approximately 90 degrees. These actions decrease the performer's (long axis) radius of rotation and thus allow the body to pirouette more quickly. Every attempt should be made to maintain the *straight-line body shape* formed by the support leg, trunk, and head.

I-J-K. By flexing the ankle, knee, and hip joints of the support leg while simultaneously extending the knee of the swing leg, the performer's total body unit is progressively lowered. The arms begin to extend to their original forward lunge position. These actions increase the performer's (long axis) radius of rotation and thus the body's turning rate substantially decreases in preparation for the upcoming lunge phase.

K-L. In addition to contacting the beam slightly *prior* to completing the double pirouette, the foot of the swing leg should also be positioned *well behind* the body. To ensure a smooth transition into the lunge, this foot placement must occur *slightly* before the performer's body weight shifts backward.

L. The final position is identical to the starting position.

8.15 Static Poses

These are but a few of the innumerable momentary static poses that can be utilized by the gymnast in the performance of a routine. A general guideline would be to select and/or create those kinds of poses (shapes) that best complement both the specific body type of the individual performer and the particular style or mood she is attempting to reveal.

FIGURE 8.15. Static Poses.

8.16 Lunge Forward Roll

A. The skill is begun from a free-standing lunge position with the arms held directly overhead and in line with the trunk. To facilitate balance and control in this position, the extended rear leg should be rotated outward at the hip joint.

A-B. By pushing off with the trail foot (right foot as illustrated) while *simultaneously* flexing the hip, knee, and ankle joints of the support leg (left leg as illustrated), the performer's body weight begins to move for-downward. Notice that the hands contact the beam at a point well in front of the support foot.

B-C-D. The support leg extends and then lines up with the lead leg, driving the hips over the hands (new base of support). Notice that, as the head ducks forward, the total body unit is being lowered onto the upper back by a controlled bending of the arms. Once the upper back touches the beam, the entire trunk begins to form a slightly curved or hollowed shape. This helps to ensure a smooth rolling action.

FIGURE 8.16. Lunge Forward Roll.

| A | B | C | D | E | F |

D-E. The slightly curved body shape literally unfolds until just prior to making leg contact with the beam. At that point the hip joints flex, causing the entire upper body to begin rotating in a for-upward direction. In addition, the knee joint of the initial support leg (left leg as illustrated) simultaneously flexes, allowing its foot to be positioned underneath the oncoming body weight. Although the hands can help guide and stabilize the performer throughout much of the actual roll phase, they should be freed from beam contact as soon as possible. In this way, they can gracefully flow laterally and upward, complementing the upswing phase of the roll.

E-F. As the performer rocks onto the initial support leg, observe that the upper body now assumes a straight-line shape and maintains an erect upright position relative to the beam. Forward momentum, rather than forward body lean, is the important factor to successful execution. The knee of the second support leg (right leg as illustrated) then flexes so that its foot can be placed in the strided position.

F. The attainment of a strided, squat-stand position represents final completion of the skill.

8.17 Lunge Free Forward Roll

A. The skill is begun from a free-standing lunge position with the arms held directly overhead and in line with the trunk. To facilitate balance and control in this position, the extended rear leg should be rotated outward at the hip joint.

A-B. By pushing off the trail foot (right foot as illustrated) while *simultaneously* flexing the hip joint of the support leg (left leg as illustrated), the performer rocks forward through a front scale position. Notice that the support leg remains slightly flexed at the knee joint, the arms move laterally, and a slightly curved or hollow body shape is being formed by the lead leg, trunk, and head.

B-C. Although the performer continues to rotate forward about the hip joint of the support leg, every attempt should be made to remain "on-balance" until the last possible moment. This helps to ensure a smoother transition into the actual roll phase. "Sighting" the beam can provide a more accurate assessment of relative body position. The arms remain free of the beam and are held laterally.

C-D. Notice that the head is ducked forward as far as is mechanically possible so that the upper back is the major body part to make contact with the beam. During this time, the entire trunk begins to form a slightly curved or hollowed shape. Such a consideration helps to ensure a smooth rolling action.

D-E-F. Except for the fact that the hands are never in contact with the beam's surface, these movements are identical in nature to the illustrations and descriptions presented in the Lunge Forward Roll, (8.16 D, E, and F).

FIGURE 8.17. Lunge Free Forward Roll.

8.18 Cast Forward Roll

Although this skill is being presented starting from an upper back resting position with a deeply hollowed piked body shape, it can be initiated from any one of a variety of sequentially related lead-in movements. And too, it is possible to execute the cast phase to the handstand prior to the actual forward roll.

A. The skill is begun from an upper back resting position with a deeply hollowed body shape. The arms are placed overhead with flexed elbows, allowing the hands to more easily grasp the beam.

A-B. By *briefly* extending out of the deeply hollowed body shape and then *instantaneously* flexing at the hip joints, the entire upper body is able to begin rotating in a for-upward direction. The arms reach in between the spreading legs en route to their upcoming contact with the beam's surface.

B-C. While the upper body continues its forward rotation, the hands are attempting to contact the beam *as soon as* is mechanically possible. Early hand contact, in addition to the deeply held straddled hip pike (legs held high relative to the beam), places the gymnast in a more advantageous position for maximizing the actual "cast phase." Note that the legs are straddled only to the degree that allows for easy hand placement.

C-D. With the buttocks and the hands serving as the base of support, the hip joints begin to extend vigorously. Just prior to attaining a straight-line relationship with the head and trunk, this rapid extension motion in the

FIGURE 8.18. Cast Forward Roll.

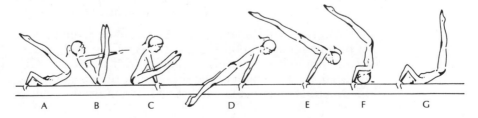

hips is instantaneously stopped, causing its momentum to be transferred into the entire body. This "stopping action" of the legs serves as the cue to begin forcefully pushing with the hands in a for-downward direction. Remember, the *quickness* with which the gymnast can execute these movements determines, to a large extent, the degree of upswing amplitude that can ultimately be realized.

D-E. Because of the forceful and steadfast push of the hands against the beam in a for-downward direction, the total body unit continues to rotate for-upward about the shoulder joints.

E-F-G. Just prior to maximizing the upswing phase of the cast, there is an increased hollowing in the shape of the total body. In addition, observe how the arms begin to flex slowly to ensure a smooth transition into the "roll phase." "Sighting" the beam prior to ducking the head forward can provide the performer with a more accurate assessment of relative body position.

Constant muscular tension throughout the entire body, particularly in the shoulder region, helps prevent the natural tendency to collapse or fold in at one's jointed and/or weaker points. The objective is to lower *gently* the rolling body onto the upper back.

G. The final illustration is essentially the same as the initial starting position. Consequently, the gymnast is again in a position to execute any of the sequentially related skills.

8.19 Backward Roll to Knee Scale

Although this skill is being presented starting from an upper back support position with a hollowed body shape, it can be initiated from any one of a variety of sequentially related lead-in movements.

A. Regardless of the selected lead-in movement, the performer inevitably proceeds through a back resting position while vigorously piking or flexing at the hips. The arms are placed overhead with flexed elbows, allowing the hands to more easily grasp the beam.

A-B. As the feet pass directly overhead, the rapid hip flexing motion is instantaneously stopped, causing its backward momentum to be transferred into the entire body. This "stopping action" of the legs serves as the cue to begin forcefully pushing for-downward with the hands against the beam.

B-C. By allowing the bend or pike observed at the hips to move progressively upward through the trunk, this deep hip pike shape begins to unfold backward into a hollowed shape for the total body unit. The continuous for-downward push of the hands serves to lift the body upward, allowing the head to begin its passage through the arms more easily.

C-D. Just as the head passes in between the extending arms, the hip joints of the oncoming support leg (right leg as illustrated) flexes, allowing the top of the pointed foot to make contact with the beam. Once this contact is realized, the knee joint of the support leg then begins to flex in preparation for the upcoming beam contact with the entire lower leg.

FIGURE 8.19. Backward Roll to Knee Scale.

Although the total body continues to unfold in a backward direction, notice that the position of the opposite leg (left leg as illustrated) relative to the beam has been established and is steadfastly maintained throughout the remainder of the skill.

D-E-F. By fully extending the arms while allowing the entire lower aspect of the support leg to rest on the beam's surface, the performer arrives in a knee scale support position.

F. The attainment of a knee scale support position with the head, trunk, and free leg forming an arched body shape represents final completion of the skill.

8.20 Backward Shoulder Roll to Knee Scale

A. The skill can be initiated from a fully extended back resting position. The longitudinal aspect of the body is positioned such that the oncoming support shoulder (right shoulder as illustrated) is in direct alignment with the beam's surface. The neck is slightly hyperextended, and the arms are placed overhead with flexed elbows, allowing the hands to grasp the beam more easily.

A-B-C-D-E. Except for the fact that the performer rotates backward over the support shoulder, these movements are essentially the same as the illustrations and descriptions presented for the Backward Roll to Knee Scale, (8.19 A through F).

E. The attainment of a knee scale support position with the head, trunk, and free leg forming an arched body shape represents final completion of the skill.

FIGURE 8.20. Backward Shoulder Roll to Knee Scale.

8.21 Piked Backward Roll Squat to Stand

A. The skill can be initiated from a pike sit position with the arms held directly overhead and in a line with the trunk. The performer extends at the hips, allowing the total body unit to rest on top of and in direct alignment with the beam's surface. The elbows are then flexed so the hands can more easily grasp the beam.

A-B. By vigorously flexing at the hip joints, the legs and feet begin to rise and rotate in a backward direction.

B-C-D. *Just as* the feet pass directly overhead, the trunk begins to flex or round, the head is ducked forward, and the arms push steadfastly downward against the beam. Appropriate timing of the arm push not only eliminates pressure on the head and neck, but it also allows the feet to be placed more closely to the hands. This latter aspect greatly facilitates "peaking" the stand-up phase of the skill.

D-E-F. Although the hip joints maintain their fully flexed position, notice that the knee joints remain completely extended and do not begin to flex *until* the feet actually make contact with the beam.

The already accrued momentum of the roll itself, the vigorous push-off action of the hands, and the timely flexion of the knee joints collectively enhance the performer's potential to execute the entire stand-up phase on the upswing side (peaking) of the vertical.

F-G. The stand-up phase should be executed such that all body segments line up with one another and with the upper vertical line at the exact same time.

G. The attainment of a fully extended standing position with the arms held directly overhead represents final completion of the skill. (The slightly strided position observed in the feet is one of several foot placement variations available to the performer).

FIGURE 8.21. Piked Backward Roll Squat to Stand.

8.22 Cartwheel Variations

1. Cartwheel
2. Lead Arm Cartwheel
3. Trail Arm Cartwheel
4. Dive Cartwheel

Except for the fact that execution is confined to the dimensions of the beam's surface, these skills are identical in nature to the illustrations and descriptions presented for the very same skills in Floor Exercise (Cartwheel 7.30; Lead Arm Cartwheel 7.31; Trail Arm Cartwheel 7.32; and Dive Cartwheel 7.33).

8.23 Walkover Variations

1. Forward Walkover
2. Backward Walkover

Except for the fact that execution is confined to the dimensions of the beam's surface, these skills are identical in nature to the illustrations and descriptions presented for the very same skills in Floor Exercise (Forward Walkover 7.6; and Backward Walkover 7.24).

8.24 Aerial Variations

1. Aerial Cartwheel
2. Forward Aerial Walkover

Except for the fact that execution is confined to the dimensions of the beam's surface, these skills are identical in nature to the illustrations and descriptions presented for the very same skills in Floor Exercise (Aerial Cartwheel 7.34; and Forward Aerial Walkover 7.17).

8.25 Standing Tucked Backward Somersault

Except for the slightly strided foot position during both the take-off and landing phases, this skill is identical in nature to the illustrations and descriptions presented for the Standing Tucked Backward Somersault (7.28) in Floor Exercise. Such a foot adjustment enhances stability and control in this as well as numerous other aerial balance beam skills.

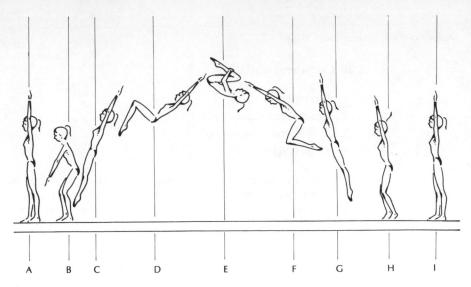

FIGURE 8.25. Standing Tucked Backward Somersault.

8.26 Backward Diving Handspring Step-out

A-B-C. Except for the slightly strided foot position, these movements are identical in nature to the illustrations and descriptions presented for the Standing Backward Handspring (7.26) in Floor Exercise.

C-D. By vigorously extending *first* the hips and *then* the lower back, upper back, and shoulders in a rapid, sequential fashion, the upper body begins to quickly rotate backward about the lower body while forming the desired slightly arched shape. At the very same time, the forceful extension of the legs against the beam's surface drives the total body unit upward and backward. (Since the movement is a *"driving"* backward handspring, maximizing vertical height or lift while proportionately decreasing rotational speed and horizontal distance is a most important objective.)

D-E. Once airborne, the performer's center of mass follows its established, perfectly regular, curved path. In addition to the body rotating somewhat slower, the actual trajectory should be comparatively higher and shorter than in the traditional backward handspring.

During the peak of the trajectory, the hip joint of the lead leg (right leg as illustrated) begins to flex vigorously in preparation for the upcoming step-out.

E-F. Notice that the fully elevated shoulder girdle is directly over the strided hands at contact while the slightly arched body shape forms a sizable angle with the vertical. The hip joint of the lead leg is fully and completely flexed at this time.

F-G. The impact of the body's momentum against the beam forces the shoulder girdle to be *momentarily* depressed. As the body continues to rotate backward, the momentarily depressed shoulder girdle immediately returns to its originally elevated position. It is this instantaneous "kickback action"

138

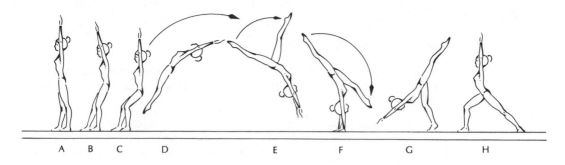

FIGURE 8.26. Backward Diving Handspring Step-Out.

(repulsion) of the shoulder girdle that "lifts" the performer into the air *prior* to making foot contact with the beam.

Although the knee joint of the support leg flexes slightly to absorb the impact of the body's momentum, the slightly arched body shape formed by the free leg (left leg as illustrated), trunk, head, and arms is steadfastly maintained throughout the remainder of the skill.

G-H. The performer continues to rotate backward about the hip joint of the support leg until arriving in a free-standing forward lunge position.

H. The attainment of a free-standing forward lunge position with the arms held directly overhead and in line with the trunk represents final completion of the skill. To facilitate balance and control, the extended rear leg should be rotated outward at the hip joint.

8.27 Standing Backward Handspring (Punch Jump)

Except for the slightly strided position of both the feet and the hands during their respective contact phases, this skill is identical in nature to the illustrations and descriptions presented for the Standing Backward Handspring (7.26) in Floor Exercise. Such hand and foot adjustments enhance stability and control in this as well as numerous other aerial balance beam skills.

FIGURE 8.27. Standing Backward Handspring (Punch Jump).

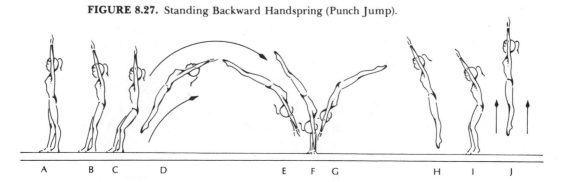

8.28 Arched Jump Dismount

A. The skill is begun from a standing position with the arms held directly overhead. Notice that this straight-line body shape is fully and completely extended.

A-B. In preparation for the jump, the arms are lowered backward (counterclockwise as illustrated) while the ankle, knee, and hip joints undergo *partial* and *very brief* flexion. As the performer assumes this open tucked position, the total body unit begins to shift forward very slightly.

B-C. By *immediately* and *forcefully* extending the legs while at the same time throwing the arms and then the entire upper body directly upward, the performer begins to rise for-upward. Although leaning slightly forward, the total body unit is fully extended at takeoff.

C-D-E. Once airborne, the performer's center of mass follows its established perfectly regular curved path. Although the body undergoes no rotation, notice the *very slight* yet *specifically timed* changes in shape: from fully extended at takeoff, into slightly arched during the ascent phase, and returning to full extension during the descent phase. (The actual trajectory should emphasize the attainment of *maximum vertical lift* rather than horizontal distance away from the apparatus.)

E-F-G. In preparation for landing, the performer maintains complete body extension until just prior to making contact with the ground. The arms remain directly overhead and in line with the trunk while the legs are stretching or reaching for the mat. Because this technique provides the largest possible distance through which to apply a stopping force, greater and more effective control in the landing phase can be realized. Notice that only the ankle, knee, and hip joints flex to absorb the impact.

G. The final position is identical to its starting position.

FIGURE 8.28. Arched Jump Dismount.

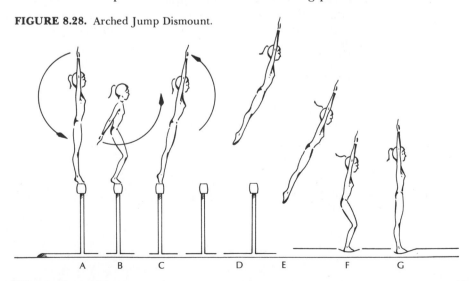

A   B   C   D   E   F   G

8.29 Straddle Jump Dismount

A-B-C-D. These movements are identical in nature to the illustrations and descriptions presented for the Arched Jump Dismount, (8.28 A through D).

D-E-F-G-H. Once airborne, the performer's center of mass follows its established perfectly regular curved path. Although the body undergoes no rotation, notice the *very obvious* and *specifically timed* changes in shape: from slightly arched during the ascent, into a fully compressed straddled pike at the peak of the airborne phase, and returning again to the slightly arched shape during the descent. (The actual trajectory should emphasize the attainment of *maximum vertical lift* rather than horizontal distance away from the apparatus.)

H-I-J-K. These movements are identical in nature to the illustrations and descriptions presented for the Arched Jump Dismount, (8.28 E, F, and G).

A B C D E F G H I J K

FIGURE 8.29. Straddle Jump Dismount.

8.30 Round-Off Dismount

A. The high step-walk pattern pictured in this illustration is one of several possible preparatory techniques that can be used to initiate the Round-Off Dismount.

A-B-C-D-E. Except for the fact that the skill is being initiated from a high step-walk pattern on the beam, these movements are identical to the illustrations and descriptions presented for the Round-Off in Floor Exercise, 7.35 A through E.

E-F. The impact of the body's momentum against the beam forces the shoulder girdle to be momentarily depressed. As the total body unit begins to assume a slightly hollowed shape, the depressed shoulder girdle immediately returns to its originally elevated position. It is this instantaneous "kickback action" (repulsion) of the shoulder girdle that lifts the body through the handstand and into the air. Notice that the performer uses only as much "hollow" in body shape as is necessary to maximize this kickback action of the shoulder girdle.

F-G-H. Once airborne, although the mass center follows a perfectly regular curved path, the performer's body undergoes *very unobvious,* yet *specifically timed,* changes in shape: from slightly hollowed just after takeoff, to slightly arched at the peak of the airborne trajectory, and returning to slightly hollowed immediately prior to landing. (Contrary to the Round-Off in Floor Exercise, the actual trajectory should emphasize the attainment of *maximum vertical lift* rather than horizontal distance.)

H-I-J. In preparation for landing, the performer maintains complete body extension until just prior to making contact with the ground. The arms remain directly overhead and in line with the trunk while the legs are stretching or reaching for the mat. Because this technique provides the gymnast with the largest possible distance through which to apply a stopping force, greater and more effective control in the landing phase can be realized. Notice that only the ankle, knee, and hip joints flex to absorb the impact.

Observe that at touchdown the total body unit forms a noticeable forward leaning angle with the vertical. Because this technique allows the performer to "check" the backward motion, additional landing control can be realized.

J. The attainment of a fully extended standing position with the arms held directly overhead and in line with the trunk represents final completion of the skill.

FIGURE 8.30. Round-Off Dismount.

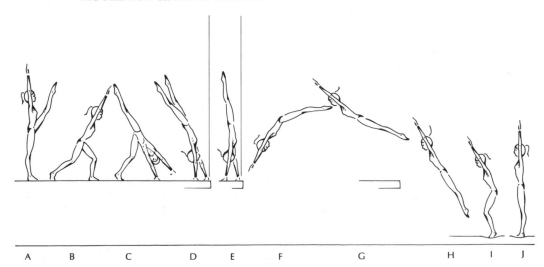

A   B   C   D   E   F   G   H   I   J

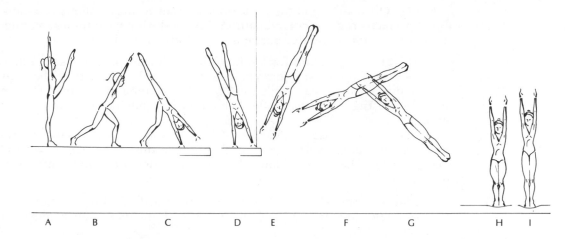

FIGURE 8.31. Cartwheel Dismount.

8.31 Cartwheel Dismount

A. The high step-walk pattern pictured in this illustration is one of several possible preparatory techniques that can be used to initiate the Cartwheel Dismount.

A-B-C. Except for the fact that the skill is being initiated from a high step-walk pattern on the beam and that only a one-quarter (rather than a one-half) turn is being initiated about the long axis of the body, these movements are identical to the illustrations and descriptions presented for the Round-off in Floor Exercise, (7.35 A, B, and C).

C-D. As the performer's hands contact the beam in a one-two sequence, notice that the slightly flexed push leg forcefully extends, causing increased sideward rotation in the total body unit. At the very same time, this impact of the body's momentum against the beam also forces the shoulder girdle to be momentarily depressed. As the push leg quickly lines up with the lead leg, the depressed shoulder girdle immediately returns to its originally elevated position. It is this instantaneous and sequential "kickback action" (repulsion) of the shoulder girdle that lifts the body sideward through the handstand and into the air. Keep in mind that these timely actions occur *prior* to the performer arriving at the vertical.

D-E. Notice that at takeoff, as well as throughout the entire airborne phase, the performer maintains a fully extended body shape with legs held together and arms placed directly overhead in line with the trunk. (Because this cartwheel movement serves as a dismount, maximizing the vertical lift from the beam while proportionately decreasing sideward rotation and horizontal distance is a most important objective.)

E-F-G. Once airborne, the performer's center of mass follows its established perfectly regular curved path. Although the body continues rotating sideward, its fully extended shape is steadfastly maintained.

G-H-I. In preparation for landing, the performer maintains complete body extension until just prior to making contact with the ground. The arms remain directly overhead while the legs are stretching or reaching for the mat. Notice that only the ankle, knee, and hip joints flex to absorb the impact.

At touchdown, observe that the total body unit forms a noticeable sideward leaning angle with the vertical. Because this technique allows the performer to "check" the sideward motion, additional landing control can be realized.

I. The attainment of a fully extended, sideward standing position with the arms held directly overhead and in line with the trunk represents final completion of the skill.

8.32 Cartwheel One-Quarter Twist Dismount

A-B-C-D. These movements are identical in nature to the illustrations and descriptions presented for the Cartwheel Dismount, (8.31 A through D).

D-E-F. By vigorously pushing for-downward with the right hand and back-downward with the left hand, the performer initiates a one-quarter twist uniformly about the long axis to the straight-line body shape. Notice, however, that this twist is *directly opposite* to the original one-quarter twist seen during the input phase of the Cartwheel Dismount. Although executing a one-quarter twist in one direction followed by a one-quarter twist in the exact opposite direction results in zero twisting, these actions often render the illusion of executing a complete one-half turn particularly since the body is also rotating. (Because this skill serves as a dismount, maximizing the vertical lift from the beam while proportionately decreasing somersault rotation and horizontal distance is a most important objective.)

F-G-H. Once airborne, although the mass center follows a perfectly regular curved path, the performer's body continues to rotate forward while also turning about its long axis. By slightly spreading the arms laterally just prior to arriving at the peak of the airborne trajectory, the natural tendency to continue twisting throughout the descent phase is, for the most part, held in check.

H-I-J. Except for the fact that the body is rotating forward rather than sideward, these movements are identical in nature to the illustrations and descriptions presented for the Cartwheel Dismount, (8.31 G, H, and I).

J. The attainment of a fully extended backward standing position with the arms held directly overhead and in line with the trunk represents final completion of the skill.

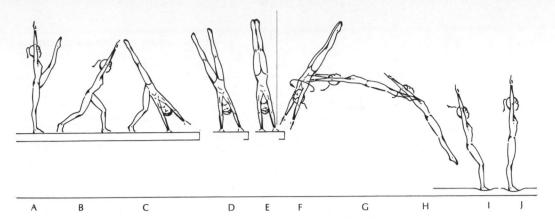

A   B   C   D   E   F   G   H   I   J

FIGURE 8.32. Cartwheel One-Quarter Twist Dismount.

8.33 Side Aerial Dismount

A-B-C-D. Except for the fact that the skill is being performed on the balance beam, these movements are identical in nature to the illustrations and descriptions presented for the Dive Cartwheel in Floor Exercise, (7.33 A through E).

D-E. Notice how as soon as possible after takeoff, the push leg (left leg as illustrated) quickly lines up with the total body unit. (Because this skill serves as a dismount, maximizing the vertical lift from the beam while proportionately decreasing sideward rotation and horizontal distance is a most important objective.)

E-F-G-H-I-J-K. Except for the fact that the total body unit is comparatively higher during the airborne phase, these movements are identical to the illustrations and descriptions presented for the Cartwheel Dismount, (8.31 E through I).

K. The attainment of a fully extended, sideward standing position with the arms held directly overhead and in line with the trunk represents final completion of the skill.

FIGURE 8.33. Side Aerial Dismount.

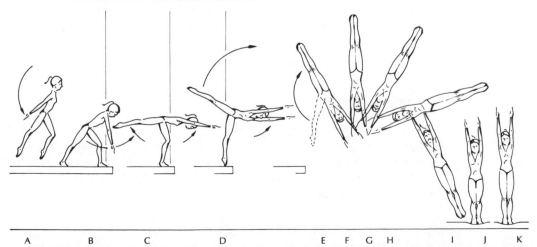

A   B   C   D   E F G H   I   J   K

8.34 Forward Aerial Dismount

A-B-C-D-E. Except for the fact that the skill is being performed on the balance beam, these movements are identical to the illustrations and descriptions presented for the Forward Aerial Walkover in Floor Exercise, (7.17 A through F).

E-F. Notice how, as soon as possible after takeoff the push leg (left leg as illustrated) quickly lines up with the total body unit. (Because this skill serves as a dismount, maximizing the vertical lift from the beam while proportionately decreasing forward rotation and horizontal distance is a most important objective.)

F-G-H-I-J-K. Except for the fact that the body is comparatively higher during the airborne phase, these movements are identical to the illustrations and descriptions presented for the Cartwheel One-Quarter Twist Dismount, (8.32 G, H, I, and J).

K. The attainment of a fully extended backward standing position with the arms held directly overhead and in line with the trunk represents final completion of the skill.

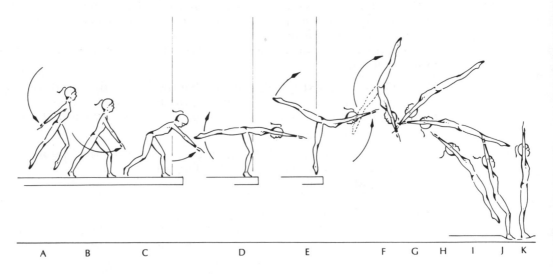

A   B   C   D   E   F   G   H   I   J   K

FIGURE 8.34. Forward Aerial Dismount.

8.35 Barani Dismount

A-B-C-D. Except for the facts that the skill is being performed on the Balance Beam, and that a one-half, rather than a one-quarter, twist is being initiated at take-off, these movements are identical in nature to the illustrations and descriptions presented for the Dive Cartwheel in Floor Exercise, (7.33 A through E).

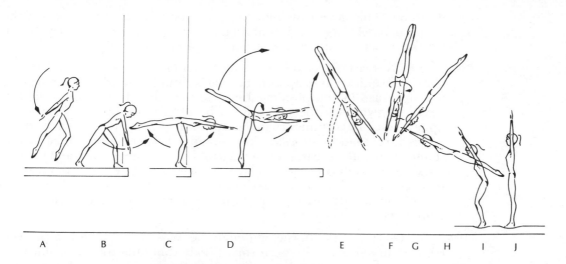

FIGURE 8.35. Barani Dismount.

D-E. As soon as possible after take-off, notice how the push leg (left leg as illustrated) quickly lines up with the total body unit. This timely shortening of the performers long axis radius of rotation serves to facilitate early completion of the one-half twist. (Because this skill serves as a dismount, maximizing the vertical lift from the beam while proportionately decreasing somersault rotation and horizontal distance is a most important objective.)

E-F-G. Once airborne notice that, although the mass center follows a perfectly regular curved path, the performer's body continues to somersault while also turning about its long axis. By slightly spreading the arms laterally just prior to completing the one-half twist, the natural tendency to continue twisting throughout the descent phase, is for the most part, held in check.

G-H-I-J. These movements are identical in nature to the illustrations and descriptions presented for the Round-Off Dismount, (8.30 G through J).

J. The attainment of a fully extended forward standing position with the arms held directly overhead and in line with the trunk represents final completion of the skill.

8.36 Roudie Dismount

A-B-C-D. Except for the facts that the skill is being performed on the balance beam and that a one and one-half rather than a one-quarter, twist is being initiated at takeoff, these movements are identical in nature to the illustrations and descriptions presented for the Dive Cartwheel in Floor Exercise, (7.33 A through E).

Notice that at takeoff, the performer has already completed a one-quarter twist about the long axis of the body. Although the arms are positioned overhead and in line with the trunk, they are also spread slightly in a lateral direction. This action of initiating a comparatively greater twist with a proportionately larger radius of rotation serves to increase the performer's twisting potential during the airborne phase.

D-E. Notice how, as soon as possible after takeoff the push leg (left leg as illustrated) quickly lines up with the total body unit. In addition, the arms are quickly pulled in and positioned next to the sides of the body. (The fully flexed elbows allow the forearms to be placed symmetrically across the upper chest.) These timely changes in body shape serve to shorten the body's radius of rotation about *both* its long axis and its lateral axis simultaneously. Consequently, the greatest percentage of both the somersault and the twist can be realized during the "peak" of the airborne trajectory. (Because this skill serves as a dismount, maximizing vertical lift from the beam while proportionately decreasing somersault rotation and horizontal distance is a more important objective.)

E-F-G-H. Once airborne, although the mass center follows a perfectly regular curved path, the performer's body continues to somersault while rapidly turning about its long axis. Notice that, as far as possible, the twist occurs *uniformly* throughout the long axis of the straight-line body shape.

H-I-J. Just prior to completing the one and one-half twist, the arms return to their original overhead lateral position. In addition to decreasing the rate of somersault, this timely change in body shape helps prevent the natural tendency to continue twisting throughout the descent phase.

J-K-L-M. These movements are identical in nature to the illustrations and descriptions presented for the Round-Off Dismount, (8.30 G through J).

M. The attainment of a fully extended forward standing position with the arms held directly overhead and in line with the trunk represents final completion of the skill.

FIGURE 8.36. Roudie Dismount.

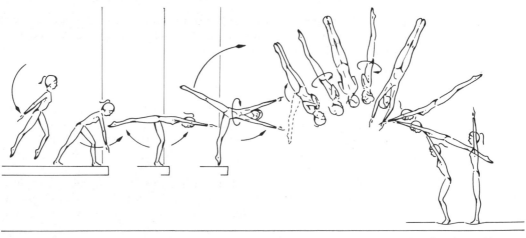

A   B   C   D   E   F   G H I   J   K   L   M

8.37 Tucked Backward Gainer Dismount

A. A fast, accelerating, and yet controlled approach is essential to maximum execution of the skill. Notice that the performer assumes and maintains an erect body carriage throughout the entire approach sequence.

A-B. The step immediately prior to takeoff should be *short* in duration, *low* to the ground, and *quick* in forward horizontal velocity. During this time the arms are being repositioned behind the trunk in preparation for their oncoming for-upward throw.

As the foot of the push leg (left leg as illustrated) makes contact with the beam, the total body unit is leaning backward, forming a sizable angle with the vertical. Because the performer is already traveling forward, this angle of input (blocking) places the body in a more advantageous position for attaining maximum vertical lift.

B-C-D. Notice that the impact of the body's momentum causes *slight* and *very brief* flexion at the ankle, knee, and hip joints of the push leg. These joints instantaneously begin to extend forcefully (kickback action) as the total body unit rocks onto and actually *beyond* the vertical reference line. During the very same moment, the swing leg (right leg as illustrated) as well as both arms and then the entire upper body are being vigorously thrown in an upward-backward direction. These actions serve to lift the performer for-upward into the air while rotating in a backward direction. (The initiation of maximum vertical lift, appropriate backward rotation, and a fully extended body shape with the swing leg rising forcefully for-upward are desirable characteristics of the takeoff.)

D-E-F-G-H. Once airborne, although the mass center follows a perfectly regular curved path, the performer's rotating body undergoes *very obvious* and *specifically timed* changes in shape: from fully open or extended (with

FIGURE 8.37. Tucked Backward Gainer Dismount.

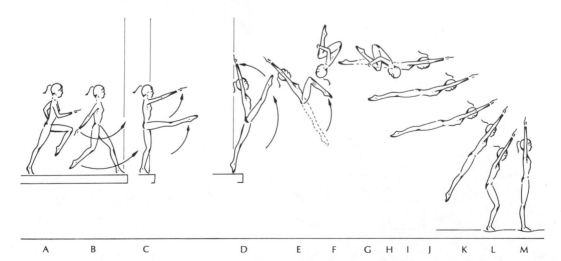

| A | B | C | D | E | F | G | H | I | J | K | L | M |

complete hip joint flexion of swing leg) at takeoff, to fully closed or tucked during the ascent phase, and returning to full extension just after the peak of the airborne trajectory.

H-I-J-K-L-M. In preparation for landing, the performer maintains complete body extension until just prior to making contact with the ground. The arms remain directly overhead and in line with the trunk while the legs are stretching or reaching for the mat. This technique provides the gymnast with the largest possible distance through which to apply a stopping force. Consequently, greater and more effective control in the landing phase can be realized. Notice that only the ankle, knee, and hip joints flex to absorb the impact.

M. The attainment of a fully extended backward standing position with the arms held directly overhead and in line with the trunk represents final completion of the skill.

9
Analysis of Core Uneven Parallel Bar Skills

Kim Peterson, University of Utah, Salt Lake City, Utah. Photo by Paul Jackson.

MOUNTS

9.1 Front Support Mount

A. The skill is begun from an erect, yet slightly forward leaning, standing position. The overgrip handgrasp on the low bar should be approximately shoulder width apart. The elbow joints are fully extended and remain so throughout the entire sequence.

A-B-C. By slightly flexing and then forcefully extending the ankle, knee, and hip joints, the total body unit begins to rise for-upward. To facilitate this motion, the performer simultaneously presses downward with the hands against the bar.

C-D. As the body approaches its maximum vertical height, the performer begins to pull inward toward the bar. Constant muscular tension throughout the entire body, particularly in the shoulder region, provides the control necessary to guide the gymnast to a front support position.

D. The attainment of a straight-line, fully extended front support position represents final completion of the skill. (The shoulder girdle should be fully depressed, allowing the upper thighs to rest upon the bar.)

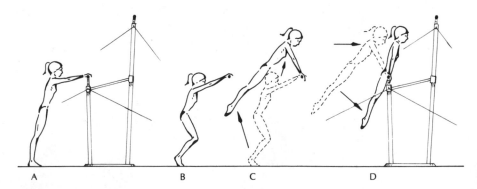

FIGURE 9.1. Front Support Mount.

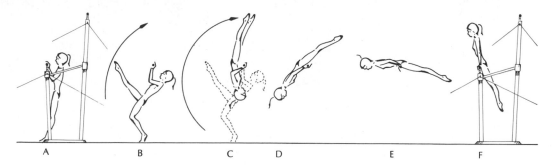

FIGURE 9.2. Backward Pullover Mount.

9.2 Backward Pullover Mount

A. The skill is begun from an erect, yet slightly backward leaning, standing position. The overgrip handgrasp on the low bar should be approximately shoulder width apart. The pronounced flexion of the elbow joints places the gymnast in close proximity to the bar.

A-B. By flexing the knee and ankle joints of the push leg while simultaneously driving the hips forward and the lead leg for-upward, the total body unit begins to rotate in a backward direction. Notice that the arms also begin to extend slightly to facilitate the initiation of this backward motion.

B-C. As the performer rotates backward underneath the apparatus, a vigorous and steadfast attempt is made to pull the bar inward toward the hips. This "pulling action" serves to lift and rotate the body about the bar. Notice that, as the legs come together, the hips are simultaneously brought closer to the apparatus. In addition, observe how the total body unit, although rotating backward, begins to extend en route to a straight line shape.

C-D. Just as the upper thighs make contact with the bar, the hands undergo a "slip-grip" motion in order to provide support for the oncoming body weight.

D-E-F. Notice how the body extends into a straight-line shape as the gymnast attains a front support position.

F. The attainment of a straight-line, fully extended front support on the low bar represents final completion of the skill. (The shoulder girdle should be fully depressed with the upper thighs resting on the bar.)

9.3 Beat Swing Straddle Mount

A. The skill is begun by executing a standing jump and grasping (overgrip hand position) the high bar such that the body, in the long-hang position, possesses an immediate potential for swinging forward. To help accomplish this, the performer stands well behind the apparatus so that the actual jump necessitates a for-upward movement.

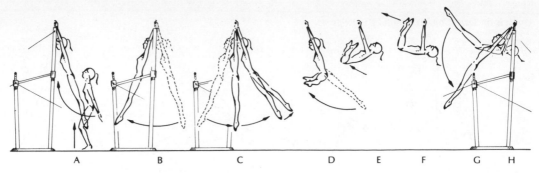

FIGURE 9.3. Beat Swing Straddle Mount.

A-B. In order to further enhance forward swing amplitude, there is a slight (scarcely observable) lifting or "scooping action" of the legs just as the performer moves through the bottom of the swing. (Throughout the entire long-hang swing, the total body unit should be fully extended with particular attention given to complete elevation of the shoulder girdle.)

B-C. As the performer moves through the bottom of the backward swing, observe how the total body unit begins to arch slightly, driving the legs and feet rearward.

C-D-E. Precise timing of the straddling action requires that it be initiated *just before* the gymnast attains the peak of the backward swing. Notice that the legs *first straddle laterally* and *then* move forward as a result of hip joint flexion. During the very same moment, the performer should be vigorously pressing for-downward against the bar. This latter action serves to hollow the trunk as well as to lift and rotate the entire body rearward about the shoulder joints.

E-F-G. Just before the performer arrives at the apex of the forward swing, the legs begin to come together again, and the total body unit undergoes a forceful extension in a for-upward direction. (Particular attention should be given to the shoulder-arm region in that this area is responsible for the vigorous rearward push against the bar. In other words, the gymnast should strive to throw the bar away, over the head, without actually letting go!)

G-H. Throughout the entire descent swing, the performer continues extending until a straight-line body shape is formed.

H. A fully extended long-hang position with the buttocks resting on the low bar represents final completion of the skill.

9.4 Glide Kip Mount (Preparation for Cast)

In the initial learning stages, this skill and any of its related variations can and should be initiated from a standing position. However, the use of a running hurdle and subsequent diving type of takeoff (especially from a vaulting board) provides greater potential amplitude for the entire movement sequence.

154

A. An accelerating run followed by a fast, low, and short hurdle trajectory are desirable prerequisites of the takeoff. As the feet make contact with the board, the total body unit is leaning backward, forming a noticeable angle with the vertical. Because the performer is already traveling quite fast in a forward direction, this angle of input (blocking) places the body in a more advantageous position for maximizing vertical lift at takeoff.

A-B. The impact of the body's momentum against the board causes *slight* and *very brief* flexion at the ankle, knee, and hip joints. As the performer transcends the vertical, these joints instantaneously begin to extend forcefully (kickback action), driving the total body unit for-upward.

B-C-D. The attainment of maximum vertical lift, appropriate forward rotation, and a fully extended body shape just as the performer grasps (overgrip hand position) the low bar are desirable end products of the take-off.

D-E-F. Throughout the entire descent phase, the basic objective is to circle about *as great an arc* as is mechanically possible. Consequently, the performer should attempt to remain away from the bar (axis of rotation) as far as possible without actually letting go and to hollow the total shape of the body only as much as is necessary to insure a minimum foot clearance from the ground.

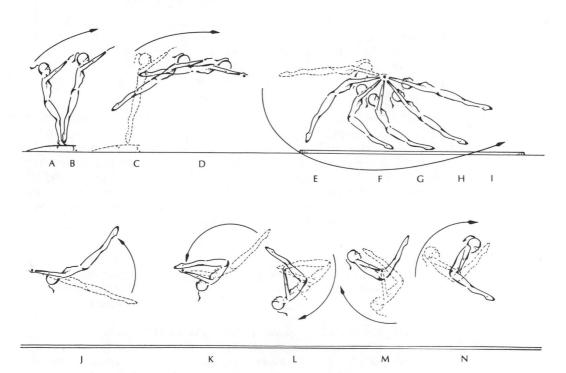

FIGURE 9.4. Glide Kip Mount (Preparation for Cast).

F-G-H-I. As the performer passes through the bottom of the swing and begins to circle and rise for-upward, notice how the total body unit progressively unfolds from its hollowed shape to a fully extended shape. (Particular attention should be given to the shoulder-arm region in that this area is responsible for the vigorous rearward push against the bar. In other words, the gymnast should strive to throw the bar away, over the head, without actually letting go, so that a maximum upswing amplitude can be realized.)

I-J-K. The actual initiation of the kip should occur *just prior* to arriving at the peak of the forward swing. By quickly hollowing first in the shoulder region and then (ever more vigorously) in the hip joints, the ankles are forcefully driven toward the bar. Note that this rapid change in body shape is timed to occur *while* the performer is *still well within* the peak range of the forward swing. In addition, bringing the body's mass center ever closer to the bar (axis of rotation) progressively improves the rotary potential of the oncoming backward swing.

Just as the ankles are about to make contact with the bar, they are instantaneously and abruptly *stopped.* It is the "quickness" of this stopping action that accounts, to a large extent, for a maximum momentum transfer from the legs into the entire body.

The appropriate combination of the above two factors—a timely shortening of the body's turning radius while simultaneously maximizing momentum transfer—is the key to effective "kipping action."

K-L-M. As the descent phase of the backward swing begins, the performer attempts to pull forcefully (with locked elbows) directly inward against the bar while, at the same moment, extending *only slightly* at the hip joints. In addition to further shortening the turning radius (and thus increasing forward rotation), these actions place the total body unit in the correct shape for executing the oncoming support phase.

M-N. The forceful inward pulling action of the arms against the bar must be continuously maintained throughout the entire upswing phase. As the performer rises and circles forward approaching the vertical, the hands undergo a slip-grip motion in order to provide support for the oncoming body weight. The shoulder girdle becomes *fully elevated* so that the bar can be maintained at hip joint level with little or, better yet, no bend in the elbow joints. Notice the slightly hollowed shape of the upper body and the approximate right angle bend of the hip joints.

N. Observe how the body is bent about the bar (cocked as in an archer's bow) with both the head-trunk and the leg-foot regions on the same side of the vertical. This body shape and position relative to the bar is essential to maximum execution of the oncoming "cast" phase. The attainment, then, of a front support cast position represents final completion of the skill.

9.5 Glide Kip Mount (Preparation for Forward Hip Circle)

A through K. These movements are identical in nature to the illustrations and descriptions presented for the Glide Kip Mount (Preparation for Cast), (9.4 A through K).

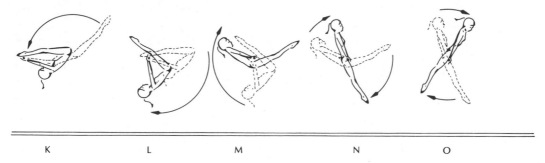

K   L   M   N   O

FIGURE 9.5. Glide Kip Mount (Preparation for Forward Hip Circle).

K-L-M-N. As the descent phase of the backward swing begins, the performer attempts to pull forcefully (with locked elbows) directly inward against the bar while, at the same moment, extending *fully* at the hip joints. In addition to further shortening the turning radius (and thus increasing forward rotation), these actions place the total body unit in the correct shape for executing the oncoming support phase.

N-O. The forceful inward pulling action of the arms against the bar must be continuously maintained throughout the entire upswing phase. As the performer rises and circles forward onto the top of the bar, the hands undergo a slip-grip motion in order to provide support for the oncoming body weight. The shoulder girdle should undergo *full depression* so that the bar can be maintained at upper thigh level with, of course, locked elbows. Notice the fully extended, straight-line shape of the total body unit.

O. Circling forward through a front support position using a straight-line body shape with the bar at upper thigh level represents final completion of the skill.

9.6 Glide Kip Catch to High Bar

A through K. These movements are identical in nature to the illustrations and descriptions presented for the Glide Kip Mount (Preparation for Cast), (9.4 A through K).

K-L-M. As the descent phase of the backward swing begins, the performer attempts to pull forcefully (with locked elbows) directly inward against the bar while, at the same moment, *instantaneously* extending the hip joints to a point such that the total body unit forms a slightly hollowed shape. Notice that this hip joint extension is *quicker* and occurs *considerably earlier* than in the previous "kip" skills (9.4 and 9.5) and, consequently, is completed just as the upper body begins to transcend the horizontal on the ascent phase of the swing.

M-N-O. Upon attaining this slightly hollowed body shape, the rapid hip joint extension is instantaneously and abruptly "stopped," causing the downward circling motion of the legs to be transferred into the upward

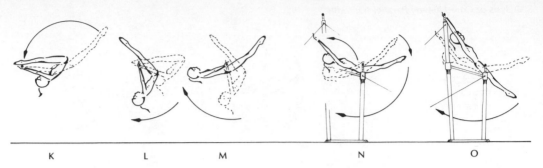

| K | L | M | N | O |

FIGURE 9.6. Glide Kip Catch to High Bar.

circling motion of the entire body. This stopping action serves as the cue for an *immediate release* from the low bar *and regrasp* (overgrip) to the high bar. (The forceful inward pulling action of the arms against the low bar must be steadfastly maintained until the actual release occurs.)

Notice that the regrasp is completed *while* the upper thighs *are still* in very close proximity to the low bar. Such a relationship provides the gymnast with a maximum potential backswing amplitude in the long-hang position.

O. The attainment of a long-hang swing position with a very slightly hollowed body shape and with the upper thighs in close proximity to the low bar represents final completion of the skill.

9.7 Glide Stoop Mount to Rear Support

A through I. These movements are identical in nature to the illustrations and descriptions presented for the Glide Kip Mount (Preparation for Cast) (9.4 A through I).

I-J-K. The actual initiation of the stoop should occur *just prior* to arriving at the peak of the forward swing. By *slightly* hollowing in the shoulder region followed by an immediate and vigorous hip pike action, the legs are forcefully driven toward the face. Note that this rapid change in body shape is timed to occur *while* the performer is *still well* within the peak range of the forward swing. In addition, bringing the body's mass center ever closer to the bar (axis of rotation) progressively improves the rotary potential of the oncoming backward swing.

K-L. As the descent phase of the backward swing begins, the continuous hip piking action drives the locked legs directly between the hands (stoop). During this time, an attempt should be made to keep the hips as far as possible away from the bar. Such a consideration not only facilitates foot clearance from the bar but also provides for greater potential amplitude in the entire backswing phase.

L-M. The hip joints are fully and completely closed (piked) once the performer reaches the exact "bottom" of the swing. The body passes through a fully piked inverted hang position with the legs held parallel to the ground.

158

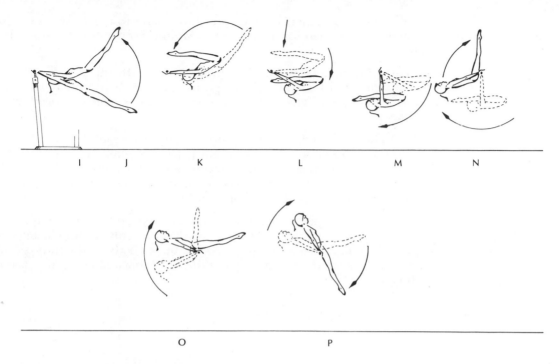

FIGURE 9.7. Glide Stoop Mount to Rear Support.

M-N-O. As the performer passes through the "bottom" of the swing, the hands forcefully and continuously press back-downward against the bar, thereby enhancing the impetus of the already existing upswing motion. Notice how during the very same time, the fully compressed body progressively begins to extend (unfold) en route to attaining a straight-line shape.

Just as the legs begin to transcend the upper vertical, the hands undergo a slip-grip motion in order to provide support for the oncoming body weight.

O-P. Once the total body unit arrives at top dead center, the back side of the upper thighs are lowered onto and rest upon the bar. Notice the straight-line shape of the total body unit.

P. The attainment of a rear support position (with a fully depressed shoulder girdle) represents final completion of the skill.

9.8 Forward Hip Circle Mount

In the initial learning stages, this skill can and should be initiated from a standing jump position with both hands already in contact (overgrip hand position) with the bar. However, the use of a running hurdle and the subsequent diving type of takeoff to a free-handed front support position enhances the aesthetic appeal of the entire movement sequence.

A-B. These movements are identical in nature to the illustrations and descriptions presented for the Glide Kip Mount (Preparation for Cast), (9.4 A and B).

B-C-D. The attainment of appropriate vertical lift, appropriate forward rotation, and a slightly arched shape in the total body unit just as the performer's upper thighs contact the low bar are desirable end products of the takeoff.

D-E. The initial free front support position reveals that the body is situated on the apparatus so that the bar (axis of rotation) lies slightly below the performer's mass center. This uneven weight distribution in favor of the upper body causes the gymnast to begin rotating about the bar in a forward direction (descent phase of the forward hip circle).

E-F. Just as the performer rotates forward beyond the horizontal, the total body unit begins to undergo a rapid and highly obvious change in shape: a deep hip pike, a slightly hollowed upper body, and hands quickly grasping (overgrip) the bar in preparation for the oncoming ascent phase of the forward hip circle.

FIGURE 9.8. Forward Hip Circle Mount.

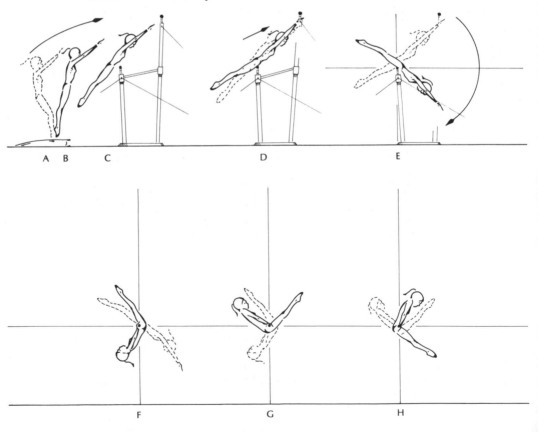

F-G. Upon hand contact with the apparatus, the arms steadfastly and forcefully pull inward so that the body (hip joints) remains in constant contact with the bar throughout the entire upswing phase.

G-H. As the performer rises and circles forward approaching the vertical, the hands undergo a slip-grip motion in order to provide support for the oncoming body weight. The shoulder girdle becomes *fully elevated* so that the bar can be maintained at hip joint level with little or, better yet, no bend in the elbow joints. Notice the slightly hollowed shape of the upper body and the approximate right angle bend of the hip joints.

H. Observe how the body is bent about the bar (cocked as in an archer's bow) with both the head-trunk and leg-foot regions on the same side of the vertical. This body shape and position relative to the bar is essential to maximum execution of the oncoming "cast" phase. The attainment, then, of a front support cast position represents final completion of the skill.

ON-BAR SKILLS

9.9 Cast to Handstand

In the initial learning stages, this skill and any of its related variations can and should be initiated from a stationary front support "cast" position. However, proper execution of some sequentially related lead-in skill (such as a Glide Kip or a Forward Hip Circle) can greatly enhance the actual "cast action" of the skill.

FIGURE 9.9. Cast to Handstand.

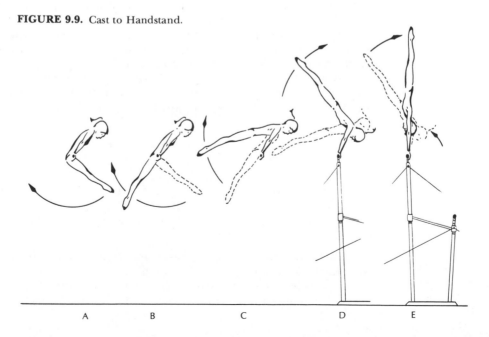

| A | B | C | D | E |

A. The skill is begun as the gymnast moves through an overgrip front support "cast" position. Observe how the body is bent about the bar (cocked as in an archer's bow) with both the head-trunk and leg-foot regions on the same side of the vertical. Because the shoulder girdle is *fully elevated,* the bar can be positioned at hip joint level with little or, better yet, no bend in the elbow joints. Notice the slightly hollowed shape of the upper body and the approximate right angle bend of the hip joints.

A-B-C. To initiate the "cast," the performer forcefully drives the legs backwards by vigorously extending at the hip joints. Just prior to the legs attaining a slightly hollowed relationship with the trunk, the rapid extension motion in the hips is *instantaneously stopped,* causing its momentum to be transferred into the entire body. This "stopping action" of the legs serves as the cue to begin the vigorous and steadfast for-downward push with the hands against the bar. Notice that, during the initial aspect of the upswing phase, the legs, trunk, and head form a fully extended, yet very slightly hollowed, body shape.

C-D-E. The forceful for-downward push of the hands against the bar continues throughout the entire upswing phase. Notice that as the legs and hips rotate for-upward, the arms and shoulders rotate back-upward so that all body segments line up both with one another and with the upper vertical at the exact same time.

E. The attainment of a fully extended handstand position represents final completion of the skill.

9.10 Backward Hip Circle to Front Support

Because of the selected starting position of the gymnast relative to the apparatus (on the low bar facing outward), the total potential amount of descent swing amplitude is obviously confined to within the height-width distance of the bar settings. Were the skill executed with the performer facing inward or, for that matter, facing in either direction on the upper rail, a maximum potential amount of descent swing amplitude could then be made available, i.e., the skill could be initiated from a fully extended handstand position. In any case, "control" of the descent phase is an essential factor.

A. The skill can be initiated from an above horizontal "cast" position with an overgrip handgrasp. Notice that the legs, trunk, and head form a fully extended, yet very slightly hollowed body shape and that the shoulders are positioned slightly in front of the hands (base of support). In order to ensure the greatest possible distance between the performer's chest and the bar (axis of rotation), the shoulder girdle should be fully abducted, i.e., rounded forward about the trunk.

A-B. By a controlled lessening of muscular tension in the shoulder region, the body unit begins to descend and rotate backward about the shoulder joints. Once it rotates past horizontal, notice how the shoulders themselves also begin to shift (rotate) backward onto and, in fact, a bit behind the

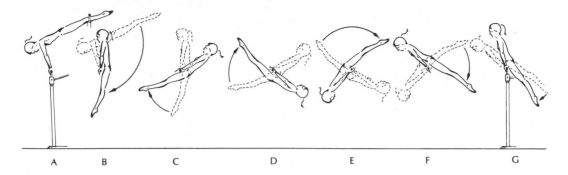

FIGURE 9.10. Backward Hip Circle to Front Support.

hands. During this time, the total body unit assumes a slightly more hollowed (foot-lead) shape.

B-C. Just prior to the upper thighs making contact with the bar, the backward rotary motion of the legs and trunk about the shoulder joints is *instantaneously* stopped, causing its momentum to be transferred into backward rotary motion for the entire body.

C-D-E. As the performer rotates backward about the apparatus, a vigorous and steadfast effort is made to maintain the upper thighs in very close proximity to the bar. This downward and inward "pulling action" of the arms is particularly critical during the "bottom phase" of the backward hip circle.

E-F. Just as the upper thighs make contact with the bar, the hands undergo a slip-grip motion in order to provide support for the oncoming body weight.

F-G. Notice how the body extends into a straight-line shape as the gymnast attains a front support position.

G. The attainment of a straight-line, fully extended front support position represents final completion of the skill. (The shoulder girdle should be fully depressed allowing the upper thighs to rest upon the bar.)

9.11 Seat Kip from Low to High Bar

A. The skill is initiated from a fully extended long-hang position (overgrip handgrasp) with the back side of the upper thighs resting on the low bar.

A-B-C-D. By slightly arching and then quickly and vigorously hollowing the shoulder, trunk, and hip regions, the legs are forcefully driven toward the bar. Note that this rapid change in body shape is timed to occur, as much as possible, *while* the performer is *still well within* the peak range of the forward swing. In addition, bringing the body's mass center ever closer to

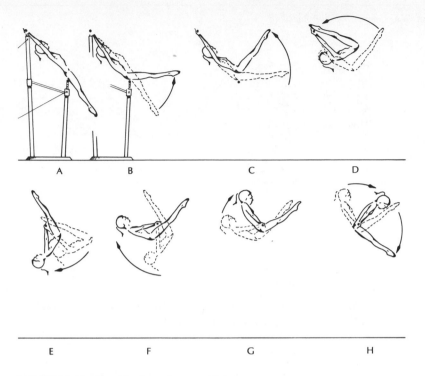

A B C D

E F G H

FIGURE 9.11. Seat Kip from Low to High Bar.

the bar (axis of rotation) progressively improves the rotary potential of the oncoming backward swing.

Just as the ankles are about to make contact with the bar, they are instantaneously and abruptly stopped. It is the "quickness" of this stopping action that accounts, to a large extent, for a maximum momentum transfer from the legs into the entire body.

The appropriate combination of the above two factors—a timely shortening of the body's turning radius while simultaneously maximizing momentum transfer—is the key to effective "kipping action."

D-E-F-G-H. These movements are essentially the same as those illustrations and descriptions presented for the Glide Kip Mount (Preparation for Cast), (9.4 K through N).

If, however, the performer intends to execute the upswing phase to prepare for an oncoming forward hip circle, refer to those illustrations and descriptions presented for the Glide Kip Mount (Preparation for Forward Hip Circle) (9.5 K through O).

9.12 Forward Seat Circle

The skill can be executed on either bar facing either direction.

A. The skill is initiated from a fully extended, rear support position with an undergrip handgrasp.

A-B-C. By rounding (hollowing) first the upper back, next the lower back, and then fully flexing the hip joints while all the time steadfastly pushing for-downward with the hands against the bar, the hips are lifted above the head and are positioned directly in line with the vertical. (This action is identical to the initial phase of a straight-arm, straight-leg press from an L-position on the floor or the beam.)

Because this fully closed body shape positions the performer's mass center both as high and as far away from the bar (axis of rotation) as is mechanically possible, maximum potential amplitude in the descent swing can be realized. Maintaining a fully compressed body shape throughout the entire descent phase cannot be overemphasized.

C-D-E. Lifting the hips in the manner just described places the body's mass center slightly off-balance, i.e., to the side of the intended direction of rotation. Consequently, the performer begins to circle forward about the bar. Notice how during this time the shoulder joints begin progressively to close, but only to a point such that an approximate right angle arm-trunk shape is formed. At the end of the descent phase the body passes through a fully piked inverted hang position with the legs held parallel to the ground.

E-F-G-H. Except for the fact that the performer is using an undergrip handgrasp, these illustrations are identical in nature to the illustrations and descriptions presented for the Glide Stoop Mount to Rear Support, (9.7 M through P).

FIGURE 9.12. Forward Seat Circle.

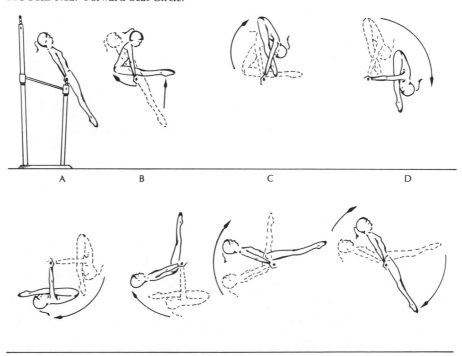

A   B   C   D

E   F   G   H

9.13 Backward (Reverse) Kip

The skill can be executed on either bar facing either direction.

A. This skill is initiated from a fully extended, rear support position with an overgrip handgrasp.

A-B. In preparation for the "reverse" throw (backward cast), the total body unit arches momentarily and then instantaneously begins to assume a deep "v-shaped" support position. This is accomplished by forceful hip joint flexion (lifting the legs and feet above the head) and by steadfastly pressing against the bar in a back-downward direction (causing full shoulder girdle depression). Because these initial movements position the performer's mass center both as high and as far away from the bar (axis of rotation) as is mechanically possible, maximum potential amplitude in the descent swing can be realized.

B-C-D. Lifting the legs and hips in the manner just described places the body's mass center slightly off-balance, to the side of the intended direction of rotation. Consequently, the performer begins to circle backward about the bar. Notice how, during this time, the shoulder joints begin to open progressively, but only to a point such that the hips can move in between and slightly beyond the arms. The end of the descent phase reveals that full body shape compression is momentarily achieved with the hips positioned in close proximity to the bar and slightly beyond the lower vertical.

FIGURE 9.13. Backward (Reverse) Kip.

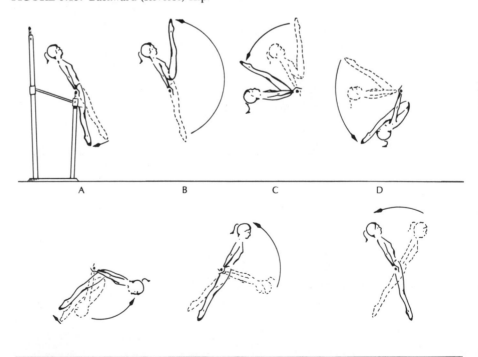

D-E-F. As the performer passes through the "bottom" of the swing, the total body unit begins to extend rapidly (unfold) en route to a straight-line shape. During the very same time, the arms (with locked elbows) forcefully and continuously press for-downward against the bar. (This latter action ensures that the back side of the uppermost thighs are immediately brought in close contact with the bar.)

As the performer approaches full extension, the hands undergo a slip-grip motion in order to provide support for the oncoming body weight.

F-G. Notice that full body extension is achieved *prior* to the performer's reaching top dead center.

G. The final position of the skill is identical to its starting position.

9.14 Backward (Reverse) Kip to Low Bar Catch

The skill is executed from a rear support position on the high bar facing inward.

A-B-C. These movements are identical in nature to the illustrations and descriptions presented for the Backward (Reverse) Kip, (9.13 A, B, and C).

C-D-E. Notice that the body attains a fully compressed (closed) shape and then immediately begins to extend (unfold) vigorously, all *prior* to the performer passing through the "bottom" of the swing. Notice also that the hips are *maintained* directly *in between* the arms to facilitate this timely unfolding of the body.

Throughout the entire extension phase, the arms (with locked elbows) forcefully and continuously press for-downward in order to lift and maintain close body (backside of upper thighs) contact with the bar. Notice how the legs rotate noticeably in a direction *exactly opposite* to the backward circling movement of the total body.

FIGURE 9.14. Backward (Reverse) Kip to Low Bar Catch.

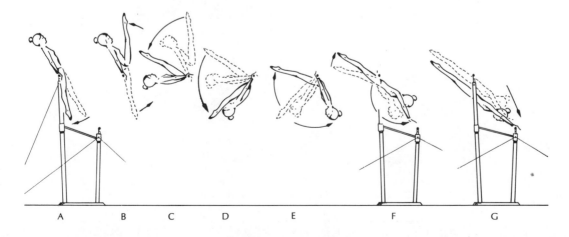

A   B   C   D   E   F   G

E-F-G. Just prior to attaining full body extension, the hands release the high and immediately regrasp the low bar. At the moment of regrasp, the fully extended body shape should be well above the horizontal. Such a consideration ensures greater potential amplitude in the oncoming descent swing.

9.15 Backward Straddle Catch

The skill is executed from a fully extended standing position on the low bar facing outward.

A. In preparation for the jump, the upper body begins to hollow while the ankle, knee, and hip joints undergo *partial* and *very brief* flexion. Notice how the total body unit shifts very slightly *backward,* positioning the performer's mass center off-balance, *behind* the feet (base of support).

A-B. By *immediately* and *forcefully* extending the legs while at the same time opening the upper body in a for-upward direction, the performer begins to rise back-upward with a small, yet perceptible amount of forward rotation.

FIGURE 9.15. Backward Straddle Catch.

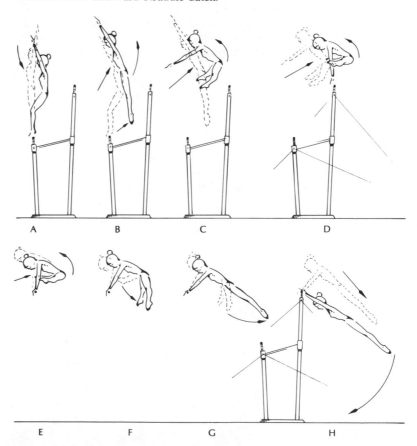

B-C-D-E. Once airborne, the performer's center of mass follows its established, perfectly regular, curved path in the back-upward direction. In addition to the body undergoing a slight forward rotation, notice the very obvious and specifically timed change in shape: from very slightly hollowed during the ascent to a fully compressed straddled pike as the performer passes over the high bar. Keep in mind that the actual trajectory should emphasize attaining *maximum vertical height just as* the performer grasps (overgrip hand position) the high bar.

E-F-G-H. Upon regrasp, the performer immediately pushes for-upward against the bar to attain a fully extended body shape (legs together) as soon as possible.

H. The attainment of a fully extended, yet slightly hollowed, total body shape in a long hang swing position represents final completion of the skill. Note the rather large amount of potential descent swing still remaining for execution of any sequentially related skill.

9.16 Cast Wrap to Backward Hip Circle

A. The skill is executed from a fully extended handstand position (overgrip handgrasp) on the high bar facing inward.

A-B-C-D. By momentarily flexing very slightly in the wrist joints, the performer's center of mass shifts outside its base toward the intended direction of rotation. Consequently, the gymnast begins to circle about the bar (axis of rotation) in a backward direction. During this time, the total body unit forms a slightly hollowed shape. Maintaining full shoulder girdle elevation throughout the entire "long-hang swing phase" cannot be overemphasized.

D-E. Immediately prior to arriving at the exact bottom of the swing, the slightly hollowed body shape is released through a fully extended and into a slightly arched shape. This "unloading" action" causes both the upper rail to be effectively depressed (bottomed) and the attached total body unit to be appropriately positioned for the oncoming "wrap phase."

E-F. To insure a smooth and effective transition into the wrap phase, the performer employs a "scooping" motion about the lower bar, going from a slightly arched and into a slightly hollowed shape with *actual bar contact* occurring *just as* the body *moves through* a straight-line shape.

F-G. It is important to notice that the bar is contacted at uppermost thigh, rather than at hip joint, level. Such a consideration will help to ensure appropriate "rail action" for this as well as any sequentially related skill.

Upon bar contact, the hip joints continue to flex vigorously, thereby wrapping the legs and feet about the bar. This deep hip joint flexion causes the upper body to hollow, both of which serve to bend (deflect) the upper and lower bars inward toward each other.

G-H-I. As the body becomes almost fully compressed (closed), the rapid flexion of the hip joints is instantaneously stopped, causing the backward rotary momentum of the legs to be transferred into the entire body. This "stopping action" of the legs serves as the cue for a simultaneous hand release-regrasp from upper to lower bar. Upon hand release, the entire body begins to rotate backward about the lower bar.

I-J-K. As the performer continues to rotate backward about the apparatus, notice how the total body unit progressively unfolds (opens) en route to attaining a fully extended shape. During the latter stage of the backward hip circle, the hands undergo a slip-grip motion in order to provide support for the oncoming body weight.

K. The attainment of a straight-line, fully extended body shape just as the performer arrives in the front support position represents final completion of the skill. (The shoulder girdle should be fully depressed as the upper thighs rest upon the bar.)

FIGURE 9.16. Cast Wrap to Backward Hip Circle.

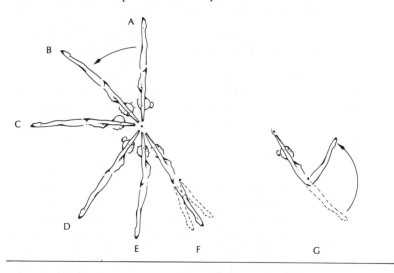

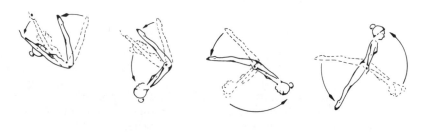

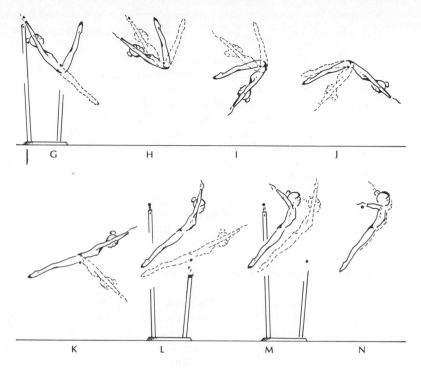

FIGURE 9.17. Cast Wrap to Eagle Catch.

9.17 Cast Wrap to Eagle Catch

A-B-C-D-E-F-G. Except for the fact that a comparatively more vigorous "scooping" motion and subsequent hip joint flexion are employed, these movements are identical in nature to the illustrations and descriptions presented for the Cast Wrap to Backward Hip Circle, (9.16 A through G).

G-H-I. As the body approaches full compression, the rapid flexion of the hip joints is instantaneously stopped, causing the backward rotary momentum of the legs to be transferred into the entire body. This "stopping action" of the legs serves as the cue to simultaneously release the upper bar. Upon hand release, the fully compressed body shape begins to rotate vigorously backward about the lower bar.

I-J-K. Once the legs transcend the horizontal, the fully compressed body shape begins to open (unfold) rapidly. This extension of the total body unit depresses the lower bar (cocked as in an archer's bow) in an out-downward direction.

K-L. Upon attaining a straight-line shape, the forceful body extension is instantaneously stopped, causing its momentum to be transferred into the total body unit. This "stopping action" of the body together with the "recoil action" of the bar lifts and rotates the performer in a up-backward direction.

It is interesting to point out that, except for the up-backward direction of takeoff, the actual mechanics for becoming airborne are identical to those presented for the Hecht Dismount (9.27).

171

L-M-N. Once airborne, the performer's mass center follows its already established, perfectly regular curved path. As the arms reach up, over, and then behind the head in preparation for the upper bar regrasp, the total body unit assumes a slightly arched shape.

The actual regrasp (undergrip handgrasp with shoulder joints in a partially dislocated position) *should occur while* the performer is *still rising* on the upswing phase of the trajectory. The relative distance between the hands should be as close together as is mechanically possible—slightly greater than shoulder width apart.

N. Regrasping the upper bar (partially dislocated shoulder position) with a noticeable forward lean in the slightly arched body shape represents final completion of the skill. (The shoulders should be at least horizontal to the bar.)

9.18 Backward Hip Circle to Handstand

Using a fully extended handstand as the initial position, the skill can be executed with the performer facing inward on the lower rail or facing in either direction on the upward rail. Whenever it is executed with the performer facing outward on the lower rail, the total potential amount of descent swing amplitude is obviously confined to within the height-width distance of the bar settings.

A. The skill is initiated from a fully extended handstand position with an overgrip handgrasp.

A-B. By momentarily flexing very slightly in the wrist joints, the performer's center of mass shifts outside its base toward the intended direction of rotation. At the very same moment, the upper body begins to shift forward of its base to partially counterbalance the backward rotation of the body about the shoulder joints. In order to ensure the greatest possible distance between the performer's chest and the bar (axis of rotation), the shoulder girdle should be fully abducted—rounded forward about the trunk—throughout the entire descent phase.

B-C. By a controlled lessening of muscular tension in the shoulder region, the body unit continues to descend and rotate backward about the shoulder joints. Once it rotates past horizontal, notice how the shoulders themselves also begin to shift (rotate) backward onto and, in fact, a bit behind the hands. During this time, the total body unit begins to assume a slightly hollowed (foot-lead) shape.

C-D. As the upper thighs approach the bar, the backward rotary motion of the legs and trunk about the shoulder joints is *instantaneously stopped,* causing its momentum to be transferred into backward rotary motion for the entire body. The timely position of the performer relative to the bar (shoulders well behind hands), the rather noticeable thigh-bar distance (body free from bar), and the hollowed foot-lead shape of the total body unit (including the rounding forward of the shoulders about the trunk) are all key considerations to an effective momentum transfer.

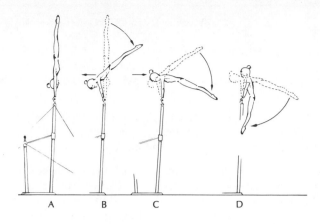

FIGURE 9.18. Backward Hip Circle to Handstand.

D-E-F. As the performer rotates backward about the apparatus, a vigorous and steadfast effort is made to maintain the existing body shape and relative distance from the bar. *Constant muscular tension* throughout the entire body, particularly in the shoulder region, helps to prevent the natural tendency to collapse at one's jointed and/or weaker points.

F-G-H-I. Because of the comparatively large amount of backward rotary motion accrued in the downswing phase, the performer is able to begin extending (unfolding) out of the slightly hollowed body shape *early* in the upswing phase. This action is initiated off the "bottom" of the swing by a forceful and continuous for-downward push with the hands against the bar. The motion is similar to "throwing the bar away," over one's head, without actually letting go! As the performer rises up the circular swing, the hands undergo a slip-grip action in order to provide support for the oncoming body weight.

At no time should any part of the body transcend the upper vertical until, of course, the actual handstand has been attained. Ideally, the skill is completed such that all body segments line up with one another and with the upper vertical at the exact same time.

I. The final position of the skill is identical to its starting position.

173

9.19 Cast Forward Somersault to High Bar

The skill can be executed from a front support cast position on the low bar facing outward.

A. Except for the fact that the performer initiates the skill from the low bar facing outward, this movement is identical in nature to the illustration and description presented for the Cast to Handstand (9.9 A).

A-B-C. To initiate the "cast," the performer forcefully drives the legs backwards by vigorously extending at the hip joints. Just as the legs attain a slightly hollowed relationship with the trunk, the rapid extension motion in the hips is *instantaneously stopped,* causing its momentum to be transferred into the entire body. This "stopping action" of the legs serves as the cue to begin the vigorous and steadfast for-downward push with the hands against the bar.

During the initial aspect of the upswing phase, the legs, trunk, and head form a fully extended body shape. In addition, notice how the *vigorous* for-downward push against the bar serves to shift and/or reposition the shoulders well behind the hands, thereby driving the total body unit in a back-upward direction.

C-D-E. Just as the thighs come in close proximity to the upper bar, the vigorous for-downward push with the hands is *instantaneously stopped,* causing the back-upward momentum of the legs and trunk to be transferred into the entire body. This "stopping action" of the cast serves as the cue to initiate the straddled forward somersault phase.

Upon releasing the lower bar, the legs straddle laterally as wide as possible (to facilitate foot-bar clearance) while the hip joints rapidly undergo full and complete flexion. Also during this moment, notice how the hands reach deeply in between the straddled legs for an immediate regrasp (overgrip) onto the upper bar. This entire somersault sequence should be initiated, executed, and completed while the performer is *still well within* the "peak" phase of the airborne trajectory.

FIGURE 9.19. Cast Forward Somersault to High Bar.

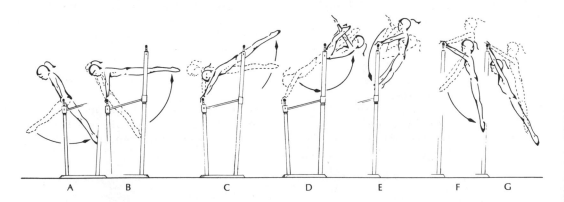

A   B   C   D   E   F   G

E-F-G. In order to maximize descent swing amplitude, the performer immediately attempts to position the total body unit as far as possible away from the apparatus by vigorously pushing for-upward against the bar. The legs come together and the body extends into a straight-line shape.

G. The attainment of a fully extended total body shape in a long hang swing position represents final completion of the skill. Upon completion, there should be a noticeable amount of potential descent swing amplitude still remaining for execution of any sequentially related skill.

9.20 Forward Seat Circle Dislocate Swing to Wrap Position

A-B-C. Except for the fact that the performer initiates the skill from the high bar facing inward, these movements are identical in nature to the illustrations and descriptions presented for the Forward Seat Circle (9.12 A, B, and C). As far as possible, the hand-width distance should be the same as in the basic Forward Seat Circle (hands slightly wider than the hips) and should remain so throughout the entire sequence.

FIGURE 9.20. Forward Seat Circle Dislocate Swing to Wrap Position.

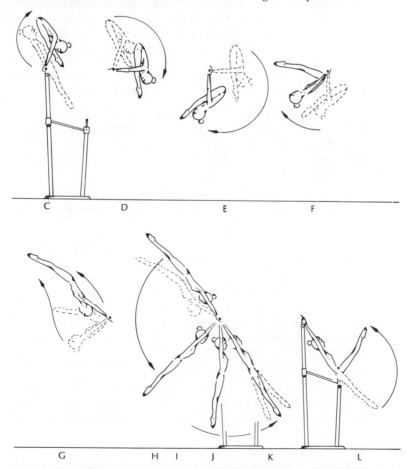

C-D-E. Lifting the hips in the manner just described places the body's mass center slightly off-balance, to the side of the intended direction of rotation. Consequently, the performer begins to circle forward about the bar. During this time, notice how the shoulder joints begin to progressively close, but only to a point such that an approximate 45 degree arm-trunk angle is formed upon arriving at the exact "bottom" of the swing. At the end of the descent phase the fully piked body shape passes through an inverted hang position with the legs tilted backward, forming an approximate 45 degree angle with the horizontal.

E-F-G. As the performer passes through the "bottom" of the swing, the hands forcefully and continuously press back-downward against the bar, thereby enhancing the impetus of the upswing motion already in progress. During the very same time, the fully compressed body progressively begins to extend (unfold) in a back-upward direction, at least above the horizontal. The continued backward opening angle observed in the shoulder joints is facilitated by means of a simultaneous outward rotation in the arms.

G-H. Immediately prior to attaining a fully extended, yet slightly hollowed body shape, the performer executes and completes the "dislocate," a 180 degree outward rotation of the arms about the shoulder joints. Notice that this action occurs during the "peak" of the upswing phase.

Upon timely completion of the "dislocate," the shoulder girdle should be fully elevated to insure that the performer's center of mass is positioned as high and as far away as is mechanically possible from the bar (axis of rotation). Such a consideration helps to ensure a maximum potential amplitude in the oncoming descent swing phase.

H-I-J-K-L. Except for the fact that the descent swing requires the performer to circle about the bar in a direction opposite to the dislocated handgrasp, these movements are identical in nature to the illustrations and descriptions presented for the Cast Wrap to Backward Hip Circle, (9.16 B through G).

L. Upon upper thigh contact with the low bar, the gymnast is ideally positioned to execute the "wrap phase" for any of the sequentially related skills.

9.21 Straddled Sole Circle One-Half Turn

This skill can be initiated from a fully extended handstand position on the high bar facing inward. Although not illustrated, the performer could maintain the fully extended body shape throughout a majority of the descent phase and then execute the actual "straddle-on action" at a point just prior to illustration B. Such a consideration would indeed serve to maximize amplitude in the entire circular swing *to the fullest possible extent*.

A. By *first* undergoing full and complete hip joint flexion (while simultaneously straddling the legs), and *then* rounding or hollowing slightly in the lower back, the upper back, and finally in the (already elevated) shoulder girdle, the performer's legs rotate laterally downward allowing the soles of the feet to be placed onto the top of the bar in a straddled position. In addition to decreasing the arm-trunk angle, the shoulders shift slightly forward of the hands (base of support) to counterbalance the body weight during the actual straddle-down.

The performer should strive to position the body's mass center as high and as far away from the bar (axis of rotation) as is mechanically possible in order to insure a maximum potential amplitude in the oncoming descent swing phase. The soles of the feet should be placed onto the bar *outside of and directly next to* the hands with the body weight positioned very slightly to the side of the intended direction of rotation.

A-B-C. Because the performer's center of mass lies slightly outside its base toward the intended direction of rotation, the total body unit begins to circle about the bar (axis of rotation) in a backward direction. Notice that the initial straddled sole circle shape is maintained not only throughout the entire descent swing but also well into the ascent swing phase.

C-D. As the legs approach the horizontal, the performer begins both to open (unfold) out of the straddled sole circle shape and to initiate the one-half turn, extending into the twist. These actions are accomplished simultaneously by extending vigorously in the total body unit (particularly

FIGURE 9.21. Straddled Sole Circle One-Half Turn.

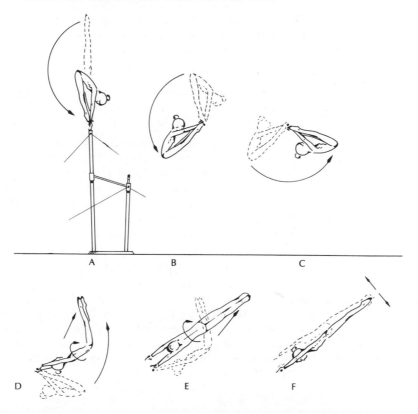

the hip joints) while forcefully pushing back-downward with the hands *in a sequential fashion* against the bar. As the hand opposite the direction of the oncoming twist (right hand for left twist as illustrated) completes its push phase, it releases the bar a bit sooner than the second.

D-E-F. Because the legs are quickly brought together while the performer is extending into a straight-line body shape, the effective turning radius (about the body's long axis) is noticeably shortened. This significantly increases the rate of twist, thereby insuring that the entire one-half turn can be initiated, executed, and completed (including the overgrip regrasp) during the "peak" of the ascent swing phase. Notice both that there is a brief moment in which the performer is completely free from the apparatus (airborne) and that the entire one-half turn occurs uniformly throughout the long axis of the total body unit.

F. A fully extended body shape with the performer positioned well above the horizontal represents final completion of the skill. At this point, the gymnast can readily execute any of the sequentially related skills.

9.22 Belly Whip Backward Uprise to Free Front Support

A. The skill is executed from a fully extended handstand position (overgrip handgrasp) on the high bar facing outward.

A-B-C. By momentarily flexing very slightly in the wrist joints, the performer's center of mass shifts outside its base toward the intended direction of rotation. Consequently, the gymnast begins to circle about the bar (axis of rotation) in a backward direction. Maintaining full shoulder girdle elevation throughout the entire descent and belly whip phases cannot be overemphasized.

Notice that the bar is contacted at uppermost thigh, rather than hip joint, level. Such a consideration helps to ensure appropriate "rail action" for this as well as for any sequentially related skill.

C-D. To facilitate a smooth and effective transition into the belly whip phase, the performer employs a "scooping" motion about the lower bar, going from a fully extended body shape at actual bar contact and instantaneously "whipping" the body into a fully compressed shape by continuing to forcefully drive the legs about the lower bar. This deep hip joint flexion causes the upper body to hollow, both of which serve to bend (deflect) the upper and lower bars inward toward each other.

D-E. Upon attaining a fully compressed body shape, the performer *immediately* begins to extend rapidly (kickback action) en route to again assuming a fully extended, yet very slightly hollowed, body shape.

It is interesting to note that the bent (deflected) bar rails, in returning to their original shape (restitution), provide increased impetus to the kickback action of the legs. And the speed of this leg action determines, to a large extent, the degree of down-inward bend in the lower rail (cocked as in an archer's bow), a consideration essential to maximizing the amplitude of the oncoming backward uprise.

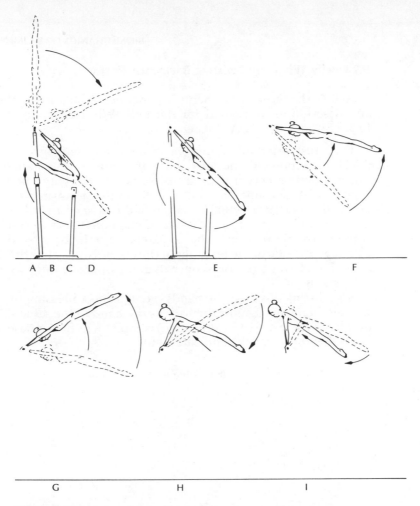

A B C D   E   F

G   H   I

FIGURE 9.22. Belly Whip Backward Uprise to Free Front Support.

E-F. Just prior to attaining a straight-line shape, the rapid extension (kickback action) of the legs about the hips is instantaneously *stopped,* causing its momentum to be transferred into the entire body. At the very same moment, the deflected lower bar forcefully recoils back to its original shape, thus adding further lifting impetus to the already rising body. During this time, the hands vigorously and steadfastly press for-downward against the upper bar. This latter action helps to maintain proper alignment (fully extended body shape) throughout the entire backward uprise.

F-G-H-I. Just prior to attaining the "peak" of the ascent swing phase, the performer begins to pull inward toward the bar, causing a noticeable decrease in the arm-trunk angle. During this time, the shoulder girdle undergoes full depression as well as abduction (rounding forward about the trunk).

I. The attainment of a free front support position represents final completion of the skill. At this point, the gymnast can readily execute any of the sequentially related skills.

9.23 Belly Whip Full Twisting Backward Uprise

A-B-C-D. These movements are identical in nature to the illustrations and descriptions presented for the Belly Whip Backward Uprise to Free Front Support, (9.22 A through D).

D-E. Just prior to attaining a straight-line shape, the rapid extension (kickback action) of the legs about the hips is instantaneously stopped, causing its momentum to be transferred into the entire body. During this very same time frame, the full twist about the performer's long axis is also initiated. In fact, the actual initiation of the twist occurs while the gymnast's legs are still in contact with the bar. Using both bars as a functional base of support, the performer is able to extend into the twist by lifting (and thus rotating) one side of the body about the other. Notice how the lead thigh lifts free of the lower bar a bit sooner than the opposite thigh as a result of the twist initiation.

Also during this time, the hands are vigorously pressing for-downward *in a sequential fashion* against the bar. As the hand to the same side of the twist (left hand for left twist as illustrated) completes its push phase, it releases the bar a bit sooner than the opposite hand.

FIGURE 9.23. Belly Whip Full Twisting Backward Uprise.

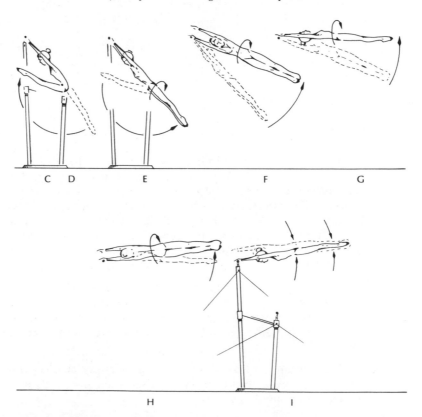

E-F-G-H-I. Although there is a brief moment in which the performer is completely free from the apparatus (airborne), the entire full twist should be initiated, executed, and completed (including the overgrip regrasp) during the ascent swing phase. Notice that the entire twist occurs uniformly throughout the long axis of the total body unit.

I. A fully extended body shape with the performer positioned above horizontal represents final completion of the skill. At this point, the gymnast can readily execute any of the sequentially related skills.

DISMOUNTS

9.24 Straddled Sole Circle Dismount

Because of the selected starting position of the gymnast relative to the apparatus (on the low bar facing outward), the total potential amplitude of the cast phase is obviously confined to within the height-width distance of the bar settings. Were the skill initiated from the high bar facing either direction, maximum amplitude in the cast phase could then be realized, i.e., casting to the handstand. In any case, attaining proper body shape and position in the actual straddle-on is an essential factor.

Although not illustrated, the performer could have delayed executing the actual "straddle-on action" until just prior to arriving at illustration C. Such a consideration would indeed serve to maximize amplitude in the entire circular swing *to the fullest possible extent.*

A. The skill is begun as the gymnast moves through an overgrip front support "cast" position. This motion is identical in nature to the illustrations presented for the Cast to Handstand, (9.9 A, B, and C).

A-B. As the legs approach the high bar, the hip joints begin to undergo a rapid flexion (while simultaneously straddling the legs) followed by a slight rounding or hollowing in the lower back, upper back, and shoulder girdle respectively.

Although these actions cause the legs to rotate laterally downward about the hip joints, notice that the hips themselves are simultaneously rotating upward about the shoulder joints. This is accomplished because the hands *continue* to push vigorously and steadfastly for-downward against the bar.

Lifting the hips well above the head provides the necessary clearance for the balls of the feet to be placed onto the bar just *outside of and directly next to* the hands, i.e., a narrowly straddled sole circle shape. Positioning the body's mass center as high and as far away from the bar as is mechanically possible helps to ensure a maximum potential amplitude in the oncoming descent swing phase.

B-C-D. These movements are identical to the illustrations and descriptions presented for the Straddled Sole Circle One-Half Turn, (9.21 A, B, and C).

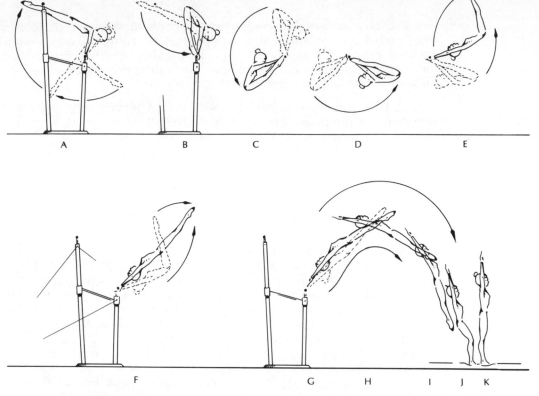

FIGURE 9.24. Straddled Sole Circle Dismount.

D-E-F. As the body rises up the circular swing with the legs approaching the horizontal, the performer begins to rapidly open (unfold) out of the straddled sole circle shape. The total body unit, *particularly the hip joints,* extends vigorously while the hands forcefully and continuously push back-downward against the bar. (This latter action is similar to "throwing the bar away, over the top and behind one's head.")

F-G. Just as the performer attains a slightly arched shape, the vigorous "extension action" of the hip joints is *instantaneously* stopped, causing the forward rotary motion of the legs to be transferred into the total body. During the very same moment, the "throw away action" of the arms is complete and the bar is released. These actions serve to initiate a forward rotary motion while projecting the gymnast away from the apparatus in a for-upward direction.

G-H-I. Remember that the amplitude realized in the airborne phase is always a direct result of the effectiveness of the preceding upswing phase. Once airborne, however, the performer's center of mass follows its established, perfectly regular, curved path (parabolic trajectory). As the body continues rotating forward about its mass center, it begins to realign into a straight-line shape.

182

I-J-K. Except for the fact that the performer is landing from a region of higher location (apparatus) to a region of lower location, these movements are identical in nature to the illustrations and descriptions presented for the Bounding Forward Handspring, (7.7 F through H).

9.25 Handstand One-Quarter Turn Dismount

A. The skill is initiated from a fully extended body shape with the hips resting on the high bar and the hands grasping the low bar in a mixed-grip. Note that the hip joints are positioned directly in line with the bar to facilitate the oncoming "cast" action. In addition, notice that the hand opposite the intended direction of turn is the one which assumes the "undergrip" position (right hand for left turn as illustrated).

A-B. In preparation for the "cast," the hip joints flex as fully as is mechanically possible about the bar and then *instantaneously* begin to undergo a rapid and forceful extension. This action causes the upper rail to bend or deflect (cocked as in an archer's bow) laterally downward.

FIGURE 9.25. Handstand One-Quarter Turn Dismount.

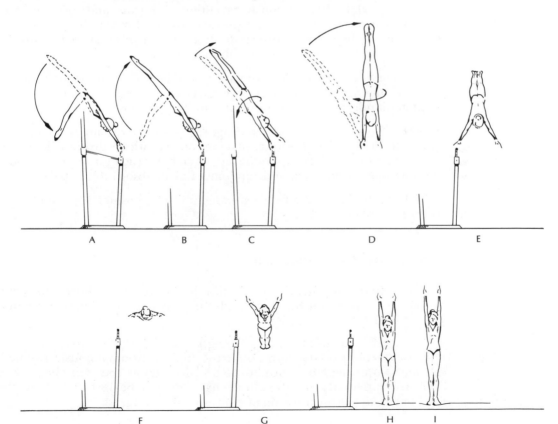

B-C. Just prior to attaining a straight-line shape, the rapid extension (kickback action) of the legs about the hips is instantaneously stopped, causing its upswing momentum to be transferred into the entire body. The deflected upper rail instantly resumes its original shape (restitution) thereby further enhancing the already existing upswing motion. Notice that the performer extends into the turn by lifting (and thus rotating) one side of the body about the other.

Also during this time, the hands are vigorously pressing for-downward *in a sequential fashion* against the bar. The overgrip hand completes its push phase instantly upon twist initiation and consequently releases the bar noticeably sooner than the undergrip hand.

C-D. The entire one-quarter turn should be initiated, executed, and completed slightly prior to arriving at the peak of the upswing phase. Notice that the entire turn occurs uniformly throughout the long axis of the total body unit.

D-E. Just as the turn is being completed, the support hand briefly pushes for-downward against the bar, causing the total body unit to begin descending back-downward alongside of and parallel to the apparatus. At that instant, the performer "snaps down" by quickly assuming a slightly hollowed body shape while simultaneously executing a vigorous and forceful hand push-off from the bar. As far as possible, the performer should strive to "spot" the landing, i.e., realize little or no travel in either a forward or backward direction as a result of the snap-down.

E-F-G. Once airborne, the arms are spread laterally to shorten the body's effective turning radius. This action increases the speed of rotation and thus facilitates landing in a more upright standing position.

G-H-I. In preparation for landing, the performer maintains complete body extension until just prior to making contact with the ground. The arms return directly overhead while the legs stretch or reach for the mat. Notice that only the ankle, knee, and hip joints flex to absorb the impact.

I. The attainment of a fully extended standing position represents final completion of the skill.

9.26 Handstand Squat Dismount

A-B. These movements are identical in nature to the illustrations and descriptions presented for the Handstand One-Quarter Turn Dismount, (9.25 A and B).

B-C. Just prior to attaining a straight-line shape, the rapid extension (kickback action) of the legs about the hips is instantaneously stopped, causing its upswing momentum to be transferred into the entire body. The deflected upper rail instantly resumes its original shape (restitution) thereby further enhancing the upswing motion already in progress.

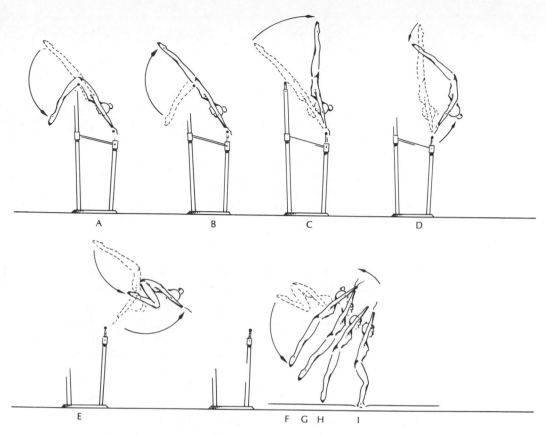

FIGURE 9.26. Handstand Squat Dismount.

C-D. As the feet approach the upper vertical, the hands briefly push for-downward against the bar causing a momentary slight arch in the total body unit. At that instant, the performer "snaps through" by forcefully pushing off the bar in a back-downward direction while simultaneously hollowing the total body unit. These actions serve both to lift the performer for-upward away from the bar while at the same time to initiate backward rotary motion.

D-E-F-G. Notice how the gymnast rapidly undergoes very obvious changes in body shape—moving instantly into a fully tucked shape and then immediately opening to a fully extended, slightly arched shape. Upon push-off from the bar, the arms should be lifted directly overhead.

G-H-I. In preparation for landing, the performer maintains complete body extension until just prior to making contact with the ground. The arms remain directly overhead while the legs stretch or reach for the mat. Notice that only the ankle, knee, and hip joints flex to absorb the impact.

I. The attainment of a fully extended standing position represents final completion of the skill.

185

9.27 Hecht Dismount

A-B-C-D-E-F-G. Except for the fact that a comparatively more vigorous "scooping" motion and subsequent hip joint flexion are employed, these movements are identical to the illustrations and descriptions presented for the Cast Wrap to Backward Hip Circle, (9.16 A through G).

G-H-I. As the body approaches full compression, the rapid flexion of the hip joints is instantaneously stopped, causing the backward rotary momentum of the legs to be transferred into the entire body. This "stopping action" of the legs serves as a cue to release the upper bar simultaneously. Upon hand release, the fully compressed body shape begins to vigorously rotate backward about the lower bar.

I-J. As the legs approach the horizontal, the fully compressed body shape begins to open (unfold) *rapidly.* This timely extension of the total body unit depresses the lower bar (cocked as in an archer's bow) in an inward-downward direction.

J-K. Upon attaining a straight-line shape, the forceful body extension is *instantaneously* stopped, causing its momentum to be transferred into the total body unit. This "stopping action" in body extension together with the "recoil action" of the depressed bar rail serves both to lift the performer for-upward away from the apparatus as well as to initiate the appropriate amount of backward rotary motion for the oncoming landing phase.

K-L-M-N. Once airborne, the performer's mass center follows its already established, perfectly regular, curved path. During this time, the total body unit maintains its fully extended shape.

N-O. In preparation for landing, the performer maintains complete body extension until just prior to making contact with the ground. The arms remain directly overhead while the legs stretch or reach for the mat. Notice that only the ankle, knee, and hip joints flex to absorb the impact.

O. The attainment of a fully extended standing position represents final completion of the skill.

FIGURE 9.27. Hecht Dismount.

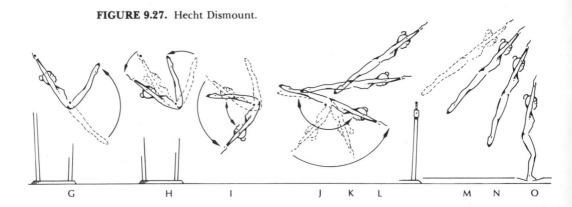

G   H   I   J   K   L   M   N   O

9.28 Hecht Full Twist Dismount

A-B-C-D-E-F-G-H-I. These movements are identical in nature to the illustrations and descriptions presented for the Hecht Dismount, (9.27 A through I). However, in order to incorporate a full twist during the "Hecht phase," an additional rotary component about the long axis of the body must be introduced at takeoff. Consequently, the arms, although still maintained overhead, are spread slightly in a lateral direction. Because this comparatively wider body shape increases the performer's twisting radius, the actual rate or speed of the twist is relatively slow and in fact scarcely observable during the oncoming takeoff phase.

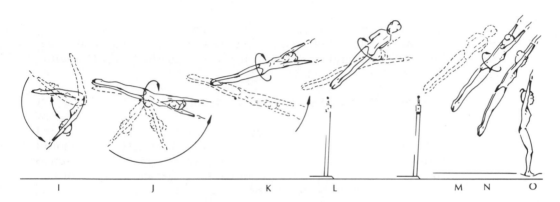

FIGURE 9.28. Hecht Full Twist Dismount.

I-J. As the legs approach the horizontal, the fully compressed body shape begins to open (unfold) *rapidly*. This timely extension of the total body unit depresses the lower bar (cocked as in an archer's bow) in an inward-downward direction.

The full twist is initiated just prior to attaining a straight-line body shape. In fact, the actual initiation occurs while the gymnast's upper thighs are still in contact with the bar. Using the lower rail as a functional base of support, the performer is able to extend into the twist by lifting (and thus rotating) one side of the body about the other. As far as possible, the twist should occur *uniformly* throughout the long axis of the straight-line body shape. In effect, the total body is seen twisting as a single unit.

J-K. Upon attaining a straight-line shape, the forceful body extension is *instantaneously* stopped, causing its momentum to be transferred into the total body unit. This "stopping action" in body extension together with the "recoil action" of the depressed bar rail serves both to lift the (now twisting) performer for-upward away from the apparatus as well as to initiate the appropriate amount of backward rotary motion for the oncoming landing phase.

K-L-M. Notice that during the airborne phase of the skill, the performer undergoes *very obvious* and *specifically timed* changes in body shape solely because of bilateral arm action. Although the actual twist has been initiated at takeoff, the total body shape is fully extended with arms held laterally overhead. As the performer rises to the apex of the airborne trajectory, notice how both arms are quickly pulled inward and positioned next to the sides of the body. (The fully flexed elbows allow the forearms to be placed symmetrically across the upper chest). This repositioning of the arms serves to shorten the body's radius of rotation simultaneously about both its long and lateral axes. Consequently, the greatest percentage of both the backward rotation and the twist can be realized during the "peak" of the airborne trajectory. During the descent phase, the arms return to an overhead *lateral* position.

M-N-O. Except for the fact that the arms are repositioned directly overhead and in line with the trunk, these movements are essentially the same as the illustrations and descriptions presented for the Hecht Dismount, (9.27 M, N, and O).

9.29 Hecht Backward Somersault Dismount

A through K. These movements are for the most part, identical in nature to the illustrations and descriptions presented for the Hecht Dismount, (9.27 A through K). However, in order to incorporate a "gainer somersault" during the airborne phase, a comparatively greater amount of backward rotary motion must be generated at takeoff. Consequently, a most forceful extension from the fully compressed body shape and the instantaneous "stopping" of this extension action once the performer attains a straight-line shape must both occur *as rapidly as possible*. (Remember, though, that the phrase "as rapidly as possible" does *not* imply "as soon as possible." In fact, the actual timing of the takeoff phase often occurs an instant *later* than in the

FIGURE 9.29. Hecht Backward Somersault Dismount.

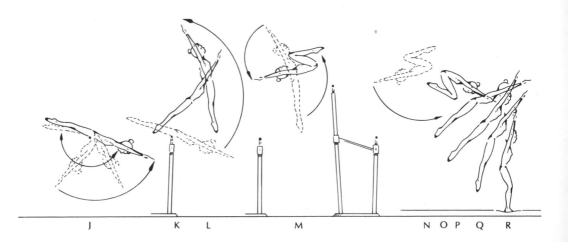

J   K   L   M   N O P Q   R

basic Hecht Dismount. This allows the performer to trade off a small portion of potential travel or distance away from the apparatus for that much needed "gainer" rotation in the airborne phase.) As a result, the performer can rise for-upward into the air while still initiating sufficient backward rotary motion to successfully execute the "gainer somersault."

K-L-M-N-O-P. Once airborne, although the mass center follows a perfectly regular curved path, the performer's rotating body undergoes *very obvious* and *specifically timed* changes in shape: from slightly arched during the initial ascent phase, to fully closed or tucked at the peak of the airborne trajectory, and returning to slightly arched in the descent phase.

P-Q-R. These movements are identical in nature to the illustrations and descriptions presented for the Hecht Dismount, (9.27 M, N, and O).

9.30 Straddled Sole Circle Forward Somersault Dismount

The skill can be executed from a fully extended handstand position on the high bar facing either direction. Although not illustrated, the performer could maintain the fully extended body shape throughout a majority of the descent phase and then execute the actual "straddle-on action" at a point just prior to illustration B. Such a consideration would indeed serve to maximize amplitude in the entire circular swing *to the fullest possible extent.*

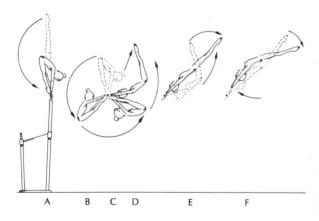

A   B   C   D   E   F

FIGURE 9.30. Straddled Sole Circle Forward Somersault Dismount.

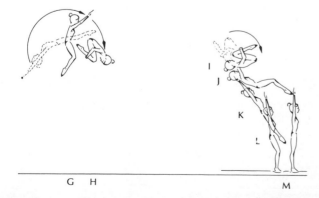

G   H   M

A. The straddle-on movement is identical in nature to the illustrations and descriptions presented for the Straddled Sole Circle One-Half Turn (9.21 A).

A-B-C-D-E. These movements are, for the most part, identical in nature to the illustrations and descriptions presented for the basic Straddled Sole Circle Dismount, (9.24 B through F). However, in order to incorporate a "forward somersault" during the airborne phase, a comparatively greater amount of forward rotary motion must be generated at takeoff. Consequently, the most forceful extension from the fully compressed straddled sole circle shape, the instantaneous "stopping" of this extension action immediately *after* performer attains a straight-line shape, and the subsequent hand release from the bar must all occur *as rapidly as possible*. (Remember, though, that the phrase "as rapidly as possible" does not imply "as soon as possible.") However, the actual timing of the takeoff phase often does occur an *instant* sooner than in the basic Straddled Sole Circle Dismount. Since the gymnast dismounts or travels away from the apparatus in the very same direction as the somersault itself, i.e., forward, a *slightly* earlier execution of the takeoff phase allows the performer to trade off a small portion of potential lift or height for that much needed forward rotation in the airborne phase. As a result, the performer can rise for-upward into the air while still initiating sufficient forward rotary motion to successfully execute the forward somersault.

E-F. Just as the performer attains an arched shape (note the rather pronounced heel lead), the vigorous "extension action" of the hip joints is *instantaneously* stopped, causing the forward rotary motion of the legs to be transferred into the total body. During the very same moment, the "throw away action" of the arms is complete and the bar is released. These timely actions serve to initiate sufficient forward rotary motion for successful execution of the somersault while projecting the gymnast away from the apparatus in a for-upward direction.

F-G-H-I-J-K. Once airborne, although the mass center follows a perfectly regular curved path, the performer's rotating body undergoes *very obvious* and *specifically timed* changes in shape: from noticeably arched upon bar release, to fully closed or tucked at the peak of the airborne trajectory, and returning to full extension in the descent phase.

K-L-M. These movements are identical in nature to the illustrations and descriptions presented for the basic Straddled Sole Circle Dismount, (9.24 I, J, and K).

10
Analysis of Core Vaulting Skills

Simone Chappuis, Acadiana Gymnastic Club, Lafayette, Louisiana.

191

THE RUN AND HURDLE PHASES

A very fast, accelerating, and yet controlled approach is essential to maximum execution of all vaulting skills. Although running tall with the head and trunk held upright, the total body unit should have a slight forward lean.

During the airborne phase of the hurdle, the body actually begins to rotate in a *backward* direction. At the very same time, the arms begin to lift *for-upward,* and the legs are extended, brought together, and placed well out in front of the body. The hurdle should be *short* in duration, *low* to the ground and *quick* in forward horizontal velocity.[1]

10.1 Squat Vault

A. Using a *fast, low,* and *short* hurdle, the performer contacts the board such that the total body unit is in an upright, yet slightly backward leaning position relative to the vertical. At impact, the ankle, knee, and hip joints undergo a slight and very brief flexion, and the arms begin to lift vigorously for-upward.

A-B. The instantaneous and forceful extension of the legs against the board "lifts" the body into the air. The forward horizontal velocity derived from the hurdle phase provides the necessary forward rotation seen in the airborne phase. Notice that the performer extends only to a point such that a hollowed body shape is formed. Every attempt should be made to *reach for and make hand contact with the horse as soon as possible.*

B-C. In order to facilitate maximum amplitude in the upcoming post-flight phase, the preflight trajectory should possess characteristics similar to the hurdle trajectory: be as fast, low, and short as is mechanically possible.

Actual *hand contact* with the horse should occur *during the ascent phase* of the preflight trajectory with the shoulder girdle vigorously moving into a

---

[1]For a more complete discussion of the Run and Hurdle phases, refer to Chapter 4: The Mechanics of Impact.

position of full elevation. Note that the shoulders are positioned well behind the hands and that the hip region is the highest part of the hollowed body shape, i.e., hip lead.

C-D-E. Immediately upon contacting the horse, the hands vigorously and forcefully *push back-downward* while the shoulder girdle instantly moves from full elevation to full depression. These "repulsion" actions serve to *reverse* the performer's roration (from forward to backward) as well as to provide *additional lift* to the already rising body.

During the very same time, the gymnast also executes the "squat action" over the horse by quickly assuming a *brief, yet fully closed* (tucked) body shape.

E-F-G-H. Once airborne, although the mass center follows a perfectly regular curved path, the performer's backward rotating body undergoes *very obvious* and *specifically timed* changes in shape: from the fully closed (tucked) shape, immediately opening into a fully extended, yet slightly arched shape, and finally returning into a slightly hollowed body shape.

H-I. In preparation for landing, the performer maintains total body extension until just prior to making contact with the ground. The arms remain directly overhead and in line with the trunk while the legs are stretching or reaching for the mat. This technique provides the gymnast with the largest possible distance through which to apply a stopping force. Consequently, greater and more effective control in the landing phase can be realized. Notice that only the ankle, knee, and hip joints flex to absorb the impact.

I. The attainment of a fully extended standing position with the arms held directly overhead and in line with the trunk represents final completion of the skill.

FIGURE 10.1. Squat Vault.

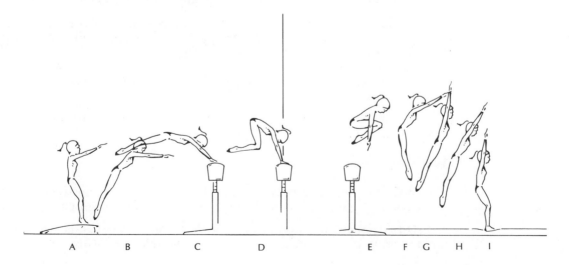

A   B   C   D   E   F   G   H   I

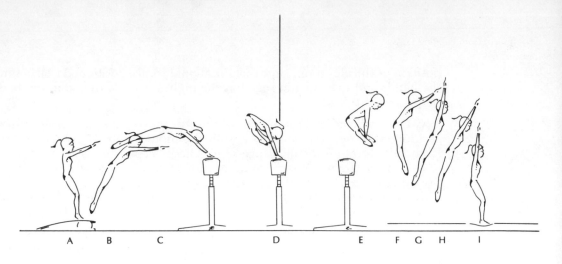

FIGURE 10.2. Straddle Vault.

10.2 Straddle Vault

A-B-C. These movements are identical in nature to the illustrations and descriptions presented for the Squat Vault, (10.1 A through C).

C-D-E. Immediately upon contact with the horse, the hands vigorously and forcefully *push back-downward* while the shoulder girdle instantly moves from full elevation to full depression. These "repulsion" actions serve to *reverse* the performer's rotation (from forward to backward) as well as to provide *additional lift* to the already rising body.

During the very same time, the gymnast also executes the "straddle action" over the horse by quickly spreading the legs laterally as wide as possible while flexing fully and completely in the hip joints. As soon as this fully compressed straddled body shape is attained, the performer immediately begins opening en route to a fully extended shape.

E-F-G-H. Once airborne, although the mass center follows a perfectly regular curved path, the performer's backward rotating body undergoes *very obvious* and *specifically timed* changes in shape: from the fully compressed straddled shape, immediately opening into a slightly arched shape (while bringing the straddled legs back together), and finally returning to a slightly hollowed body shape.

H-I. These movements are identical in nature to the illustrations and descriptions presented for the Squat Vault, (10.1 H and I).

10.3 Stoop Vault

A-B-C. The movements are identical in nature to the illustrations and descriptions presented for the Squat Vault, (10.1 A through C).

C-D-E. Immediately upon contact with the horse, the hands vigorously and forcefully *push back-downward* while the shoulder girdle instantly moves

194

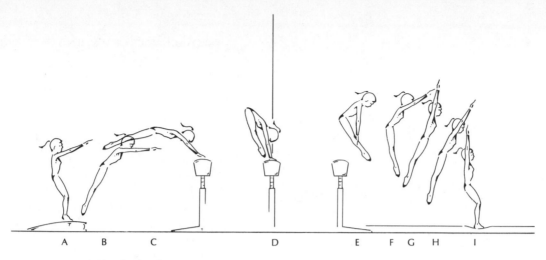

A   B   C   D   E   F G H   I

FIGURE 10.3. Stoop Vault.

from full elevation to full depression. These "repulsion" actions serve to *reverse* the performer's rotation (from forward to backward) as well as to provide *additional lift* to the already rising body.

During the very same time, the gymnast also executes the "stoop action" over the horse by quickly flexing the hip joints as fully and completely as possible. (Note how the performer strives for a maximum hip-hand distance in order to facilitate clearing the horse with straight legs.) As soon as this fully compressed piked body shape is attained, the performer immediately begins opening en route to a fully extended shape.

E-F-G-H. Once airborne, although the mass center follows a perfectly regular curved path, the performer's backward rotating body undergoes *very obvious* and *specifically timed* changes in shape: from the fully closed piked shape, immediately opening into a fully extended, yet slightly arched shape, and finally returning into a slightly hollowed body shape.

H-I. These movements are identical in nature to the illustrations and descriptions presented for the Squat Vault, (10.1 H and I).

10.4 Layout Squat Vault

Because "layout" vaults require a more extended body shape (longer radius) during preflight as well as a greater body angle (relative to the horizontal) upon hand contact with the horse than do the "basic" vaults, comparatively greater amounts of both *lift* and *forward rotation* must be generated at takeoff. Increasing these components of the preflight phase can be accomplished by: (1) maximizing the forward horizontal speed of the run and hurdle phases; (2) standing as tall as is mechanically possible during impact; and (3) minimizing the amount of time on the vaulting board (by instantly and forcefully extending the total body unit upon actual board contact).[2]

[2]For a more complete discussion of the Impact and Takeoff phases, refer to Chapter 4: The Mechanics of Impact.

195

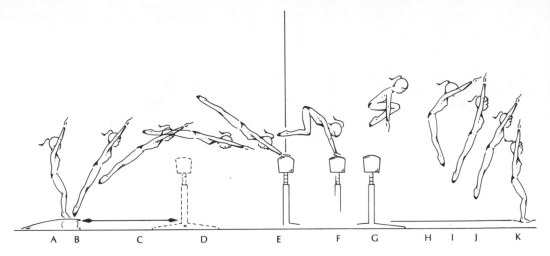

FIGURE 10.4. Layout Squat Vault.

A. Using a *fast, low,* and *short* hurdle, the performer contacts the board so that the total body unit is in an upright, yet *very slightly* backward leaning position relative to the vertical. At impact the ankle, knee, and hip joints undergo a slight and very brief flexion and the arms begin to lift vigorously for-upward.

A-B. The instantaneous and most forceful extension of the legs against the board "lifts" the body into the air. *Maximizing* the forward horizontal velocity of the run and hurdle phases as well as *minimizing* the angle of block at touchdown provide the necessary forward rotation seen in the preflight phase. Notice that the performer extends to a straight-line body shape. Every attempt should be made to *reach for and make hand contact with the horse as soon as possible.*

B-C-D. In its motion characteristics, the preflight trajectory should be very similar to the hurdle trajectory—fast, low, and short. Although realizing considerable forward rotation, note that the *straight-line body shape is steadfastly maintained.*

D-E. Actual *hand contact* with the horse should occur *during the ascent phase* of the preflight trajectory with the shoulder girdle vigorously moving into a position of full elevation. Note that the foot region is the highest part of the straight-line body shape and that the total body unit is well above the horizontal.

E through K. Except for the fact that the body is fully extended (laid out) and positioned well above the horizontal upon hand contact with the horse, these movements are identical in nature to the illustrations and descriptions presented for the basic Squat Vault, (10.1 C through I). However, proper execution of the "layout" technique generally has the potential to realize a slightly greater postflight amplitude.

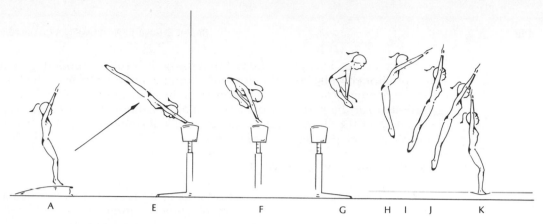

FIGURE 10.5. Layout Straddle Vault.

10.5 Layout Straddle Vault

A through E. These movements are identical in nature to the illustrations and descriptions presented for the Layout Squat Vault, (10.4 A through E).

E through K. Except for the fact that the body is fully extended (laid out) and positioned well above the horizontal upon hand contact with the horse, these movements are identical in nature to the illustrations and descriptions presented for the basic Straddle Vault, (10.2 C through I). However, proper execution of the "layout" technique generally has the potential to realize a slightly greater postflight amplitude.

10.6 Layout Stoop Vault

A through E. These movements are identical in nature to illustrations and descriptions presented for the Layout Squat Vault (10.4 A through E).

FIGURE 10.6. Layout Stoop Vault.

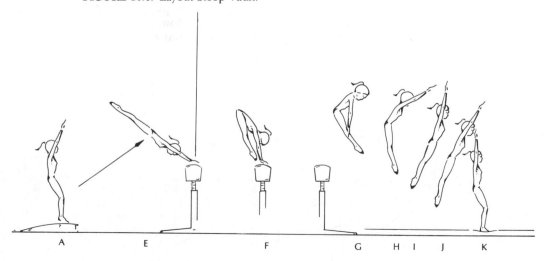

E through K. Except for the fact that the body is fully extended (laid out) and positioned well above the horizontal upon hand contact with the horse, these movements are identical in nature to the illustrations and descriptions presented for the basic Stoop Vault, (10.3 C through I). However, proper execution of the "layout" technique generally has the potential to realize a slightly greater postflight amplitude.

10.7 Forward Handspring Vault

In order to execute successfully "handspring-type" vaults (particularly those characterized by some form of somersaulting in the postflight), *maximum* amounts of both forward horizontal speed and forward rotary motion must be generated at takeoff. Taking full advantage of the introductory guidelines presented in 10.4 for "layout-type" vaults as well as minimizing the distance of the board setting to the horse are necessary, if not essential, to all advanced vaulting skills.

A through E. These movements are, for the most part, identical in nature to the illustrations and descriptions presented for the Layout Squat Vault, (10.4 A through D). The basic difference centers on generating significantly greater forward rotary motion while using a *comparatively flatter* (lower) preflight trajectory. In so doing, maximum amplitude in the postflight trajectory can then be realized.

E-F. Actual hand contact with the horse should occur during the *ascent phase* of the preflight trajectory with the shoulder girdle vigorously moving into a position of full elevation. Note that the foot region is the highest part of the fully extended, yet very slightly hollowed body shape and that the total body unit forms a noticeable backward leaning angle (blocking action) with the vertical.

FIGURE 10.7. Forward Handspring Vault.

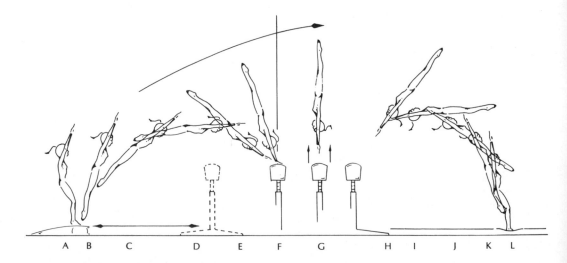

F-G. Immediately upon contacting the horse, the vigorous and forceful for-downward push of the hands (shoulder girdle repulsion) helps to rotate as well as to *lift the already rising* body through the handstand and into the air.

In addition, notice the very discreet change occurring in the shape of the total body unit—from very slightly hollowed at contact to a fully extended straight-line shape upon "lift-off." Although this timely fluctuation in body shape is essential to the dynamics of the movement, it should be as minute and unobvious as possible.

G-H-I-J. Remember that the postflight amplitude is always the direct result of the preceding run, hurdle, takeoff, preflight, and repulsion phases respectively. Once airborne, however, the performer's center of mass follows its established, perfectly regular, curved path. Although the body continues rotating forward about its mass center, *note that a fully extended shape is steadfastly maintained.*

J-K-L. Except for the fact that the gymnast is landing from a region of higher location (vaulting horse) to a region of lower location (landing mat), these movements are essentially the same as the illustrations and descriptions presented for the Bounding Forward Handspring in Floor Exercise, (7.7 F through H).

10.8 Cartwheel Vault

A through E. Except for the fact that a one-quarter twist is initiated at takeoff and executed during the preflight phase, these movements are essentially the same as the illustrations and descriptions presented for the Forward Handspring Vault, (10.7 A through E). Notice that the actual twist occurs uniformly throughout the long axis of the straight-line body shape. In effect, the total body is seen twisting as a single unit.

FIGURE 10.8. Cartwheel Vault.

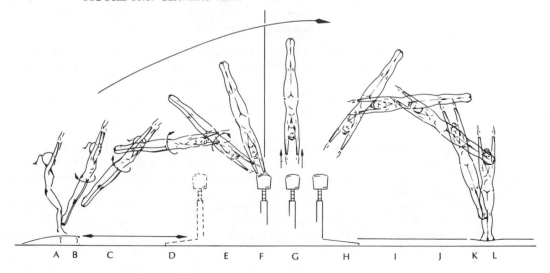

E-F. Actual hand contact with the horse should occur in a rapid one-two sequential fashion during the *ascent phase* of the preflight trajectory. The shoulder girdle is vigorously moving into a position of full elevation. Note that the foot region is the highest part of the fully extended body shape and that the total body unit, although rotating sideways, forms a noticeable angle (blocking action) with the vertical.

F-G. Immediately upon contacting the horse, the hands (in a rapid one-two sequential fashion) are vigorously and forcefully pushing (shoulder girdle repulsion) both downward and to the side of the intended direction of the postflight. These timely actions help to rotate as well as to *lift the already rising body* through the handstand and into the air. Note that during this time the *fully extended body shape is steadfastly maintained.*

G through L. These movements are essentially the same as the illustrations and descriptions presented for the Cartwheel Dismount in Balance Beam (8.31 E through I).

10.9 Handspring Forward Somersault Vault

A through E. These movements are, for the most part, identical in nature to the illustrations and descriptions presented for the Forward Handspring Vault, (10.7 A through E). The basic difference centers on generating even greater forward rotary motion while using a comparatively *flatter* (lower) and *shorter* (further minimizing the distance of the board setting to the horse) preflight trajectory. In so doing, maximum amplitude and forward rotary motion can be realized in the postflight phase.

E-F. Actual hand contact with the horse should occur during the *ascent phase* of the preflight trajectory with the shoulder girdle vigorously moving into a position of full elevation. Note that the foot region is the highest part of the fully extended, yet slightly hollowed body shape and that the total body unit, although rotating vigorously forward, forms a noticeable backward leaning angle (blocking action) with the vertical.

F-G. Immediately upon contacting the horse, the hands vigorously and forcefully push (shoulder girdle repulsion) in a for-downward direction to a point such that a slight, but noticeable, arched shape (heel lead) is briefly assumed in the forward rotating body. These timely actions help to rotate and lift further the already rising body through the handstand and into the air.

G through M. Remember that maximizing postflight amplitude while maintaining sufficient quantity of forward rotary motion is always the direct result of the preceding run, hurdle, takeoff, preflight, and repulsion phases respectively.

Once airborne, although the performer's mass center follows a perfectly regular curved path, the forward rotating body undergoes *very obvious* and *specifically timed* changes in shape: from slightly arched (heel-lead) at lift-off,

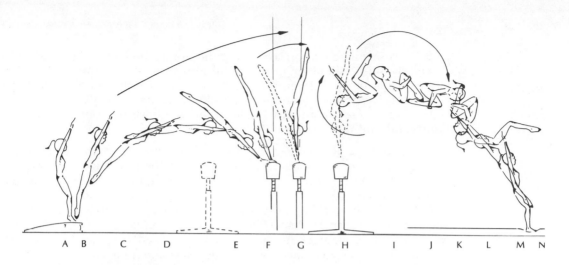

FIGURE 10.9. Handspring Forward Somersault Vault.

moving instantly into a fully closed or tucked shape for a majority (approximately one and one-quarter) of the somersault phase, and then opening to full extension immediately prior to landing. (Keep in mind it is the "quickness" with which the "heel-lead action" can be *stopped* and the "tuck action" can be *started* that accounts for maximum transfer of rotary motion from the legs and into the entire body.)

M-N. Except for the fact that the gymnast is landing from a region of higher location (vaulting horse) to a region of lower location (landing mat), these movements are essentially the same as the illustrations and descriptions presented for the Tucked Forward Somersault in Floor Exercise, (7.14 H through J).

10.10 Tsukahara Vault

Many aspects of the preflight phase are quite similar to the input phase of the basic Round-Off in Floor Exercise (7.36).

A through E. Except for the fact that a one-half twist is initiated at takeoff, executed during the preflight, and completed upon hand contact with the horse, these movements are essentially the same as the illustrations and descriptions presented for Handspring Forward Somersault Vault, (10.9 A through E). Note that the actual twist occurs uniformly throughout the long axis of the straight-line body shape. In effect, the total body is seen twisting as a single unit.

E-F. Actual hand contact with the horse should occur during the *ascent phase* of the preflight trajectory with the shoulder girdle vigorously moving into a position of full elevation. Note that the foot region is the highest part of the *slightly arched body shape* and that the total body unit, although rotating vigorously backward, forms a slight, but noticeable, forward leaning angle (blocking action) with the vertical.

201

F-G. Immediately upon contacting the horse, the hands vigorously and forcefully push (shoulder girdle repulsion) in a for-downward direction while the trunk and hips quickly flex to a point such that a hollowed shape (foot-lead) is briefly assumed in the backward rotating body. These timely actions help to rotate and lift further the already rising body through the handstand and into the air.

G through L. Remember that maximizing postflight amplitude while maintaining a sufficient quantity of backward rotary motion is always the direct result of the preceding run, hurdle, takeoff, preflight, and repulsion phases respectively.

Once airborne, although the performer's mass center follows a perfectly regular curved path, the backward rotating body undergoes *very obvious* and *specifically timed* changes in shape: from hollowed (foot lead) at lift-off, moving instantly into a fully closed or tucked shape for a majority (approximately one and one-quarter) of the somersault phase, and then opening to full extension immediately prior to landing. (Keep in mind it is the "quick-ness" with which the "foot-lead action" can be *stopped* and the "tuck action" can be *started* that accounts for maximum transfer of rotary motion from the legs into the entire body.)

L-M. Although the gymnast is landing from a region of higher location (vaulting horse) to a region of lower location (landing mat), these move-ments are essentially the same as the illustrations and descriptions presented for the Standing Tucked Backward Somersault in Floor Exercise (7.28 G through I). Notice, however, that the total body unit forms a slightly forward leaning angle with the vertical at actual touchdown. Because this "blocking action" helps to "check" the backward horizontal and rotary motions of the postflight phase, a more effective control of the landing can be realized.

FIGURE 10.10. Tsukahara Vault.

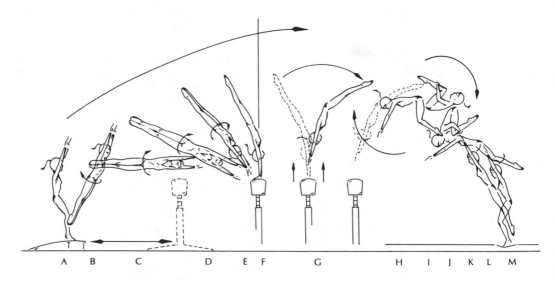

A   B   C   D   E   F   G   H   I   J   K   L   M

11
Spotting and Safety Procedures

Candice Greene and Gary Smith (coach), Acadiana Gymnastic Club, Lafayette, Louisiana.

203

The term "spotting" can be defined as "any form of physical assistance that a gymnast receives during the execution of a skill or a series of skills." Its applications are observed in most training and competitive situations, at all levels of performance, and with varying degrees of effectiveness. As is the case with any type of assistance, the value of the technique is dependent upon the way in which it is employed.

Spotting should serve *primarily* as a teaching aid and *secondarily* as a protective measure. It is of utmost importance that teachers and coaches understand this sequence of application. Although protection is *always* a product of effective teaching, the opposite is not necessarily the case. To demonstrate the point, we need to look at cause-effect relationships inherent in motor skill performance. For example, protecting a gymnast from under-rotating a somersault is essentially a procedure after-the-fact. Because the skill was performed incorrectly, assistance from the spotter becomes necessary to prevent the possibility of injury. Although commendable and often times necessary, this rather limited and inverted use of the spotting process is basically a last-ditch attempt to salvage the "effect"—underrotation. Little has been accomplished, however, in terms of controlling the "cause" of underrotation—takeoff, rotational mechanics, etc. The implication here is an obvious one. Spotting becomes most effective when used *first* as a teaching aid to pinpoint and correct the source, the causative factors, the controllable variables that affect successful performance. Always keep in mind the axiom: "Control the cause—and the effect will be your slave."

The two basic methods used in spotting are *manual manipulation* (e.g., hand contact) and *mechanical manipulation* (e.g., spotting belt). Each method has distinct advantages and disadvantages depending, of course, upon the nature of the skill in question and the purpose for the spot. Generally speaking, manual spotting is superior to belt spotting because it holds far more potential as a *teaching* aid.

Consider, for example, the relative merits of each method of assisting the Backward Walkover shown in figure 11.1. The first series of illustrations demonstrate that belt spotting merely serves to support the body weight during execution of the skill. By comparison, the spotter in the second series of illustrations is seen manually assisting and guiding the gymnast throughout the entire movement sequence. In addition to providing a built-in measure of protection, this procedure allows the performer an opportunity

204

FIGURE 11.1. Two methods of spotting a Backward Walkover: (1) Mechanical manipulation; (2) Manual manipulation.

to actually "feel" each of the critical positions essential to proper execution of the skill. The manual manipulation method, appropriately applied, generally offers the best of both worlds.

However, in highly complex skills involving aerial rotation and twisting mechanics, manual spotting sometimes becomes more difficult to execute than the skill itself! The pendulum of concern begins to shift in favor of greater emphasis for performer safety. This is why the complex skill should initially be divided into easily workable components with each part being (hand) spotted separately. As these components are properly mastered, they can be progressively combined into ever larger units. Ultimately the skill can be reconstructed and effectively spotted in its entirety. Spotter performance and gymnast performance should be viewed as mutually developmental in that both require sufficient time and experience in the learning process for improvement.

The mechanical manipulation method, by its very nature, is limited in capability to lifting, lowering, directing and/or stabilizing the gymnast during a performance. Since the basic techniques remain essentially the same regardless of skill complexity, they are *easier to learn* than hand spotting techniques. Spotting belts provide a means whereby *continual* assistance and protection can be given throughout an entire movement sequence. Although its use in facilitating learning should not be underestimated, this type of assistance provides more for *performer safety* than for teaching purposes. It often ensures that added dimension of protection so necessary to learning many of the high risk skills.

205

Regardless of which method is used, which skill is attempted, or (for that matter) which apparatus it is attempted upon, the very same movement variables characterize every spotting situation. From a biomechanical standpoint, effective spotting becomes a matter of learning how to refine "brute force."[1] Understanding the delicate interplay of the following factors affecting force is an important first step to success as a spotter: (1) *amount* of force (how much help is required); (2) *direction* of force (what space or area the skill should cover); (3) *point* of force application (where the assistance is needed); (4) *sequence* of force application (what the logical order of events is in spotting the skill); and (5) *time* of force application (how long and when the force should be applied).

At first glance, these variables may appear difficult to comprehend and perhaps even impossible to control. Yet experience has shown that this is not the case. Relatively little time is required to gain an insight into basic mechanical principles, especially when studied from the perspective of practical application. With this in mind, let us consider how each of these movement concepts affects the quality of gymnastic spotting.

Amount of Force

Force is simply the pushing or pulling effect one body exerts upon another. Although there may be force without motion, motion cannot occur without force. The amount of force necessary to assist a performer properly varies according to the objective of the skill and the gymnast's own effective effort. In any case, it is advisable to provide a reasonable amount of *overassistance* during the *initial skill learning*. As skill performance and spotting proficiency increase, the amount of spotting force needed should correspondingly decrease.

In many instances, the inexperienced spotter finds difficulty in generating enough force to assist a performance effectively. This is particularly true in those skills that require considerable lifting and/or holding assistance. Since more potential force is available from strong muscle groups than from weak ones, it stands to reason that the wise spotter will primarily depend upon the large leg muscles rather than the smaller back and arm muscles to obtain maximum force. *Spreading* the feet (greater base stability), *bending* sufficiently at the hips and knees (increasing the distance through which force can be applied), and maintaining *close* physical contact with the performer throughout the entire skill (increased arm-shoulder leverage) all significantly improve the amount of force that a spotter can develop. Compare the "ready" positions for spotting a standing Backward Somersault shown in figure 11.2. Obviously, greater amounts of force can be generated using the latter technique.

A popular concern voiced by teachers and coaches deals with the problem of how to spot the large or heavy performer effectively. How can a spotter,

[1]John W. Bunn, *Scientific Principles of Coaching* (Englewood Cliffs, N. J.: Prentice-Hall, 1964).

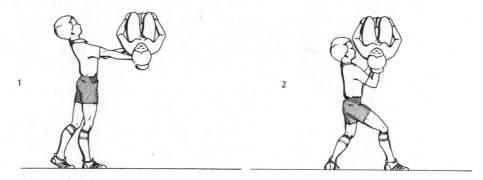

FIGURE 11.2. Two techniques for hand spotting a Backward Somersault: (1) Poor technique; (2) Good technique.

especially one who is small in stature, adequately assist and protect the large gymnast who is attempting a difficult skill? Although this sometimes can be a real and justifiable dilemma, it usually results from allowing a gymnast, regardless of size, to attempt those types of skills that are too complex for her present ability level. Because skill difficulty varies according to performer readiness, the almost universal solution can be found in the judicious use of related skill progressions. Mastering the appropriate lead-up skills is a necessary first step to establishing performer readiness. *Thus, it is not a question of differences in physical size between spotter and gymnast. Rather, it is a matter of taking the appropriate steps to equate performer capability with task difficulty.* In so doing, the amount of force (effort) then required to assist in the performance of any skill remains well within the potential of most spotters of any size.

Direction of Force

The nature of force serves either to produce motion, alter motion, or influence a body's tendency toward motion. Whatever the effect, force always acts in the exact direction in which it is applied. Having a clear understanding of the skill's movement pattern then is essential to appropriate use of force direction. For instance, a correctly executed aerial cartwheel should have an observable upward flow in its movement pattern.

FIGURE 11.3. The manual manipulation method for spotting an Aerial Cartwheel.

Consequently, the spotter, shown in figure 11.3, attempts to help the performer attain this objective by applying an upward (vertical) force. Not only does this assistance enhance the skill's aesthetic appeal, but also it gives the performer an opportunity to "feel" the correct force trajectory characteristic to aerial movements.

Whether the spotting objective is to lift, lower, direct, stabilize, rotate, or some combination, the assistance given is almost always initiated from some point *underneath* the bulk of the performer's body. This guideline is critical to spotter effectiveness because it is the only reasonable way in which the downward pull of gravity can be controlled.

The angle at which force is applied to the performer also determines the effectiveness of the spot. As shown in figure 11.4, three different angles of stopping force are being applied to control the descent phase of a Long-Hang Swing on the Uneven Parallel Bars. Since force is most effective when applied at an angle of 90 degrees to the plane of the body, the most appropriate assistance is revealed in the first example. Selecting a greater or lesser angle of assistance not only reduces spotter effectiveness, but also it interferes with proper skill mechanics.

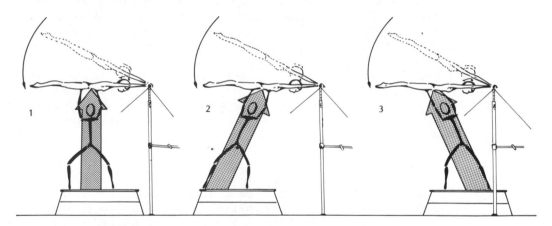

FIGURE 11.4. A comparison of three angles of stopping force for hand spotting the descent phase of a long hang swing on the Uneven Parallel Bars: (1) Proper technique; (2,3) Improper techniques.

Point of Force Application

The quality of spotter assistance is, to a large extent, determined by applying force at the most appropriate place/s on the gymnast's body. As long as the performer remains attached to the apparatus during execution of a skill, any application of external force on any part of the body always affects rotary motion. However, certain points of force application are more advantageous than others. Consider the three illustrations of spotting a Cast on the Uneven Parallel Bars presented in figure 11.5. Because the spotting force in the first example is being applied too close to the performer's

FIGURE 11.5. A comparison of three points of force application for spotting a Cast on the Uneven Parallel Bars: (1, 2) Improper techniques; (3) Proper technique.

shoulder joints (axis of rotation), an unrealistic amount of effort is required to assist properly. In addition, observe how such a force application tends to distort the natural body line of the gymnast. A similar situation also occurs in the second example, this time because the spotting force is applied at a point too far away from the performer's axis of rotation. Although considerably less effort is required, still an undesirable break in the body line usually results. By applying force at the appropriate vantage point (in this instance on the front portion of the middle thighs), the spotter in the third example has sufficient leverage to adequately assist in the lifting phase of the skill without affecting the desired straight-line body shape of the performer. Understanding how different points of force application affect body motion as well as body shape is an important factor in selecting the appropriate spotting technique.

The nature of force application on spotting airborne skills is perhaps best demonstrated by reviewing the two sets of illustrations presented in figure 11.6. Whenever a force is applied directly through the center of mass of a freely movable object, straight-line (linear) motion will result. Notice in the first set of illustrations that every part of the object as well as of the performer's body is moving the same distance, in the same direction, in the same amount of time. This observation is especially useful in those spotting situations which require lifting, lowering, directing, and/or stablizing the gymnast. However, many instances also require some control of a skill's rotational aspects. As seen in the second set of illustrations, application of force at some point other than through an object's mass center causes rotary (angular) motion to occur. In fact, the further away from an object's center of mass that the force is applied, the greater will be the resulting rotation. Observe how, to assist in the postflight phase of a stoop vault, the spotter takes full advantage of this principle by applying the appropriate amounts of force at two strategic points—through the performer's mass center (waist) for controlling the rate and direction of descent and at a point well away from the mass center (arm) for regulating the rate and degree of body rotation.

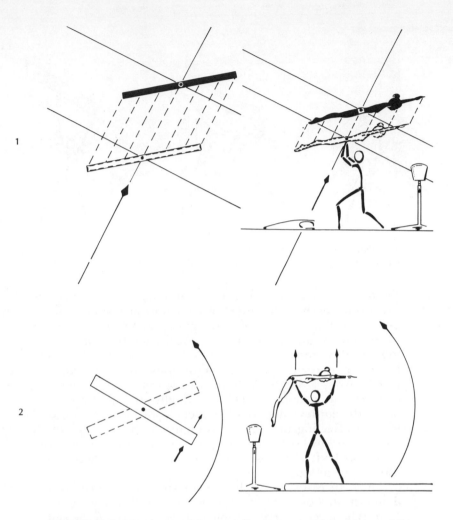

FIGURE 11.6. The nature of force application on spotting airborne skills:
(1) Straight line or linear motion; (2) Rotary or angular motion.

Sequence of Force Application

Since each and every skill must first be *initiated,* then *executed,* and finally *completed,* the *logical order* for applying spotting force naturally follows the *very same pattern*. Yet assistance is not necessarily required throughout an entire skill. It all depends upon the nature of the movement and the specific needs of the individual gymnast. In any case, the correct sequence for applying spotting force is always determined by the mechanical characteristics of the given skill.

When spotting airborne skills, it is particularly important to consider the order of priority in which assistance should be rendered. Keep in mind that a spotter possesses only a given amount of available force. As more and more of this force is used to control the rotational aspects, less and less force remains available to assist in the lifting, lowering, and/or stablizing the body in flight. Because the gymnast is forever confronted with overcoming gravity, these later components must take precedence over rotational aspects. Consequently, the wise spotter will ensure that the performer *first* attain sufficient vertical amplitude (height) and then take the appropriate measures to facilitate the required angular movements (rotation).

Time of Force Application

Knowing what procedures are needed for spotting a skill is of little practical value without also being keenly aware of *when* they are needed. Obviously, one must have a clear understanding of how the performer produces force to initiate, control, and terminate the skill. What is perhaps not quite so obvious deals with how to develop an acquired "feel" for the tempo of a movement. Although experience has no substitute, there are certain guidelines that readily apply to proper timing in virtually all spotting situations.

Application of spotting force should occur *simultaneously* with the *initiation of the performer's movement.* To demonstrate the point, attempt to further lift a gymnast performing a simple standing vertical jump *after* she has left the floor (while airborne). Now repeat the procedure except this time provide the lifting assistance *during* the actual jumping movement (prior to becoming airborne). The second approach is certainly more effective than the first. Whenever the forces generated by both spotter and gymnast occur at the exact same time, a smoother and more powerful movement is generally the result.

When attempting to control dismounts, landings, or, for that matter, the descent phase of any skill, the basic guideline for proper timing of force application remains essentially the same: *The sooner the spotting force is applied, the greater will be the resulting control.* Observe the two examples of spotting an Underswing Dismount on the Uneven Parallel Bars presented in figure

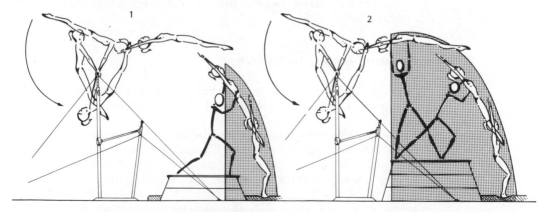

FIGURE 11.7. A comparison in "timing" the spot for an Underswing Dismount on the Uneven Parallel Bars: (1) Late timing; (2) Early timing.

11.7. Just as the gymnast passes through the peak of the airborne trajectory, downward momentum begins and continues to increase unless some force acts to alter this chain of events. In other words, the skill's total landing force (impact) will be sustained by the performer unless the spotter provides an opposing force. The amount and direction of this opposing force is partly dependent upon *when and through what distance* it is applied. Consequently, the spotter must slightly *anticipate* each movement in the skill in order to gain maximum advantage. Obviously, the potential for greater spotting force and control are realized in the second example.

The act of spotting is a "skill" in itself. It is somewhat unique, though, because two people (spotter and gymnast) are jointly involved in a coordinated effort to attain a single, individual performance. This sometimes precarious interrelationship, perhaps best described as a "sacred trust," places specific requirements on both the spotter and the gymnast. It is therefore essential to the success of the learning experience that a workable set of guidelines be established and carefully followed.

GUIDELINES FOR THE SPOTTER

Objective of the Skill

It is vitally important to have a thorough knowledge of the mechanics involved in the execution of the skill. This includes:

1. An accurate concept of the full potential of the skill. (Having an *ideal model concept* promotes effective spotting.)
2. A thorough understanding of how the performer *initiates* the skill (produces force or momentum), *controls* the movement phase (appropriate use of body segments), and *completes* the skill (recovery).
3. An awareness of the more *critical aspects* of the skill. (This insight helps the spotter make better use of both teaching and protective techniques.)

Knowledge of Spotting Techniques

Although spotting techniques may vary somewhat, there are certain key points applicable to all skills that should be remembered:

1. Be sure that the *difficulty level* of the skill is *appropriate* to the *capabilities* and *experiences of the performer*. Seemingly impossible spotting situations indicate that the skill in question is too complex for the gymnast's ability level and implies the necessity of lead-up skills and progressions.
2. Learn to spot effectively the most *basic skills first*. As the gymnast increases in performance capability, the spotter's ability to assist and protect will correspondingly improve.

3. Establish a clear, accurate *communication link* with the performer. Standardize communication so that both parties know exactly what, when, where, how, and why the skill is to be performed and spotted.

4. Use the nature and objective of the skill itself as the guide for *proper positioning* of both spotter and performer.

5. Regardless of whether the objective is to lift, lower, stabilize, rotate, or some combination, the assistance given is primarily initiated from some point *underneath* the bulk of the performer's body.

6. In order to provide the appropriate kind and amount of assistance, the spotter should maintain *close physical contact* with the performer.

7. During *initial learning* of difficult skills, provide *continuous assistance* throughout the entire skill. On the other hand, avoid undue over-spotting (overassistance) so that the gymnast can acquire a *feel* for the skill.

8. As skill proficiency increases, the role of the spotter should diminish accordingly.

9. Always be keenly aware that a prime consideration is protection of the performer's head and spinal column.

10. Learn what to expect from each gymnast. Make every effort to read individual weaknesses.

GUIDELINES FOR THE GYMNAST

Performer Readiness

Human performance is similar to computer performance in that both require a certain set of preexisting conditions to function effectively. Gymnastics performance is by no means an exception. In this light, let us review some important guidelines that can significantly enhance performer readiness.

1. Have a thorough working *knowledge* of the *ideal model concept* of the skill. This includes an understanding of the critical areas affecting success.

2. First *visualize the skill* in its entirety, and then break it down into workable parts. Mentally piece together each of these parts to reestablish the total concept of the movement.

3. *Physical readiness* is fundamental to correct technical execution. Factors such as adequate flexibility, strength, power, endurance, and timing are directly related to successful skill learning.

4. Once a skill or a component of a skill has been initiated, always *follow through* to the completion of the movement.

5. Follow a *definite progressive pattern* in skill learning. Master first those basic skills that have the broadest application to the more complex skills. Experience the widest possible range of simple movement patterns before moving on to the more complex ones.

6. The *early part* of each class or *training session* should be reserved for *attempting new and/or particularly difficult skills.* Avoid working with physical handicaps, injuries, undue fatigue, etc.

7. *Dress* in terms of the learning situation. Use chalk, rosin, handgrips, body padding, etc. where appropriate.

8. Insure that the *apparatus* is in good working condition, is properly aligned, and is adjusted according to individual needs. Also, it is important to have adequate and properly placed matting.

9. Practice sessions should always be *supervised.* Judicious use of the "buddy system" often promotes effective skill learning.

10. Develop a healthy respect for the potential hazards involved in gymnastics. This, in itself, serves as an excellent "fail-safe" mechanism for both short- and long-range protection.

GUIDELINES FOR ALL TEACHERS, COACHES AND EDUCATORS

Gymnastics Safety Certification

Developing sound knowledges, principles, and practices for safe and effective spotting is an essential ingredient to any successful gymnastic program. Of equal importance, however, is the need for virtually every gymnastic professional to participate in any one of the innumerable Gymnastic Safety Certification Programs offered throughout the nation by the United States Gymnastics Safety Association for the expressed purpose of obtaining official "Safety Certification."

In fact, the President's Council on Physical Fitness and Sports recognizes the need for and wholeheartedly endorses the objectives of the Gymnastics Safety Certification Program. Such certification is essentially for the purpose of:[2]

1. Helping reduce accidents and their severity;

2. Providing an independent recognition system for those who are actually qualified to instruct safely;

3. Proving to school officials and board members that gymnastics has a positive safety program;

4. Putting coaches in a legally defensible position in the event of an unfortunate accident; and

5. Making gymnastics the first organized sport to establish Safety Certification of coaches for the protection of athletes.

For specific information regarding the U.S. Gymnastics Safety Certification Program, contact:

Mr. Raleigh DeGeer Amyx, Executive Director
United States Gymnastics Safety Association
424 C Street, N.E. Capitol Hill
Washington, D.C. 20002   (202) 543-3403

[2]Conrad, C. Carson, Executive Director, The President's Council on Physical Fitness and Sports, Washington, D.C. 20201.

Suggested Readings

BARHAM, JERRY N. *Mechanical Kinesiology.* St. Louis, Mo.: C. V. Mosby, 1978.

BOWERS, CAROLYN. et al. *Judging and Coaching Women's Gymnastics.* Palo Alto, Ca.: National Press, 1972.

CARTER, ERNESTINE. *Gymnastics for Girls and Women.* Englewood Cliffs, N.J.: Prentice-Hall, 1978.

COOPER, PHYLLIS. *Feminine Gymnastics,* 2nd ed. Minneapolis: Burgess Publishing Co., 1973.

DYSON, GEOFFREY. *The Mechanics of Athletics.* London: University of London Press, 1971.

GEDNEY, JUDITH M. *Tumbling and Balancing: Basic Skills and Variations.* Englewood Cliffs, N.J.: Prentice-Hall, 1977.

GEORGE, GERALD, ed. *The Magic of Gymnastics.* Santa Monica, Ca.: Sundby Publications, 1970.

HAY, JAMES G. *The Biomechanics of Sports Techniques.* Englewood Cliffs, N.J.: Prentice-Hall, 1973.

HENNESSY, JEFF. *The Trampoline . . . As I See It.* Lafayette, La.: International Publishing Co., 1969.

LOKEN, NEWTON and WILLOUGHBY, ROBERT J. *The Complete Book of Gymnastics.* 3rd ed. Englewood Cliffs, N.J.: Prentice-Hall, 1977.

MILLER, DORIS I., and NELSON, RICHARD C. *Biomechanics of Sport.* Philadelphia, Pa.: Lea and Febiger, 1973.

MURRAY, MIMI. *Women's Gymnastics—Coach, Participant, Spectator.* Boston, Mass.: Allyn and Bacon, Inc., 1979.

NORTHRIP, JOHN W., LOGAN, GENE A., and McKINNEY, WAYNE C. *Biomechanical Analysis of Sport.* Dubuque, Iowa: Wm. C. Brown Co., 1974.

O'QUINN, GARLAND, JR. *Gymnastics for Elementary School Children.* Dubuque, Iowa: Wm. C. Brown Co., 1967.

SALMELA, JOHN H., ed. *The Advanced Study of Gymnastics.* Springfield, Ill.: Charles C Thomas, 1976.

SCHMID, ANDREA, and DRURY, BLANCHE. *Gymnastics for Women.* Palo Alto, Ca.: National Press, 1977.

SZYPULA, GEORGE. *Tumbling and Balancing for All,* 2nd ed. Dubuque, Iowa: Wm. C. Brown Co., 1968.

TAYLOR, BRYCE, BAJIN, BORIS, and ZIVIC, TOM. *Olympic Gymnastics for Men and Women.* Englewood Cliffs, N.J.: Prentice-Hall, 1972.

WETTSTONE, EUGENE, ed. *Gymnastics Safety Manual.* University Park, Pa.: The Pennsylvania State University Press, 1978.

Index